Wise Women

Wise Women

REFLECTIONS OF
TEACHERS AT MIDLIFE

EDITORS

PHYLLIS R. FREEMAN
JAN ZLOTNIK SCHMIDT

ROUTLEDGE
NEW YORK   LONDON

Published in 2000 by
Routledge
29 West 35th Street
New York, NY 10001

Published in Great Britain by
Routledge
11 New Fetter Lane
London EC4P 4EE

Copyright © 2000 by Routledge
Printed in the United States of America on acid-free paper.

Library of Congress Cataloging-in-Publication Data

Wise women: reflections of teachers at midlife / Phyllis R. Freeman
    and Jan Zlotnik Schmidt, editors.
        p. cm.
    Includes bibliographical references.
    ISBN 0-415-92302-6 (hard). —ISBN 0-415-92303-4 (pbk.)
    1.Women teachers—United States—Attitudes. 2. Middle
age—United States. 3. Feminism and education—United States.
I. Freeman, Phyllis R. II. Schmidt, Jan Zlotnik.
LB2837.W58 2000   99-42363
371.1'0082—dc21—dc21   CIP

Contents

PART III FEISTY ❧ GIRLS

PART IV TEACHING in TIME

Preface

VIRAGO, ELDER, WITCH, HEALER, CRONE, HAG, OLDER WOMAN, LA
LOCA, THE CRAZY WOMAN, TRIBAL STORYTELLER, TEACHER

We began work on this volume because we were both turning fifty, confronted by these characterizations and stereotypes of menopausal women.
We asked ourselves if these words in any way named us. Were we doomed
to be hags, witches, or crones? How were we going to face the issues confronting us as middle-aged women? Would we be able to deny the messages
that the culture was sending us about our aging bodies? And how did our
changing senses of identity have an impact on our own personae and
stances as teachers in the academy?

   We decided to begin our progression toward our fiftieth birthdays by
scheduling lunches as a kind of ritual gathering, as a way to discuss how we
would mark this milestone year in our lives. We did not wish the year to pass
without considering its importance, without marking it in some way, without thinking about how we would spend the next fifty years of our lives! As
we began our conversations, we also were acutely aware that because the
baby boomers were nearing fifty, women's middle passage, after years of
neglect, was suddenly the subject of intense scholarly scrutiny. We noticed,
however, that despite an array of volumes focusing on either menopause or
on midlife for women, no single work anthologized autobiographical,
reflective narratives of midlife teachers. We wondered if we were vastly different teachers at fifty than we were at thirty. We wondered what distinguished our teaching practice—how had we changed? We realized that we
were entering uncharted territory. Thus the idea of this volume took shape.
We gathered women in midlife from different disciplines, stages of their
careers, institutions, and regions of the country to join us in this midlife
journey. We read drafts of their essays, held e-mail conversations with many

members of the group, and also asked the contributors to comment on each other's work. We wanted the volume to be a collaboration. As editors, therefore, we decided not to create a scholarly essay assessing patterns of experience of midlife, but, instead, to comment briefly on noteworthy motifs in the introduction and then let the essays stand unmediated by our scholarly perspectives. We did not want to stand apart from the contributors; instead, we wanted to value the reflective narratives of the participants. We agreed with Margaret Lock (1993), who asserts that "we cannot measure subjective experiences but must narrate them"(xxxix).

We hope that we have created a work that invites readers to participate and to engage in autobiographical reflection and writing. In this spirit, each section is prefaced by evocative quotations. Finally, we have incorporated a selected bibliography of relevant research on the menopause and midlife transitions for women and on autobiographical writing in the hope that readers will be encouraged to continue exploring their midlife passages. In this way we hope to create a communal vision of women living, working, and teaching in the academy.

This book reflects much of what we have learned and received in a quarter century of teaching. Therefore, we have a circle of teachers, students, and friends in and out of the classroom to thank:

We thank the administration of SUNY New Paltz for the gifts of our separate sabbatical leaves when first the concept and then the work of this book took shape. To Ilene Kalish, Krister Swartz, and Shea Settimi at Routledge for their faith and expert support of this project, we send our sincere thanks. To the memory of our colleague and dear friend, poet Carley Rees Bogarad, our continuing recognition of how much she has taught us both about the teaching life.

Phyllis wishes to thank the following people:

To more than twenty-five years of undergraduate and graduate students in psychology, especially Julian Keenan and Michelle Warfield, my appreciation for helping me become the person and the teacher I am. To my parents, Helen and Mel Freeman, my first teachers, my continuing love and respect. To my nieces Lori and Lani, my hope that they both will remain "feisty girls." To my old friend, George S. Lechner, for our many conversations about reflective teaching and *charis*, my deep appreciation for the gifts of his knowledge and his friendship. And most especially to my husband,

David Krikun, my great gratitude and love for twenty-three years of being the wind beneath my wings.

Jan wishes to thank the following people:

I wish to acknowledge the students whom I have taught in both undergraduate and graduate writing courses—their words have nourished me and enriched my life; I hear their voices in my dreams. And I wish to thank those whose friendship has nourished me throughout the years: Barbara and Michael Adams, Arthur Cash, Judith Dorney, Carole Levin, Patti Phillips, Deborah Roth, and Robert and Kappa Waugh. Most of all I thank Mary Gordon, my trusted friend, reader, and critic of twenty-five years, and my family—Mae and Harold Zlotnik; Marilyn Zlotnik, Peter Hultberg, Samantha and Gabriel; Adrienne and George Todd and Mechelle, Jared, and Dylan; Gayle Guistizia, Segev, and Yotam. Family means so much to me. Finally, I thank my husband, Philip Schmidt, and my son, Reed Schmidt, for their unending gifts of love. Their love has sustained me.

We hope that this anthology returns, in small part, some of the pleasures that we have received from our relationships with these special people.

Introduction

Menopause suddenly is "in." Its treatment as a disorder is big medical business, and its consideration as a discrete phenomenon by popular and academic presses is a big industry. In the biomedical literature, in popular culture texts, on the Internet, in anthropological explorations, in feminist polemics, and in daily conversation women's aging body is discussed, debated, problemitized, publicized, and politicized. Not since the 1960s have the bodies of women of our generation received so much attention. Intellectual controversies and personal choices seem to abound: is menopause a time of potential pathology (a "staggering catastrophe"—Robert A. Wilson 1966), of crisis ("a woman is often unhinged at the change of life"—Edward Tilt 1870), or of opportunity? At midlife are we "dangerous women" or women of power? Do we face aging and menopause with bitterness and dread, as wrote Simone de Beauvoir, or with "zest" (attributed to Margaret Mead)? Will this stage bring us a "partial death" (Helene Deutsch 1945)? Now at last will we experience the emergence of our "true selves" (Germaine Greer 1992)? Or is this really adolescence in reverse as others have claimed? Should we face it naturally or with a little help from hormones?

What about those of us who have spent our professional lives as academics? Coming of age with the women's movement, many of us gained access to power through our professional choices; we achieved academic successes; some of us nurtured families; and many of us juggled community and political commitments as well. Now suddenly (it seems) we are middle-aged. We face aging partners and aged parents, departing children, younger faces at faculty meetings, increasingly younger faces in the classroom, and for the most part, financial stability and reasonable health. Experienced in reflective practice in other aspects of our professional lives, we now feel committed to examining this transition in our own lives as well. But where are our models of aging at midlife? And if we are without these models, how do we face this next chapter of our working lives? What fears and hopes are present for us, what changes and transformations await us? And what legacy do we wish to leave for our junior colleague-sisters? Having so far negotiated a settlement between the life we were capable of and the one we chose (Grumet 1988), we ask what this next life chapter will bring. Is this transition likely to be "much rougher" than that of our male colleagues who, some claim, seem to "mellow" in midlife (Apter 1995)?

Why pay attention to a bodily process at all? Isn't there something unseemly or undignified about exploring reproductive status and menopause, especially in relationship to our professional roles? Furthermore, hadn't many of us, particularly in the sciences, long ago worked hard to banish any hint of softness (read: subjectivity) from our thinking, intent on being taken seriously by our male colleagues? Would a serious scholar/teacher risk all by considering a taboo subject such as this one? But what is the cost of continued silence? Perhaps as Audre Lorde wrote in *The Cancer Journals* (1980), self-conscious living, living without silence, is a tool to combat powerlessness and separation from other women.

This silence pervades the issue of developmental change in adult learners in the academy. The work on cognitive and ethical positions held by college students through their first-year postgraduation by Perry (1970), Belenky et al. (1986), Baxter-Magolda (1992), and others has changed how many of us engage our classes and bring students along to more advanced positions during their college careers. Yet this literature remains strangely silent on the developmental changes of teachers themselves.

Although there is some literature on changes in intellectual orientation in teaching assistants and in beginning teachers, most schema end with categories called "mastery" or "expertise" as if when this level is once achieved, it need never be surpassed. But teaching is after all a "work in progress." There is always some new road to travel, some new goal to aim for, some teaching pinnacle just out of reach. Some other cognitive position might better serve in one class than in another or when encountering one kind of material rather than another. Furthermore, perhaps teaching professionals achieve new cognitive positions as they age. Even Chickering and Havinghurst's (1981) widely cited chapter on developmental issues facing college students from ages eighteen to sixty-five fails to consider whether teachers too face developmental challenges at midlife. Surely middle-aged women (and men) have developmental issues that have an impact on their teaching. Menopause is not a unitary point in time or in space, but rather a process occurring over several years that likely affects myriad aspects of women's lives. So too the process of becoming a good teacher takes years and is affected (and affects) not only our cognitive processes, but also our physical body, our emotions, our self-image, our relationships, our spiritual selves, and our worldview. Is there a "felt sense" of teaching, a bodily awareness or an internal sense that encompasses teaching (Gendlin 1981, 32), and if so, how is it affected by menopause? A developmental perspective might yield insight into this whole-body, inside-out aspect of teaching practice in a way that up to now mostly has been absent in the teaching literature.

QUESTIONS, ISSUES, CHALLENGES

Many women at midlife suddenly do feel free to consider just these kinds of questions, to give voice to this material, and to explore areas that would have been unthinkable at earlier career and life stages. Isn't this part of the promise of midlife, to be freed from those constraints and concerns of youth and inexperience? Furthermore, as Banner and Cannon point out in *The Elements of Teaching* (1997), committed teachers recognize that "we animate inert knowledge with qualities of our own personality," with our "spirit" and with the dimensions of our character (2). As teachers, we are called on to draw on those parts of ourselves that can enhance and accommodate our students' learning. And this teaching character must be "authentic" (113). As we age and mature, so too must our teaching. Authentic teaching requires reflective practice. Teaching personalities that fit at twenty-five are not those that are authentic at fifty.

As we considered these issues, we asked ourselves questions about our own developmental struggle as midlife women teachers. We began a conversation through a journal exchange. In our journals several themes emerged: accepting aging bodies; facing time, change, loss, finitude; living zestfully. Our discussions led us to wonder how other women were negotiating this midlife passage. We looked for models in other women's words, but, instead, we found works discussing menopause, visions of aging, and a few autobiographical accounts of midlife transitions. But few works directly explored what life is like for women at midlife teaching in the academy. This anthology evolved, then, out of our desire for an extended dialogue among a varied group of midlife teachers. We asked each participant to the volume to create a self-reflective, autobiographical essay prompted by the following questions:

- As women professionals we are unlikely to be immune to the assumptions, debates, and competing discourses on midlife that swirl around us in our culture. What images represent our menopausal experiences?
- How do the controversies about midlife manifest themselves in our personal and public lives? In the views of our aging body? In our work in the academy?
- Who are we in the classroom at midlife and what metaphors now shape our teaching experiences?
- What is life like for a woman faculty member at midlife? Is there a local culture of the professional office/academy comparable to what cross-cultural investigators uncover? Are our work worlds separate territories with rules and conventions, language, and social norms that shape not only conceptions of teaching but of life at midlife as well?
- Are the midlife experiences of historically underrepresented women teachers different from those of other teachers?
- What special challenges face women entering the profession at midlife?
- Have women claimed a territory, a place of centeredness, an outlook that sustains them in the face of change, loss, opportunity, and finitude?

We wondered what kind of patterns would emerge from the diverse writers' consideration of these questions. We realized that these might be our questions framed to fill our needs at this time in our lives. What would other midlife women decide were the most important issues for them? We were surprised often in the process of asking women to write with us: some women refused to contribute because they were uncomfortable about the autobiographical format; others were insulted at being considered middle-aged; and others agreed to participate despite reservations about either the time commitment or the prospect of writing in a form quite different from their usual academic work.

We present here the words of those who accepted our challenge to reconceive their pasts, to do that "second living [that] is both spiritual and historical" that Patricia Hampl (1993, 601) suggests is at the heart of the autobiographical journey. The journeys for these women writers took on many forms—meditative, narrative, critical. However, what connects them is the impulse to scrutinize the experience of teaching at midlife, to "[reach] deep within the personality" and "[seek] ... narrative form" and to represent "the life-of-the-times" (1993, 601), the life of the academic woman teaching in the academy.

Thematic Perspectives

We found as we reread the essays that thematic strands emerged in the fabric of our texts. One of the most striking themes is the reconceptualization of living in the female body at midlife. Instead of viewing the menopause and midlife transitions in Helene Deutsch's terms as a phase of "general dissolution" (1945), many of us have experienced a resurgence of physical, sexual, emotional, and psychic energy. In this spirit, Lynne Taetzsch accepts such inevitable physiological manifestations of her "aging body" as loss of memory as she also declares that she wants to "differentiate [herself] from the group named *older women*": she "could still be outrageous and cool." Similarly, Mimi Schwartz, confronting aging and the prospect of retirement, represents this time as fulfilling as epitomized in her intimate, tender relationship with her husband and in her desire to emulate her neighbor Mary and be a "risk-taker" in old age. For Patricia Phillips and Marlene Schiwy midlife is a time to reconfigure body space and the space of teaching as a fluid, open, dynamic place of change—an open space suggestive of Chantal Chawaf's (1980, 177–78) place of "linguistic flesh" where "the corporeality of language" and body reminds us that "life is of the utmost importance." As Jan Schmidt suggests, we struggle to live bounteous lives. It is a place where, as Patti Phillips reflects, "recursive" rhythms of stasis and change create an open, dynamic teaching environment—a space, in Schiwy's terms of feminine energy, where "heart and mind and soul all nourish each other." In this space of teaching, Mary Gordon reflects, "the girl" in us is resurrected. Instead of seeing the face of the mid-forties woman in the mirror, Gordon sees the figure of her youth, the portent of both past and future time.

As living in the body is reenvisioned, so too are midlife transitions. Instead of viewing midlife as an inevitable time of psychic diminution, many of us pose the question asked by Genia Pauli Haddon: How do we in menopause "confront death while there is still time to live"? (Haddon 1991, 349). How do we accept limits, the concept of finitude, what Christine Downing calls "the central task of menopause": "There are limits to what the heroic spirit can achieve, some obstacles which no amount of courage or energy can overcome...and the hero goes on anyway, knowing this" (Downing 1987, 84).

Many of us confront the concomitant, inevitable losses of middle age: career crises, illness, life after children, the evisceration of youthful idealism;

and we gain renewed strength from turning inward, from self-exploration and understanding. A repeated theme in the volume is the rejection of what Jane Tompkins calls the "world of rows," obedience to external authorities, characteristic of the "first part of life," and the discovery of sources of strength and authentic selfhood through turning inward.

One of the realizations expressed in many of the essays is that we cannot "do it all." We lose the sense that we are able to be "superwomen," and we realize what passions need to be nourished and what we must give up. Thus, Julia Alvarez reveals that out of an "anguishing process" of examining "impossible choices," she finally decided to leave a tenured position, fulfilling work with students, and a world of education that has defined her life in order to devote more energy and time to writing. "Part of being older and wiser," Alvarez contends, "is learning to work with the nature I've been given." Not only do we accept limitations imposed by the demands of our own natures, but several of the essayists also express a loss of a youthful idealism borne out of the social turmoil of the 1960s. Gayle Pemberton's reflections represent a recurring motif in the volume. Her younger self believed that "activism would come in teaching well...all or some of the wonderful writers, white and black, from this side of the Atlantic." She desired to work for an expansive literary canon and "real equity in North American society." And although she recognizes "there is very little progress or commitment to real equity" and that "after twenty-five years [she is] beyond exhaustion in fighting for real fairness," she still believes in teaching and affirms that "literature is more important than it ever was. Its message is more urgent."

Gail Griffin, too, voices a loss of faith in students, teaching, feminism, yet despite this loss of idealism, she affirms a cycle of ripening: "a clearing of space, a falling away of old structures to make room for something new but ancient-seeming: a deep sense of process and cycle, a certain stillness at the heart of constant motion." As a result of this process of ripening, a new-born sense of rootedness and strength emerges. Diane Glancy's metaphor for this process mirrors stances depicted in many of the essays: "daubing"—a reiterative process of scrutiny, spiritual meditation, patient industry, and fixed shaping of a life. She explains: "I kept singing my work a song to live."

With this sense of rootedness comes a concomitant feeling of empowerment: a drive for the visibility that Audre Lorde (1980, 20) believes "without which we also cannot truly live." Embracing visibility, for example, leads Tikva Frymer to declare herself a "first woman"— a "pioneer...the lead goose, breaking the wind for others." Diane Halpern provides a vision of "academic courage"; she urges readers to "believe in your own research and work even when you are presenting 'unpopular conclusions,' your work is being attacked, and . . . you are [being] vilified." She counsels readers to have the "courage to ask the tough questions and conduct the tough research." "Academic courage" also prompts several other contributors to confront the racism and sexism of the academy. In her essay, Paula Gunn Allen announces her decision to retire from academia and presents her disgust with a "system of the invidious." Finally, Dean Falk critiques the sexism of the "traditional, male-oriented publish-or-perish arena" and suggests that the more qualified, the more powerful a woman is in the academy, the more likely she is to become a target and to be viewed as an academic "witch," to be "burnt alive at the stake." Perhaps we were most unprepared for the vehemence and anger of the positions taken in these essays. But the anger does not consume or paralyze these women; rather, it fuels action and self-reflection.

This sense of power also shapes models of transformative pedagogy. Prevalent throughout the volume are visions of teaching that Christa Walck suggests are a "way of being and doing that construct who [we are]." We do not present ourselves as objectified, depersonalized figures in the classroom who impart knowledge; rather, an intersubjective, interactive, dialogic process takes place in which our identities as teachers are continuously constructed and reshaped by our encounters in the classroom. As Walck reveals, her previous "persona," prior to her awakening, "seemed not to be [her] but someone else [she] had constructed to do the teaching. She set up experiences for others, manipulated the action, provided information, and in doing so, set herself aside under the guise of interaction." As Walck describes how she "be[came]" an "artist" in the classroom and reimagined syllabi, the physical space of the classroom, assignments, encounters with the subject matter of the course, she realizes that she has become the "explorer" in the classroom, capturing the "life of the spirit." This spirit of embodied teaching is apparent in many of the reflections. The classroom, according to Judy Scales-Trent, brings together "fragment[s] of identity" and is a place to be "centered," as opposing worlds of "home" and "school," "poetry" and "legal texts," "love and work," are connected and reintegrated.

Another sustained theme is the movement, in Margaret Matlin's words, from a "lecturer/banker" to "midwife teacher," signaled by a classroom dynamic that features "mutual engagement" (hooks), mutual passion for ideas, a critical and dialogical exchanges of ideas, and a mutual responsibility for the creation of learning. Esther Chow's essay presents a methodology echoed in our approaches to teaching: a process of "critical consciousness that redefines the purposes, the process, and the outcomes of teaching and learning"; that values the "lived experiences of class members" and the connections of self and knowledge; and that acknowledges students' "multiple voices" and perspectives and engages them in participatory education. Implicit in many of these models of feminist teaching is an expression of political activism, as bell hooks describes it, "an openness of mind and heart that allows us to face reality even as we collectively imagine ways to move beyond boundaries."

Moving beyond established institutional boundaries is also a concern voiced in this volume. Jean O'Barr stresses the need for women to "speak truth to power"—to challenge institutional norms and practices, to forge new visions of community that will transform the institutional milieu. Sue Rosser challenges established curricular and institutional norms to create an integrative, interdisciplinary vision of women's issues and science. Judith Dorney explores how understanding and expressing sources of anger may empower women and give them the ability to work communally to change the institutions that they work in. Finally, bell hooks acknowledges the importance of mentoring, the importance of female role models, as a force to "change the direction of our students' lives." These forms of generativity have the potential to create a more humane society, one in which life-giving values are affirmed.

What emerges in these essays in different ways is an ethos of what Phyllis Freeman names *charis*: a "cycle of giving, receiving, and returning." What many of us hope to create in our worlds in the academy is what Jane Roland Martin calls a "schoolhome": an environment in which "core values of care, concern and connection" are developed; a desire for "authentic public spaces [that] bridge public and private . . . where ordinary citizens can act with dignity, independence and vision" (cited in Belenky 1996). These homeplaces nurture body, mind, heart, intellect, and soul and offer the possibility of active transformations of learning into communal actions that sustain the human spirit and enlarge a sense of human endeavor.

We hope this volume gives readers a homeplace: a space to contemplate and to negotiate midlife passages and come to a greater understanding of what Patricia Hampl calls the "mystery" of living and teaching in time.

PART

I

Body & Time

AT MENOPAUSE LIFE CAN TURN INTO ONE LONG PREMENSTRUAL EXPERI-ENCE. HORMONES SLAP YOU UP AGAINST THE DOORS OF YOUR UNFINISHED BUSINESS.

Maura Kelsea

THE CHANGES THAT TAKE PLACE IN THE BODY OF A CLIMACTERIAL WOMAN HAVE THE CHARACTER NOT ONLY OF THE CESSATION OF PHYSIOLOGIC PRO-DUCTION BUT ALSO OF GENERAL DISSOLUTION. WOMEN'S BIOLOGIC FATE MANIFESTS ITSELF IN THE DISAPPEARANCE OF HER INDIVIDUAL FEMININE QUALITIES AT THE SAME TIME THAT HER SERVICE TO THE SPECIES CEASES. . . . [E]VERYTHING SHE ACQUIRED DURING PUBERTY IS NOW LOST PIECE BY PIECE; WITH THE LAPSE OF REPRODUCTIVE SERVICE, HER BEAUTY VANISHES, AND USUALLY THE WARM, VITAL FLOW OF FEMININE EMOTIONAL LIFE AS WELL.

Helene Deutsch

IT IS PERHAPS ONLY IN OLD AGE, CERTAINLY PAST FIFTY, THAT WOMEN CAN STOP BEING FEMALE IMPERSONATORS, CAN GRASP THE OPPORTUNITY TO REVERSE THEIR MOST CHERISHED PRINCIPLES OF "FEMININITY."

Carolyn Heilbrun

I

Teaching Where I Was Taught

Coming Home

MARY GORDON

On the fourth floor of Barnard Hall, where English classes are, and have always been, taught at Barnard College, there is a full-length mirror to the right of the elevator. Generations of women have—anxiously, joyously, distractedly—examined their reflections here. When I had a young body, an eighteen-, nineteen-, twenty-, and twenty-one-year-old body, I looked at myself in the mirror. I was coming from English class, the place where I felt at once exhilarated and protected, the place where I was finding myself and my new life. Thirty years later, I still look at myself in that mirror several times a week. But what I see now is a fifty-year-old body, and I am the teacher now.

I first came to Barnard in the spring of 1966. My two friends and I had just been admitted to Barnard, and we were coming to look in on some classes on a day off from our Catholic school in Queens. It must have been a Holy Day of Obligation, otherwise there would have been no reason for Barnard to be in session while we were free. Perhaps it was Holy Thursday or the Feast of the Ascension. Perhaps we lied to our parents and said we would go to Mass first.

Was it punishment for that lie that led us to get off the subway at the wrong 116th Street, 116th and Lenox? The man in the token booth took one look at our clothes and faces and guessed our mistake without our having to say anything. "This isn't Broadway, girls," he said, as if we were hick starlets with straw valises. He told us to take the subway back down to 42nd St, then the shuttle, then the West Side train uptown. We didn't listen. We walked across 116th Street, through Harlem, through Morningside Park, fearless, pretending we felt at home, knowing that our parents would be appalled.

When I arrived in September, a commuter, traveling back to my mother's house each night, I felt that I had finally discovered my true home. A country where each experience was vivid, and I often felt my head swam. I discovered the Romantic poets were not romantic and that I did not like them, except for Keats, that I preferred the Renaissance, so, after reading Sidney and Donne and Herbert and Marvell and the Revenge Tragedians, I took a course on Tasso and Ariosto, taught by an Italian, and on Ronsard, taught by a Russian Jew brought up in France. I heard a snatch of Hindemith and spent the day in the library listening to his music, earphones on my ears like a radio announcer. I discovered the paintings of Van Eyck and took the bus crosstown on Friday afternoons to the Metropolitan to see for myself. I could sense the material of my mind thinning, spreading, growing transparent; sometimes I was feverish with the excitement of what I was learning and the skin around my eyes felt abraded, and my eyes felt lashed, and after hours studying in the library, I would go outside and the color of the sky at six o'clock on an October evening—slate blue, shot through with black—seemed as inviting and dangerous as if I were a child playing too late too hard and at any minute I might be called in. But I was not called in; I was told to stay out later, to travel farther, the world of ideas was mine, I belonged here, I could inhabit any region of it. I knew myself a poet, but I didn't want to be a fake, like some I suspected, so I set myself tasks so that I could honor my calling: I wrote villanelles and curtal sonnets and translated from the Italian and revised all night. A teacher suggested that I might really be a fiction writer and I said, no of course I'm not, I'm a poet: I am, (can't you see) in love with form and its restrictions, so different from the unrestricted life, which as a poet, I intended to live.

In the spring of my freshman year, the time of the Columbia Riots, I got where I wanted to be, but where I wanted to be changed radically in a few days, and this change made the distance my friends and I traveled even greater.

Only now do I understand the speed at which we then were forced to travel. In six months we went from processions where we crowned a statue of the Virgin with a wreath of flowers to linking hands with strangers, learning what to do in case of tear gas or cops run amok. The same girls who in the spring had been singing, "O Mary we crown thee with blossoms today / Queen of the Angels, Queen of the May," were chanting the following autumn, "Hey, hey, LBJ, how many kids did you kill today?"

A year earlier I had been presiding over student council meetings where we had to decide on an appropriate punishment for girls who'd been caught getting into a car with a boy WHILE STILL IN UNIFORM; now I was sitting in on teach-ins on the lawn in front of Butler Library where we contemplated "burning the whole fucking place down."

People dropped out, or at least stopped going to classes, but I never did, except during the riots when the teachers I liked canceled classes or excused us from attending. But except for those weeks, I entered the buildings of Barnard, which offered a solidity—their smell, the width of the staircases, the cool stone of the banisters. I was taught by women, who told me I was gifted, wellborn women with hair hanging down their backs or coiled in blond knots at their napes, elegant men in houndstooth jackets who smoked pipes and told me of people I never heard of whom I got confused: Arthur Henry Hallam, Arthur Hugh Clough. One summer, one of these teachers arranged for me to have a summer grant, which meant that for the first time since I was fifteen, I didn't have to work at an office job all summer. I went to Harvard and studied Italian. I walked through Harvard Yard instead of to a mimeograph machine.

So when I stand in front of the mirror as a teacher at Barnard, I am very conscious of repaying a debt. I cannot repay it directly. I am not one of those wellborn men and women with a knot at the nape of my neck or a herringbone jacket. I bring my own history, my own gifts, to the project of my teaching. And the students are both similar to me, and, because of the accidents of the outside world, quite different.

This semester I have two small classes. One is what we call a senior seminar; each senior is required to write thirty pages on a topic connected to the seminar she is taking. She, it is always a she: Barnard is a women's college, and no Columbia students (male or female) are allowed into senior seminars. This seminar is my ideal teaching situation: I can teach books that I love; teaching them requires a close reading on my part, and this close reading will nourish my own writing. I am teaching a new course this semester; I've called it "Lyrical Prose." I'm trying to trace what I believe is a firm but undernoticed pattern in American literature, a tradition of sensuous writing that adheres to the most rigorously classical standards of sentence construction and formal arrangement. I will teach Willa Cather, Katherine Ann Porter, Jean Stafford, Eudora Welty, Elizabeth Bishop, and

Louise Bogan. At the beginning of the semester, the students have never heard of Stafford or Bogan; they may have read one story of Porter's in high school; they vaguely know that Welty is old, southern, and still alive. By the end of the semester, the students are on fire with enthusiasm for these women writers. Why are their books out of print, they cry, their voices full of fighting spirit. They speak of these women's courage, their aesthetic daring, their way of following an image, staying with it until it is saturated. They are alive with their own sense of discovery and kinship with these women who have gone before them, marking a place that time and fashion have allowed to become overgrown. But they will clear the place, they will tell their friends to read these wonderful books, and if they themselves teach, they will teach them to their own students.

I teach this class both similarly and differently from the way I was taught. I was never taught literature by practicing writers; the practicing writers taught me only in writing workshops. So I have a kind of stake in this writing that my own professors didn't have—not to say that they didn't have a stake, but it was a different one. I also, being of a different temperament and with a different history (I am of another generation and I am not Protestant), feel free to vent about the injustice of these writers being virtually unread, two of them nearly out of print. What I learned from the teachers I had was the importance of close reading, and the leading of students to a faith in their own God-given right to look at language hard, to unpack it of its meanings, to coax it to reveal its treasures and its charms.

My other class is a fiction-writing workshop. In my own writing workshop of thirty years ago, we wrote very differently. Virginity and its loss were major topics. We wrote nothing positive about our mothers; our mothers were the wardens of our sexuality; they were our enemies; we had to conceal things from them. In my students' stories, there are lines like, "Mom, can you please close the door when you and your boyfriend are fucking?" They can use the word "fuck" in class, and we can discuss whether or not it is an appropriate level of diction, and whether the explicit sexual descriptions are good or bad as plot devices. Many of them are the children of western Europeans, but many are not. How I identify with their struggles not to disappoint parents who have struggled too hard so that they can be here! Their parents tell them stories about Korea, of Taiwan, of an Ireland torn apart by the IRA, of the experiences and pressures of being the recipients of affirmative action. These stories have the same shapes, create the same conflicts, as the ones my friends and I had. Parents, brought up in scarcity and danger, want only safety and prosperity for their children. A writer's life is not conducive to safety and prosperity. Whereas, in my generation, parents might have wanted their daughters to marry a doctor or a lawyer, these parents want their daughters to become doctors or lawyers. The pressure on us was to give up writing and marry: on these young women, it is to give up writing and go to med school. But I cannot say to my students, even looking at the good fortune of my own life, that writing will bring safety and prosperity. I must tell the truth: writing will open you up to all sorts of literal and metaphoric risks. I can try to support the decision to take the risks, but I cannot minimize them in my accounts of my own life, a life they look to as a model. I can't quite believe it, that I'm not one of them, that they look at me and see someone, if not old, then no longer young, someone whose life is more than half over, someone whose life has already been substantially shaped. What happened to the girl in the mirror? How does she connect to the woman at the podium, at the head of the seminar table, giving out Kleenex and praise during conferences and office hours? Where did this girl go?

Educated in a women's college, dominated by a female faculty, I have a prejudice in favor of single-sex education, but it's not one I can quantify or support with details. I only know the difference in atmosphere when I teach a class of all, or primarily, women. There is an atmosphere of ease, of lightness in the room, which isn't there when there are more males. Not that the males are, one by one, more aggressive or less generous spirited. So I cannot justify my assertion, except by observation: women among women speak more freely, more expansively. They are jokier, bolder. They allow each other to experiment, to fail, and to revise. They are less afraid; perhaps they aren't worrying about being attractive.

I believe that in my teaching I am passing on a torch that too many people believe is dying with my generation: the torch that is set aflame by the burning love of literature. My students love the books they read as I loved them; they see in them a promise, a possibility, a richness of life they can find nowhere else. Even though they have MTV and the Internet, they would rather read these books than do these or many other things of far greater profit to themselves and, perhaps, the families who pay for their being able to study with me. People say to me: Doesn't your teaching take away from your writing? It is, of course, time-consuming and physically exhausting. But it gives me what many of my writer friends do not have: a sense of hope. The belief that what we love will not die with us. This is worth losing sleep for.

Isn't it better to lose sleep reading a student's work than to lose sleep afraid that what you do in the world is meaningless?

And so, when I look at my older, tireder body in the mirror, I am grateful for the opportunity to so joyously repay the debt to those teachers who opened a world for me, a world I would not without them have believed I had the right to inhabit. Standing with my students, waiting for the elevator, all of us pretending not to look at our own images, I am more able than otherwise, I think, to keep the girl alive.

2

Game Plans

MIMI SCHWARTZ

Yesterday a friend told me that she quit her twenty-five-year job as fashion editor on a New York magazine because she couldn't compete with all those thirty-year-olds, so eager, so pretty. "They make me feel like a hundred and six!" she said, slumped into the corner of our lunch booth and eating french fries instead of her usual salad, dressing on the side.

"You're ridiculous! You look terrific!" I said, but, in fact, Carole looked older than she did six months before when she was working twelve-hour days, plus commuting to Manhattan. Her blond hair had turned almost imperceptibly gray, and she seemed smaller somehow, weighed down. Maybe it was because she'd just cleaned all her kitchen cabinets for the first time in twenty years and was starting on her closets. To simplify, that's her game plan, she said. But her energy level kept dropping, even if her high blood pressure did not.

I'll never retire, I told myself two hours later while in a department meeting at my college. We were discussing plans for our program's five-year self-study. "Who will do the assessment chapter?" asked Jack, a cheerful, smooth-faced man younger than I (but he has less hair), who became program coordinator after me.

"I'd love to, Jack, but . . ." It was Pam, looking fifteen instead of thirty-six, shaking her pixie face. "I'm swamped." She used to be my student not that long ago. "Me too!" said Linda—was she forty yet?—pleading that she had to run a conference. "Let's not do it!" said Penny, our rebel, just turned fifty. She was making her case based on principle, while I was looking at myself on the wall of faculty photos to my right. Not so bad: long cascading hair, come-hither smile, trim plaid suit of a new assistant professor raring to go at thirty-nine. Was that a freed-jailbird look in my smile (this was my first full-time job after eighteen years as Mom and Mrs. Schwartz), or just the pleasure that came from being around people who didn't ask, "What's for dinner?"

"Mimi, how about it?" I heard dimly, just as I realized how old that photo was. I gave that suit away, along with my favorite gray sweater dress, when I hit fifty and developed new muscles from lap swimming. Nothing more, I had assured myself, despite a few extra pounds, well, maybe eight or ten extra. "So Mimi?" Jack kept pressing, the other pipsqueaks eyeing me, some fingers tapping. My God, I was the oldest one in this room! "Okay, okay," I said, dumbfounded. Maybe Carole was right.

Three hours later I was slumped in the last row of a poetry reading given by an old high school buddy turned poet. The audience was crammed with young women, drawn to his black satin vest, dare-me smile, and way of making love with his voice. He, at fifty-five, is in his prime, and I am old, I fumed, crossing my arms to cover a belly stuffed with too many of Carole's french fries. A girl with a deep cleavage and ringed nose arched her back before him, as he stroked his graying beard, reading about tenderness: "it's a word I see now/you must be older to use" (Stephen Dunn, "Tenderness").

I was sitting next to a young guy with random curls and the kind of broad shoulders I fell for in my husband a hundred years ago. Random curls and I accidentally bumped elbows, and I whispered, "Sorry!" all set to smile, but he looked right past me. So I pictured him with a black eye that he'd later say some old lady gave him—and felt like the woman in Doris Lessing's *Summer before the Dark* who, when her hair suddenly turned gray, wanted to shout to everyone: "I'm here, can't you see? Why don't you look at me?" But my roots are totally covered (unlike the poet's graying beard) and always will be, thanks to Pam at Metropolis Salon. No fair, no fair.

"Even if I won a Pulitzer Prize, men wouldn't line up like sitting ducks for a woman over fifty," I said over the celery dip at the reception after the poetry reading. I was talking to the poet's editor, a woman close to seventy, maybe more, who had driven two hours from Manhattan for this celebratory evening. We were talking about women in the workplace, and I mentioned how Carole and other women I knew (not me, of course) were feeling too old to compete.

"Nonsense," said this five-foot platinum blonde with a smile that demolished her wrinkles. "I love to be around young people. Except for Stephen, my authors are all twenty, thirty, forty years younger than I am, and we still pal around together." She had just been in the Rockies hiking with one, as a matter of fact.

Indeed, she was surrounded by people, men and women, young and old. Two were aspiring writers, hoping for discovery, but the others included somebody's husband, who was a plumber, and one of my students, a biology major who had come for extra credit. They had no agenda other than good talk with a peppy woman who made everyone feel like the only one in the room: How interesting! No, no, you must do it! I'm so glad you told me that! She beamed nonstop. I straightened my shoulders and made room for a young woman in a minidress. She had my old haircut, long and loose, without the split ends that made me cut mine to neck length when I was forty-eight, shorn as a femme fatale, a woman who could wear favorite sweater dresses without a second thought.

But male faculty still flirted, and my students (unlike my two teenagers at home) actually listened to me! So what if I wasn't a cool big sister like pixie-faced Pam, never went to a Dead concert, and used Tylenol as my drug of choice? I could still teach them a thing or two, my students believed, and that made me march through the back door of my home at night in triumph: I'm here! Can't you see? And my family did; they saw Mim, Professor Schwartz, Mom, Hon, all rolled into one woman I loved being.

After the poetry reading I drove home on an almost empty road with oncoming headlights few and far between. Yes, my cabinets would stay messy because—my eyes started closing until I opened the windows and began singing with the Golden Oldies on WRDR—because... *"That old black magic has me in its spell"*... because... What was I thinking? *"Those icy fingers up and down my spine"*... Oh... that I wouldn't retire even if my hair was now ear length and I wore big sweaters over stirrup stretch pants. Unlike my mother and friends, I refused to squeeze into a lifetime of girdles to hide a few lumps and bumps.

And if I did eventually quit my job... *"Down, down, down, I go"*... someday I would be like my neighbor Mary, not like Carole. When she wasn't cleaning cabinets, Carole was granny nanny for two working daughters: Mondays in Manhattan, Thursdays in Philadelphia, and on call the rest of the week. No wonder she was tired. Or was it fear of forgetting the fine editor she was, all that status gone? I pulled into the driveway of a dark house. My husband, Stu, had gone to sleep already.

But Mary wasn't tired or afraid. Last week, at seventy-nine, she nailed a FOR SALE sign on the lawn of her house, a pleasant gray ranch with a huge oak for shade and daylilies conferring like friends under two large picture windows.

"You're moving?" I asked, amazed. This trim, green-eyed Smith graduate with silver hair and polished apple cheeks has lived on our block forever. She was always upbeat and on the go to concerts, bridge, and volunteer work, and if she ever worked for a salary, I don't remember what she did; it never mattered.

"Yes, I'm off to Merrick Gardens. The house is too much."

"But you're managing so well!"

"I'm rattling around without Mac. Besides, if my right eye goes like my left one, what then? I'm stuck at home with a homecare aide, feeling sorry for myself. At Merrick, I'll have a lovely, sunny apartment and meals downstairs so I don't have to cook." She patted my shoulder. "There'll be plenty of bridge games and company when I want it. And when I don't, I'll just shut the door." She laughed. "I'll be fine."

She spoke as if she were about to take off for Borneo, Antarctica, or the Sudan, the way she and Mac did every summer until he dropped dead two years ago mowing the lawn. Mary had mowed ever since, making the half acre seem like nothing for her. Now, still smiling, she was leaving a half century of memories in one house behind, afraid or not.

Now she is a risk taker, I decided at 2:13 A.M., throwing off the blanket to cool a hot flash while Stu snored. Usually the sound lulled me into a rhythm, but not when I began imagining myself not as Mary, but as the woman in my student's essay:

> My grandma baked the best cookies, her bent back over the oven door, testing for doneness. Her withered hands were always ready with a hug for me, her wrinkled face smiling with love.

Nothing unusual about it—love and oldness, like all the grandma essays in this autobiography class—until she mentioned her grandmother's age: sixty! I've always pictured these sweet old things as ninety, like my Tante Elsa (who's actually eighty-two, but sees herself as one hundred plus). Her world keeps shrinking because it's either "too hot outside" or "too cold" or "too far to go with her arthritis."

"You should go to the Senior Resource Center! It's a block away and you could get a hot lunch for a dollar," I say every time I visit, because her refrigerator is always empty ("Food Mart is delivering later..."). The blinds are also drawn, and I want to let the Manhattan skyline back in, but all I am allowed is one turn of the three-way switch on her table lamp.

"I don't know anyone there."

"You'll meet them."

"Maybe in a few weeks." Her jaw becomes set. "I have everything I need right here." She surveys her graying walls and spotted carpet that she no longer sees. "But believe me," she advises, "enjoy yourself now. Growing old is not for sissies."

Tante Elsa will let Fate decide her future—a fall in the tub, a stroke, a nursing home unchosen—rather than reinvent herself in any way. The woman who once plied me with *apfel kuchen* and Time's optimism—"When you grow up," she'd assure me regularly at her kitchen table, "the growing pains in your legs will stop." And later, "Your baby fat will disappear and boys will love you." And later, "Your daughter's colic will stop . . . Your son won't be afraid of robbers . . ."—now sits in dark rooms of regret that let no future in.

I will not let my walls close in on me, I vow as the woodpecker starts hammering against our brick chimney the way he does every May morning. I move toward my husband's belly as I have for thirty-seven years and wonder what he'll do if I die first. Sell the house? Lose thirty pounds and move to Malibu Beach—his fantasy for years—to surf the big waves with young blondes in shoestring bikinis cheering him on? I wish him luck; the dead don't get jealous easily.

If he dies first, I'll stay put for a while—drawn to the brightness of my kitchen windows and the way mornings here surprise me: the changing hues of the maple tree, the way hemlocks lean in the rain, and the squirrels finding new ways to raid the bird feeder. I might even clean my kitchen cabinets in between writing time and running a newspaper for inner-city youth (something I've been meaning to start for years). Maybe I'll hire a young handyman with dragon tattoos to admire or get a boyfriend like Mary, who is dating an old flame who is eighty-seven. And when I bake cookies with my grandchildren, it'll be in stretch pants and four-inch-heeled boots, no bent back and Easy Spirit shoes for me, no way. Unless, of course, my back gives out, which it won't because I'll be swimming laps daily and playing tennis in the Senior League. It has ninety-year-olds in it, I hear. And yes, okay, I'll sign up for Merrick Gardens when it's time (it takes years to get in and you don't have to go), so I won't end up like Tante Elsa—or her father. He sat alone for years in his black armchair by a darkened window, imagining locomotives flying over treetops to a world he could not reach.

Yes, that's my game plan, I vow as the digital clock reads 6:06 A.M. the sound of woodpecker fades. It'll work, just keep looking forward, I say, and I stop hearing Henry Miller's words: "I believe everything you tell me but I know it will all turn out differently." The vines on the wallpaper blur and someone is murmuring that I'm a dynamo, real sexy in jeans, and I dance barefoot on grapes in firelight to shouts of Olé—just as the alarm clock (Who set that?) goes off. Stu's side is empty (Where is he?) so I curl into my own warmth, but then the comforter disappears, hands pull me from my dream, and I hear, as my pillow slips beneath me, "How come I still love you when I'm up and you're still lying in bed?"

3

"Pregnant with [Myself], at Last"

Images of Midlife/A Journal Entry

JAN ZLOTNIK SCHMIDT

> THE WOMAN WHO IS WILLING TO MAKE THAT CHANGE MUST
> BECOME PREGNANT WITH HERSELF, AT LAST. SHE MUST BEAR HER-
> SELF, HER THIRD SELF, HER OLD AGE, WITH TRAVAIL AND ALONE.
>
> *Ursula Le Guin, "The Space Crone"*

As I work on this project with Phyllis, reread my journal from the past year and a half, the time between forty-nine and fifty-one, I am awash in images of midlife that crystallize like iconic inscriptions in miniature and suggest so many experiences collapsed in single moments.

First I see the figure of Degas's ballet dancer. Her round belly jutting out, her feet awkwardly placed in third position in front of her, she strains for movement. And I think of my early years in the classroom—a time marked by my earnest anxiety about performance. I often asked myself: Was I doing well enough? As I strained toward the students, tension and insecurity shaped my posture and the texture of my days.

Then I see a thin Monet poplar—a yellow-brown trunk and blue-violet feathery leaves. The tree reminds me of the scraggly white birch, the tall lean trees in the forest that I adored as a child. A child scratching designs on the bleached white, parchmentlike skin of the tree. I knew then as I do now that I wanted to teach; wanted to create; wanted to write. Now I see myself as a woman "pregnant with herself." No longer as unnerved by her interactions with students; less worried about approval; more able to connect, to listen; to give herself over to the pleasure of others' stories, I am more able to enjoy and feel renewed by the task of teaching the young.

And yet there are many losses. I see my body resembling a Giacometti bronze—skeletal, perilously close to falling, yet mysteriously solid. I have experienced those deaths that mark middle age. My aunt starved herself to death, closing her lips to food; my mother-in-law died in my arms as I tried to revive her through artificial respiration—she spit her last breath into my mouth; three close friends all died suddenly in their fifties; my son has left for college (the day after he left I went into his empty room and sobbed, relishing the slight, vestigial odor of his tennis shoes and powder); my husband has taken a job in another city (our life in our one-hundred-year-old farmhouse near the river gone forever); and finally, the university and society at large seem so much more inhospitable if not downright destructive to those feminist values and issues of social justice that I have believed in fervently—beliefs borne out of the social upheaval of my college years in the 1960s. I feel dispossessed. All my homes are lost to me.

And my own home in my own body forsakes me. The doctor calls after a checkup to tell me that my blood tests indicate that I definitely am menopausal. I yearn for periods, for the rhythms of a youthful body that I pretty much took for granted, and dashed are my mythical hopes for a new baby—a little girl. Wonderful Mary Cassett portraits of mothers and young children float before my eyes: the baby's rosy flesh, the pink hue on the mother's cheeks as she encircles the baby with her arms; the light warm touch of air. That life is gone.

Now when I look at myself in the mirror, I realize I am going to miss the manifestations of my youthful body. Even though I have known my whole life that I was not a beauty, I still felt that I could count on a certain attractiveness—coolness, thinness. Now I see my dyed brown hair—strands of gray peeking through; lines under my eyes; my double chin; the large forearms of my grandmother; and my slightly paunchy midriff. As my students call me their "mother away from home," I know that I am entering a new phase of life.

Well, the girl is gone, and an older, wiser woman is inhabiting her body. I want to face middle age with zest, with a sense that daily life still provides moments of beauty and pleasure, that I still can ask for bounteousness. And I realize that part of this sense of bounty is a belief in kindness—in compassion—in caring relationships with others. I still believe that caring and teaching can reduce the toxins of the world. I see a Matisse still life: the lovely blue-green fish vertiginously swimming in air, the incandescent orange and red curves and shapes of the background.

And I am aware that I have changed. I have come from feeling empty, from living in what in a poem of mine from last April I called "a single room / a single room / with a window / broken by light," to a place of light and warmth and hope. How did this happen? What will happen next? I think that the journal exchange with Phyllis, the scrutiny of these changes in midlife, the challenge of facing these feelings, have given me an internal strength that I didn't possess two years ago. I know now that I must accept change and live in moments, moments of light and warmth. At the end of that poem from last April I write: "I want to say / I come from here . . . a world of white light / and green shadows / and warm yellow stones." From the perspective of middle age, I still am hungry for experience, ready for a world colored by "yellow warmth and shadow." And I want to give myself to this world as I am renewed by relationships, friendships, students, writing, and teaching.

4

"Saturating Language with Love"

Variations on a Dream

MARLENE A. SCHIWY

FEMININE CONSCIOUSNESS IS ROOTED IN THE HEART. THE FEEL-
ING COMES WITH THE THOUGHT, AND AS THE THOUGHT IS SPO-
KEN, THE HEART OPENS AND FEELING FLOWS TO DEEPER, RICHER
LEVELS.

Marion Woodman, Leaving My Father's House

Leafing back through my journal in search of clues to my recent entry into midlife, I discover a dream I had recorded in April, shortly before I received the invitation to write this piece. In my dream an anonymous and disembodied voice says, "The only way to practice God is to saturate language with love." As I hear the words being spoken, I know they are true. I feel urgently that language must be taken apart and permeated with a whole new dimension and color—the dimension of love—before it can be reassembled and made whole. In the dream I don't doubt that this is possible.

I know that an impersonal voice heard in a dream carries archetypal weight. And I knew in April and know now that this dream holds something important for me.

The night before that, my graduate modern European literature class had been discussing Christa Wolf's concept of the "living word," wherein language might be reunited with the knowledge of the senses rather than continuing in the service of Western culture's three-thousand-year-long "dangerous experiment with abstract rationality" (1984, 268). Instead of producing more heroic narrative, Wolf proposes, the living word would "greet with a smile the wrath of Achilles, the conflict of Hamlet, the false alternatives of Faust," preferring instead "to name the inconspicuous, the precious everyday, the concrete" (270–71). The feminine realm, in other words.

And there is another likely thread of meaning tied to the dream. My Wednesday evening Women's Journal Workshop had been immersed in the work of Jungian analysts Marion Woodman and Helen Luke, who tell us that feminine consciousness is rooted in the heart and manifests itself as an unfailing courtesy and kindness toward everything in life. "To hear the feminine," Woodman tells us, "we have to dare to open our receptors to old words with new meanings. Love spoken from the mind is one thing; love whispered from a volcano is another" (1992, 124).

I know immediately that these threads, with their common theme of language, are interwoven. But what kind of transformation would it take to rescue words from disembodied abstraction, to restore their concreteness and eroticism, to render language thick and fleshy, pulsing with vitality and life? And what would it mean to "saturate language with love"? Perhaps there is a clue here that I can follow—in my life, and in these early midlife reflections. I turned forty-five in October.

INTERNAL GESTURES

In the early years of teaching, my anxiety level rose as the time to walk into class approached. My breathing was quick and shallow, and often a headache accompanied me through the door. I felt the terrifying responsibility of maintaining control over myself, my words, my body, and not least, the class. My sense of self was tenuous. At the worst of times I felt it could at any moment leave my body, fly out through the top of my head. It took an enormous effort to "pull myself together" and hold my bodily space. Even while I yearned for freedom and ease of movement in the classroom, I felt the need to protect my boundaries. If I let go and relinquished control for even a moment, who knows what might happen?

It took voice lessons and a Gestalt course in group process to bring me back into my body. As I learned how to breathe deeply instead of cutting sensation off below the neck, I began to trust that there was enough oxygen and that the ground beneath my feet would support me; that I would neither "fall apart" in front of the class if I relaxed, nor float away or be obliterated by anxiety when things did not go as I'd hoped. To the contrary, my body, when I breathed deeply into it, felt solid and firmly centered. It wasn't going to leave me or go anywhere. For several semesters that became my mantra as I walked to class: "My body is heavy and solid on the earth." As I said the words, my breathing slowed down and deepened, and I felt my all-too-solid flesh become my ally, my friend, my support.

That is the first internal gesture I remember making in the classroom. There have been others over the years, perhaps most important among them, remembering to keep my heart wide open.

My Heart, Wide Open

In my work with the Women's Journal Workshop I have felt a great and unprecedented freedom to use myself exactly as I am—imperfections and all—as an invitation to intimacy, and to express the love I feel for the women who come and the material we explore together. I know that over the years the workshop has called on all that is best in me. My ability to listen with focused and loving attention. Warmth and readiness to nurture. Embodied presence and willingness to serve others. Sensitivity and discernment, intuition and spontaneity, empathy and love of beauty. For almost a decade now, the workshop has kept my heart wide open. Here I have been able to teach effortlessly from the deepest center of my being, where heart and mind and soul all nourish each other. From my journal:

> I am reading Helen Luke in preparation for Wednesday's workshop. It is always so good, so important to be reminded to dwell in the feminine realm, to value what is receptive, responsive, quiet, and hidden as much as the outward heroic quest of the masculine. Luke writes about "receptive devotion" and "creative resonance" as quintessential feminine qualities that are not recognized, much less valued in this culture. I love the term "creative resonance" because it evokes the vital receptivity and active responsiveness that can "hear women into their own speech," in the words of Nelle Morton. A listening ear had to be present in order for the Word to be received, and Morton sees here, "a complete reversal of the going logic ... a depth hearing that takes place before speaking—a hearing that is more than acute listening. A hearing that is a direct transitive verb that evokes speech—new speech that has never been spoken before." At best, this is what takes place in the workshop.

This is the most holistic and satisfying work I have ever done, from preparing original handouts and arranging the living room chairs in a circle to choosing the music we will write to that evening and baking the cakes we'll enjoy before the night is out. There is serenity and comfort in knowing that every Wednesday the house will hold a circle of women quietly exploring their inner realms, writing their lives, laughing and sometimes crying together. Comfort for me, as well as for those who come.

I like the ease of bodily movement, the spontaneity and naturalness, the humor and empathy that have come so readily in the workshop. And, over time, this freedom has gained a steadier foothold in my college classes as well. There, too, I began to make that gesture of consciously opening my heart—a gesture that has its own distinct bodily component. Another journal entry:

> Last night I remembered to open my heart in my Modern Culture class. It always feels as if invisible ripples of energy are flowing out from my body into the classroom, as if I'm inwardly blessing them. This seems to create a field of energy that contains us all, both individually and collectively, so that we're not just a group of discrete and isolated individuals anymore but a shared body of learners. The difference is palpable. I'm not sure how the class picks up the blessing from my body, but every time I remember to make the gesture, they do. It's as if the muscles around my heart relax and a barrier I didn't even know was there, dissolves and falls away. I think my entire being softens and expands. My sense of self is no longer behind the desk or in front of the class, and there's no more sense of "my space" and "their space." We are all of us everywhere in the room. And the room feels full.

Sylvia Ashton-Warner described a similar process in different terms. "When I teach people, I marry them," she reflected. "To bring them to do what I want them to do they come near me, I draw them near me, in body and in spirit. They don't know it but I do. They become part of me, like a lover" (1963, 210–11). I send myself out to them. She draws them near herself. The end is the same.

My own internal gesture affects every dimension of my teaching. Style and content subtly shift. Lecture turns into discussion, and questions become conversations. Students begin to turn to each other, not only toward me. My vocabulary and syntax become more concrete and immediate, more active and engaged. Abandoning the safety of professorial disembodiment, I am no longer an abstraction to my students. I am present to and with them in this particular moment, in this particular female body. A body kindred with theirs, of the same kind. There is kindness here, a quality for which I have increasing respect. Not with its customary watered-down connotations of a subtly condescending benevolence, but in the sense that Helen Luke intends when she writes, "The word 'kindness' is so deep because it means, for me, kinship with every person, every animal, every plant—the entire creation. Everything is kin" (1995, 183–84).

Embodiment

If my teaching can be embodied, perhaps my students' learning can be as well. Maybe they will recognize sooner than I did that understanding occurs not only in the deep dark recesses of the brain's left hemisphere, but in every cell of the body, that the body resonates in its own way as it recognizes what is authentic and important.

My most dramatic experience of this occurred when I discovered the work of Marion Woodman some years ago. At first it seemed I had stumbled across a new language and syntax, one which my mind was not sure it understood. My body, on the other hand, prickled with excitement. It reverberated to the tuning fork of her words and recognized them as shockingly true, even familiar. Reading on, I felt comforted and nourished, as if some hidden hunger were at long last being satisfied. More mysteriously, my body felt accepted and loved as I continued, page after page. Here were words that burned through to my soul. Here was my life inscribed on every page, my anguish illuminated with such compassion that I could see past the neurotic subterfuges of my ego to the authentic suffering they attempted to suppress. This was not meaningless suffering, it turned out, but to the extent that I was willing to enter it consciously, an experience that could open my heart with compassion for others in recognition of our vulnerable common humanity. Woodman tells us,

> It may help to remind yourself that if you have no experience of the wisdom of the conscious body, you are in unknown territory listening to your mother tongue. Its rhythms beat with the heart, with the emotions that circle and repeat and again repeat with totally new vibrations of feeling. Its vocabulary is simple; its knowing deep. This is not the language of polished English prose. It is heart language calling out to other hearts. (1992, 124)

The French feminists claim that language has long been cut off from its origins in the body and the earth, and that we must make our way back to those roots. "We need languages that regenerate us, warm us, give birth to us," urges Chantal Chawaf. "The word must comfort the body" (1981, 177).

This would be a living word indeed, a word that would arise out of language saturated with love.

"The feeling comes with the thought, and as the thought is spoken, the heart opens and feeling flows to deeper, richer levels" (Woodman 1992, 116). That's how it feels to me these days. An endless love affair between feeling and thinking, each feeding the other and neither attempting to dominate. How can I bring this more vividly into the college classroom?

CROSSING THE MIDLIFE THRESHOLD

Before forty, you live your persona.
After forty, you live your own life.

Halfway through the decade that Victor Hugo referred to as "the old age of youth" (while the fifties are "the youth of old age"), who is this self assumed in my writing? If there is a felt sense, an "internal aura that encompasses everything [I] feel and know" (Gendlin 1978, 32) about my life as a woman crossing the threshold into midlife, what is it ? And how can I put it—elusive, nebulous, fluid, holistic, kaleidoscopic—into words?

I am younger than I expected to be at forty-five. We all are, I suspect, but that doesn't diminish my surprise. Physically stronger and healthier than ever, I attribute my overall well-being to regular exercise and vitamins, healthy eating and a comparatively low stress level, and, not least, to my life-long "journal habit" and a loving and stable primary relationship. At forty, a variety of minor but annoying physical symptoms served warning that if I did not change my ways, I could expect more ominous problems before long. To my credit, I paid attention. I changed my diet and gradually lost fifty pounds, resumed jogging, and stopped feeling guilty about not setting the alarm clock.

Here I am, then, frequently delighted and somehow a little surprised that things have worked out as well as they have, so far. The sporadic depressions and fierce fears of eternal aloneness that haunted me during my twenties are gone. There is fulfillment in many directions, and gratitude, too, that I have been able to find a rhythm that accommodates my need for independence, creative freedom, and a meaningful community of women. The fluid balance of teaching, writing, and conducting workshops I've engaged in for the past decade has served me well. Heading off to London at age thirty to take up my British Commonwealth Fellowship, I wondered how I would ever parlay a Ph.D. in German literature into a viable career when the last thing I wanted to do was teach endless sections of German 100. How strange, now, to see how the various threads of choice and circumstance continue to cross in meaningful patterns that make up the tapestry of my life. Everything I do feeds into everything else.

My adjunct status at the College of Staten Island places me both inside and outside the academy. My responsibility to my students—at least as I conceive it—is the same as that of my full-time tenured colleagues. I generally teach twenty hours a year to their twenty-two, but receive one-third or less of their salary and none of the benefits. Under these conditions, the usual scholarly challenge to both teach well and publish—at least for those adjuncts who hope to secure a tenure-track position in the future—is complicated by the need to generate other income. Given the dangerous and shortsighted trend toward part-time labor (adjuncts outnumber full-time faculty two to one in our department), I am constantly forced to ask myself: What am I prepared to do—beyond giving my best in the classroom and holding unpaid office hours—if I am also to resist participating in the growing institutionalization of exploited academic labor? My answer, never satisfactory, changes from one semester to the next.

On the brighter side, being underemployed has its distinct advantages. A gypsy scholar is exempt from the usual round of administrative duties and committee work, and the pressure to publish is generally self-imposed rather than a condition of employment. I have more control of my time and energy than most people I know. From a work in progress:

October 29th.
I just filled my huge new black café au lait cup with strong Colombian coffee. Albinoni is rippling joyously in the background and sunlight is touching everything in the room with gold. It's my favourite kind of morning, when everything seems possible and nothing is more precious than this freedom I have to get up at leisure and contemplate how to shape the day.

There's something wonderful—and privileged, I know—in waking up without an alarm clock and determining the day's rhythm. Often I'll spend a quiet half hour writing in my journal, followed by three or four hours of work. The house is quiet, or I play music that suits my mood. When I'm grading student papers, I spread out at the dining room table, put a load of laundry in the washer or a pot of soup on the stove, and work away at various tasks at once. In the late afternoon, it's out to the boardwalk for a run, or a walk with Steve. Each day has its own rhythm.

Even after thirteen years with Steve, I'm still often surprised to have found my soul mate. Not a day goes by that I take the sweetness of his presence for granted or fail to realize that our quiet days together are gifts, each one, and that I don't feel the bittersweet joy of our fleshly bond that will one day end. Throughout my twenties and early thirties I vowed that even if I never formed a lasting bond with a man, I would create a rich and meaningful life for myself. And I know I would have. But once my life grew intertwined with Steve's, even with all the uncertainty and conflict of the early years—could I ever get used to New York and his children? would we get married? have a child? relocate to Vancouver?—I began to know the richness of having a companion in life and of gaining a new perspective, at once double and shared. During the thirteen years since we met, I have not experienced that penetrating loneliness of old, that nagging thirst for intimate relationship that builds intensity like the absence of cool water in an unrelenting heat spell. Over the years, I have discovered an elegant simplicity in our shared commitment to create a life encompassing with equal weight of importance the needs and desire of us both.

Meanwhile, on a more prosaic note, after three decades of alternately craving and resenting the male gaze, I am both annoyed and amused now to observe myself hoping I haven't experienced the last of it just yet. How ironic it is that this in recent years frequently described and much celebrated sexual invisibility (see Greer 1992 and Heilbrun 1997, among others) should loom ahead just as I begin to revel in my own appearance. After too many years of assessing my reflection with the coldly objective eye of a real estate agent or an auctioneer, I find myself well pleased, at last, with my own flesh.

The body is the beloved home in which the soul dwells. Perhaps that is what embodiment is: acceptance and love of our own sacred matter. So many of us spend our whole lives struggling to get there. In the sorrow of a midlife miscarriage earlier this year, I was overwhelmed with tenderness and gratitude for this body that tried so hard to give me what I have wanted for so long. Even as it was filled with grief, my body comforted me.

I experience much more tenderness, in general, these days. Tenderness, I think, is not much suited to the frenetic rhythms of youth. It's a slow-growth emotion that feeds on careful observation and painstaking sensitivity toward others, the humbling recognition of one's own flawed nature, and the sense that everything that lives is fragile and yearns for recognition and love. I feel it growing in me. I feel more of everything, in fact, and have far greater respect for what the Jungians call the feminine feeling-function, so ruthlessly disparaged throughout my twenty-six years of formal education.

Authority and Authorship

Obtaining my Ph.D. at the University of London a decade ago granted me a certain measure of formal authority within the academy. But writing my book—one that, like a love child, was created out of desire, passion, and a lifelong love affair with women's journals—provided me with a sense of personal authority far more authentic and potent. Here, at last, was something I had created not to satisfy an external requirement or stake out my intellectual turf, but simply because it was replete with personal meaning. Gradually—and the publication of the book caused a quantum leap in this process—my tenuous sense of official entitlement to the role of college professor has been replaced with the growing confidence of my own experience and authorship, providing an authority that no diploma could afford.

In women's studies and creative writing classes where students read my book, the effects have been eye-opening. Because it is such a personal book and includes excerpts of my own journal, there is nowhere to hide. Once my students know that I have struggled with self-doubt, depression, and body image just like themselves, adopting a conventional professorial pose would be inappropriate, if not impossible. Women students in particular tell me time and again that they never before felt such intimacy with a professor's life. And although they have the right to staple off-limits in their own class journals anything they deem too personal for my eyes, I find very few staples when I sit down to read at the semester's end. My own self-disclosure invites theirs, I suspect.

I wrote *A Voice of Her Own: Women and the Journal Writing Journey* to celebrate the power and beauty of women's journals and to reclaim the quiet voices that speak within them—including my own, too long stripped of its subjectivity, its many registers and feeling-tones, by the streamlined, impatient demands of academic discourse. That women would write to tell me they recognize themselves in my words has been an unexpected gift.

Mother / Virgin / Crone

In my Jungian Women workshop series, we have been focusing on the three dimensions of the mature or "Conscious Feminine": the archetypes of

Mother, Virgin, and Crone (Woodman 1990). They manifest recurrently in our lives, and overlap one another as they do, rather than appearing in linear succession. In my personal life over the past half dozen years or so, it is this archetypal material that resonates most powerfully. The women in the workshop, too, respond with fierce interest.

Our quest in the second half of life is to bring all three archetypes within ourselves into conscious relationship with each other. The maternal impulse to nurture is powerful in me; it always has been. The Virgin, too, has been there all along, urging me to refuse the safety of a comfortable pre-fabricated life, whether that of the German Baptist immigrant community in which I was raised and which promised a traditional marriage, children, a stalwart community, and heaven itself, or more recently, that of a high-level achiever with a prestigious and well-paid nine-to-five career. The challenge to grow into the loving energy of the Crone —who stands at the crossroads of the transitory and the eternal and speaks the truth with love because she has nothing to gain and nothing to lose—is one I gladly accept for the years to come. I want to know the Crone in myself.

So here I am, in the middle of my life. I never expected to get here so soon. In a year and a half, Steve will take early retirement and we will relocate to Vancouver; meanwhile, I still want a child. I thought I'd be wiser and have more answers to my questions by now. I'm very grateful for the invitation to put these words on paper. Awake, I'm still not sure exactly what it would mean to saturate language with love, but I still have time. Perhaps I'll have another dream.

I would like to dedicate this essay to the women in my Women's Journal Workshop, with loving gratitude for everything you have shared with me over the years. For his sensitive editorial eye, my thanks, as always, to Steve.

5

The Time of Our Lives

The Public Life of Teaching

PATRICIA C. PHILLIPS

FIRST, HOW LONG IS EPHEMERAL? TWO WEEKS, TWO YEARS, FIFTY
YEARS, OR TWO THOUSAND YEARS? BEYOND THAT, WHAT DO WE
HAVE? ... AND WHAT TIME/SPACE RELATIONSHIP ARE WE TALKING
ABOUT WHEN IT COMES TO ART? ALL WORKS SHOULD ATTEMPT TO
BE EPHEMERAL. THIS SHOULD BE THEIR AMBITION. IN THIS SENSE,
EPHEMERAL MEANS NOT TO HAVE PRODUCED SOMETHING WHICH
IS OF INTEREST TO ANYBODY WHATSOEVER TODAY. ... IT MEANS TO
ACCEPT OUR LIMITATIONS, OUR SPARSE KNOWLEDGE, OUR TIMES,
OUR MISERY ... IT'S TO ACCEPT THAT A BOLT OF LIGHTNING CAN BE
IMPRESSED UPON OUR MEMORY JUST AS STRONGLY AS A PYRAMID.

Daniel Buren

It is fascinating how apparently insignificant incidents maintain a vivid resonance. Having arrived in my mid-forties with an expectant, sometimes
stormy combination of relief and anticipation, I am frequently—virtually
daily—perplexed by the unruly intricacies of memory. Perpetually surprised by experiences that remain indelibly inscribed over time, I find it disturbing to fathom those passages that have darkly receded, only to be
unpredictably, partially, and momentarily retrieved through conversations,
sights, smells, or other sensations.

For still inexplicable reasons, I periodically flash back with stunning
recall to a moment in eighth grade. One of my most memorable, challenging, and engaging teachers (who I would have again as we both advanced
into high school and continue, to this day, to remember with fondness)

suddenly and explosively interrupted the class activities and loudly and (seemingly) interminably exhorted me for watching the clock.

While I think that I might have been dreamily or distractedly looking at the clock on the wall, I generally was unconscious of my activities and astonished that my passive behavior could ignite such a severe response. Even through college I was a quietly responsive and sufficiently productive student. I didn't shine, but I inconspicuously abetted rather than under-mined the general culture of classes I attended. I generally encountered mild appreciation rather than sudden anger.

The teacher was livid. I was mortified. Given the triumphs and atroci-ties of many people's school memories, this incident can only be described as unremarkable, if not dismissible. Life progressed uneventfully as my friends and I looked forward to high school. But these few moments endure as a vivid recollection. I felt bad and betrayed. I suspect that the teacher per-ceived my upward gaze as rejection or boredom. And I recall only glancing furtively and anxiously at the clock for the remainder of the year.

Time remains a constructive metaphor for teaching and learning. Sequences, recursive patterns, new encounters, and repeated habits form the cartography of time, travel, and exchange in territories of teaching. If unceasing, time is negotiable, offering opportunities and obstacles, shared encounters and privileged moments. As I remember this moment in 1965, the dynamic, ever-changing reinscription of private desire and public con-duct in the classroom may be the most trenchant impression. Who does control the time of learning? In what ways? And what are the consequences?

More than thirty years later, I remain acutely, if sometimes ambiguously, aware of the public life—the conventions of control, regulation, and the less calculable orchestrations of the collective time and space of the classroom. Of course, time is never simply the reliably inaccurate clock on the school wall. It is the deeply embedded, profoundly evocative dynamics of social, intellectual, creative, visceral, and biological forces that constitute the pub-lic space of teaching. How do teachers become agents or adversaries of time? When—in what ways—is time a pedagogical resource?

Two decades after time was temporarily suspended for me in an eighth-grade social studies class in suburban New Jersey, a friend who is an archi-tect suggested that I read J. G. Ballard's short story "Chronopolis." Never a science fiction fan, I became attracted and repulsed by his ghastly urban environments—how architecture and infrastructure (such as in *Concrete Island* and *Crash*) serve as metaphors for the perils of injudicious progress, human isolation and aggression. "Chronopolis" is a sublime mise-en-scène that takes place in an enormous but eviscerated metropolis that had condemned and banished time thirty-seven years earlier. What led to this expulsion?

In order to manage a burgeoning population, multiple shifts of workers, and daunting demands on services, over thirty million citizens were assigned to particular time zones and color groups that regulated times they could travel, go to the bank, shop, or use the telephone. Time had surpassed any imaginable regulatory role. Whereas the sophisticated management of time had once supported a smoothly functioning, rapidly growing city, it ultimately became a repressive instrument. The therapeutic solution was withholding and denial; time was found guilty and forever suspended. All clocks were stopped at 12:01 and removed from public spaces; wristwatches were confiscated and destroyed. In fact, anyone found to have a watch was subject to severe admonishment and possibly penalty of death.

The psychological development (or decline) of characters in Ballard's story is mildly interesting, but it is the rendering of a depleted urbanism and vacant public life of "Chronopolis" that remains startling and disquieting. Time was the adhesive that held the city hostage. Ultimately, this temporal dictatorship inspired a complete social upheaval. But when time was outlawed, the city began to decline until it too ceased to exist. Center city was abandoned. Transportation systems stopped. Public space became as vacant as time. First obsessively present and then alarmingly absent, time in this macabre urban morality tale is both symbolically and instrumentally a dynamic that animates and sustains an idea of public life—and public lives. Without this—and the concomitant themes of development, aging, and change—any notion of working together to construct a creative vision of the future is perpetually thwarted.

If Ballard was primarily interested in time as a social instrument, the final passage of "Chronopolis" describes its psychological insinuation. Alone in a prison cell, Newman (the main character) anticipates his future. In his frantic quest in the abandoned metropolis for the meaning of time, a murder occurs for which he is mistakenly accused. Resigned to the charges of murder and violation of Time Laws, he accepts the sentence of twenty years' imprisonment. He is bemused and comforted to discover a clock on the wall of his cell. But his pleasure pales. Within just two weeks, the incessant ticking has become a disquieting, irritating invasion.

If not a maddening distraction, arrival at my mid- and late forties has introduced an urgent, if inaudible, summons of time's insistence. An intriguing concept, midlife is a unique time of resignation and expectation.

Without sudden announcements, there are evidential physical signs and emotional transformations to suggest that a threshold has been approached and entered. But this is a passage that does not clearly distinguish departure from destination, or past from future. Midlife is a deeply connective, integrative experience. Often detailed with regret, there is also an emerging, but palpable narrative structure of prospect. Resignation and expectation. There are new rhythms of acceptance and acknowledgment and of promise and optimism.

In the lives of women, there are harshly ambivalent responses to midlife and entering middle age. Regardless of gender, class, background, or ethnicity, "midlife crisis" is a vernacular concept that is widely understood and administered as an explanation for a stunning range of physical, psychological, and emotional experiences. It has become an aphorism for those quietly disturbing, mysteriously unnerving feelings and behaviors that mark significant transitional moments.

The changes, of course, are too glibly and tidily ascribed to time, offering a vaguely comforting justification without any implication of a constructive response. Platitudes often console and dismiss. This too will pass. Time heals everything. For many, midlife signifies an arrival that paradoxically summons the imminence of decline. It is a pictograph of life as a pristine silhouette of a single mountain. The first part of life is spent in assent, but the moment that the summit is reached, a slow, inevitable descent, a foreboding passage of depreciation and diminishment, is inevasible.

An aphorism, "the glass of water that is half empty or half full," also illuminates commonly held perceptions of midlife. For women, in particular, the image of the body as vessel has been both an empowering and debilitating metaphor. Conception. Pregnancy. Women are bearers of new life, who may often feel exalted and entrapped by these biological possibilities. In middle age, are women perceived as becoming slowly depleted, or still actively seeking a fullness—a nurturing vision of unexpected replenishment?

At midlife, I find myself involved in an absorbing reconciliation and rejuvenation of myself as a teacher, administrator, writer, critic, mother, and woman. For the past ten years, I have acknowledged a connection between doing and being, my writing on art, architecture, and public life and a developing pedagogy. With the exception of those moments of tremendous pressure—of the frenetic, vertiginous sensations of accepting multiple roles and occupying many spaces virtually simultaneously—I have never felt that my life's commitments and passions have been adversarial.

I have always suspected (and genuinely hoped) that teaching, research, observation, writing, and my life within a family have mysteriously but unmistakably enhanced each other. Admittedly, this optimism has often required a creative negotiation of facts and faith. Regrettably, a high level of energy and a legendary work ethic too frequently have made this kind of self-analysis a low priority (that I did not require) or an extraordinary privilege (that I did not deserve). I had located a site of potential resources, but hadn't dedicated myself to the cultivation, excavation, and synthesis required to identify and release these reserves.

For the past twenty years I have written about contemporary art, architecture, and landscape. A particular interest has been public art—art and artists who are intrinsically connected to a particular community or ideas of public life. Resolutely troubled by a (primarily) Western notion that sees art in some state of pure isolation from life, I have advocated for artistic practices that are interrogative of and entwined with issues of contemporary life. These inquiring, transformative processes ask—even insist—that viewers become active partners or participants in the invention and apprehension of art.

In contrast to the long-standing, if unsubstantiated, equations of importance and endurance, or value and stability, that have given art meaning, a great deal of new work is defiantly ephemeral. Calculatedly short-lived, it often engages time as an agent, material, subject, or methodology. Generally sited and deployed in cities, the work embraces a place or community as "a site of transformations and appropriations, the object of interventions, but also a subject continually being enriched by new attributes" (Michel de Certeau 1985).

As Daniel Buren suggests, the late twentieth century raises new questions about time and expectation, change and value, passing and lasting impressions. It is an accelerated, acquisitive, and yet acquiescent period in which the presence and dependability of enduring objects is as quixotic as time itself. The visual environment transforms as rapidly as the actions of the eye and mind. In both public and private life, the phenomenological dimensions of indeterminacy, instability, and temporality require spirited assimilation, not because they are grim, inescapable forces, but because they suggest prospective ideas and productive metaphors for the biological and social, the individual and public body.

A critical inquiry into the temporary—the ephemeral in art—has led to an intellectual curiosity about time in general, and how it effects the production and perception of art. Transient works often encompass an urgency, topicality, and timeliness. Whether in an installation, public project, or landscape intervention, there has emerged a geography of impermanence, a volatile spatiality for which questions of time are consequential, if not instrumental, to the process and understanding of art.

What are the connective metaphors between the ephemeral, often insurgent art practices that are a critical, political, and aesthetic preoccupation, my work as a teacher, and my life as a woman in her mid-forties? Generally, by midlife a series of patterns and reiterative practices congeals in life and work. They offer a level of comfort, confidence, and stability. To some extent, they define who we are—those reliable qualities or loathsome habits.

A reflective pedagogy represents—and requires—dependable strategies and introspective dimensions. Like the conscious and unconscious rhythms of the body, there is a corporeal and visceral texture to teaching. There are lineaments that are profoundly familiar, if inexplicable. Teaching is sustained and stabilized by the recognized images that repeated reflection offers—the predictable academic sequences and settings of communication and exchange.

But these recursive patterns of content and methodology—the cycles of learning—need to be periodically interrupted and suspended in order to exploit moments and movements of change, when reflection moves from the dependable to the unexpected. How does reflective teaching embody the private and public, the purposeful and enigmatic, the enduring and ephemeral, the pyramid and the lightning bolt—not as dichotomous concepts, but as coexistent, conditional phenomena?

In *The Sphinx in the City: Urban Life, the Control of Disorder, and Women* (1991), Elizabeth Wilson explores the relationship of feminism and the city. In spite of a tradition of ambiguity, if not hostility (cities are perceived as threatening and dangerous for women), she suggests how both the pleasures and dangers of the city have emancipated women. Citing Marcel Proust's descriptions of Venice, she writes:

> Here, the texture of the city is both natural—crystalline matter—and the substance of dreams, which are the involuntary workings of the mind. Perhaps we should be happier in our cities were we to respond them as nature or dreams: as objects of exploration, investigation, and interpretation, setting for voyages of discovery. The "discourse" that has shaped our cities—the utilitarian plans of experts whose goal was social engineering—has limited our vision and almost destroyed our cities. It is time for

a new vision, a new ideal of life in the city, and a new "feminine" voice in praise of cities. (11)

And Rosalyn Deutsche writes in *Evictions: Art and Spatial Politics* (1996),

> The loving grip of a good society (citing Claude Lefort) warns us of the seemingly benign fantasy of social completion, a fantasy that negates plurality and conflict because it depends on an image of social space closed by an authoritative ground. This image is linked to a rigid public/private dichotomy that consigns differences to private realm and sets up the public as universal or consensual sphere.... It is this security of public/private divide, which shelters the subject from public space, that art informed by a feminist critique of the image has so forcefully challenged by insisting that identity and meaning are formed in public space. (326–27)

At midlife, I seek a teaching environment that is as explicit and unpredictable as a city. Full of pleasures and dangers, I want to expand my role in "publicizing" the expectancy and risk of learning and inquiry, of difference and conflict. This kind of environment acknowledges and supports the vicissitudes of time and space so that students can be coprotagonists—creators and collaborators of new, often unanticipated meanings. Involved in the shifting sands of contemporary art, I am perpetually confronted with a restless content that invokes an imminence without any critical or academic authority. And as art and artist transgress accepted boundaries (especially in the public realm), teaching always involves "interdisciplinarity... when the solidity of the old disciplines breaks down—perhaps even violently" (Roland Barthes).

The classroom or studio is a social space. Loved and loathed by both students and teachers, it is unquestionably one of our most fascinating and ubiquitous public spaces. In a less polemical but poetic level, artist Ann Hamilton's reflections on her passion for making installations suggest how time and space ignite discovery:

> An installation surrounds you, absorbs you into it. You are part of it the minute you step in—it can get closer to breaking down the separation between you-the-viewer and it-the-object. In an installation, an object only has meaning as a part of a series of relationships to the skin of the surroundings. You become implicated as an agent in the relationships that make the work. It's like the interior/exterior condition we live with in our

bodies—the skin creates illusions of separation, but it's a permeable membrane that goes both ways. (1991)

At midlife, teaching is an increasingly embodied activity. While there may be a growing familiarity, it does not engender an easy optimism. As teaching becomes slowly corporealized, its impressions on the social body of past, present, and future students is a daunting prospect. There is never a clock in sight where I teach, but I feel (as never before) how the time of teaching affects the environment of learning. Acceptance and anticipation. Like the transformations of my own life at midlife, teaching, too, is something that I will always fear and desire. There is the weight and buoyancy of responsibility—the perils, possibilities, and privileges of the life I have chosen.

Ripening ❧ Rootedness

I WANT TO ALLOW MENOPAUSE TO BE A SOUL EVENT, WHICH MEANS LETTING IT BE TRANSFORMATIVE, WHICH MEANS LETTING IT HURT, WHICH MEANS REALLY LETTING GO OF SOME STILL CHERISHED OLD WAYS, ACCEPTING THAT SOME THINGS ARE REALLY OVER——THOUGH I MAY WISH THEY WEREN'T AND MAY KNOW I DID NOT LIVE THEM AS FULLY, HONESTLY, OR COURAGEOUSLY AS I WISH I HAD.

Christine Downing

TWO OR THREE THINGS I KNOW FOR SURE, AND ONE OF THEM IS WHAT IT MEANS TO HAVE NO LOVED VERSION OF YOUR LIFE BUT THE ONE YOU MAKE.

Dorothy Allison

AGE IS A DESERT OF TIME——HOURS, DAYS, WEEKS, YEARS PERHAPS——WITH LITTLE TO DO. SO ONE HAS AMPLE TIME TO FACE EVERYTHING ONE HAS HAD, BEEN, DONE; GATHER THEM ALL IN: THE THINGS THAT CAME FROM OUT-SIDE, AND THOSE FROM INSIDE. WE HAVE TIME AT LAST TO MAKE THEM TRULY OURS . . . . YOU NEED ONLY CLAIM THE EVENTS OF YOUR LIFE TO MAKE YOURSELF YOURS. WHEN YOU TRULY POSSESS ALL YOU HAVE BEEN AND DONE, WHICH MAY TAKE SOME TIME, YOU ARE FIERCE WITH REALITY.

Florida Scott-Maxwell

6

Reverie

JANE TOMPKINS

In my mind's eye I keep seeing rows. Rows of desks, running horizontal across a room, light yellow wooden tops, pale beige metal legs, a shallow depression for pencils at the far edge, and chairs of the same material, separate from the desks, movable. The windows—tall and running the length of the classroom—are on the left. Light streams through.

The rows are empty.

Now the desks darken and curve. They're made of older, grainier wood; they're the kind with a surface that comes out from the back of the seat on your right and wraps around in front. The desk top is attached to the seat where you sit, which is clamped to the seats on either side or to those in front and in back. The desks metamorphose in my mind. Now they are hinged, tops brown and scarred; they open to reveal notebooks, textbooks covered in the shiny green-and-white book covers of Glen Rock Junior High; there's a bottle of mucilage and a pink eraser. On top, there's a hole for an inkwell, black and empty. The seat, when you stand, folds up behind.

Sometimes the desks are movable; more often they're clamped down. Always they're in rows. And empty. The teacher's place is empty, too, another desk, or tablelike thing. Sometimes it's a podium on a platform. The blackboard behind.

The scenes are all mixed together—grade school with graduate school—but always the windows along one side of the room, and always the desks in rows.

After babyhood we spend a lot of time learning to sit in rows. Going from unruly to ruled. Learning to write on pages that are lined. Learning to obey. There is no other way, apparently. Even if the desks were arranged in a circle, or were not desks at all but chairs or ottomans, still they would have to form some pattern. We would have to learn to sit still and listen.

The first part of life goes on for a long time. The habit of learning to sit in rows doesn't leave off when the rows themselves are gone. Having learned to learn the rules, you look for them everywhere you go, to avoid humiliation. You learn to find your seat in the invisible rows.

The last part of life, though, is different. It is no longer automatic, your walking in and sitting down. When you see a row, your gorge rises, or you are simply indifferent. When the command comes to be seated, you don't obey. All of a sudden, survival no longer depends on getting to your desk in the ten seconds after the buzzer sounds. It depends on listening only to your inner monitor, which says: You'd better go while the going's good. Time to give up the security of rows.

'Cause you're not *in* the classroom anymore. There is no blackboard with equations on it, no teacher with her pointer to point out what you need to know. No test, no assignment. No three o'clock when the bell for dismissal rings. No after school.

No smell of chalk dust and freshly sharpened pencils, no fragrances of different kinds of paper, gray and white and yellow, blank pages, lined and unlined, inviting you to prove something, yourself... I can do this problem, spell that word, name the capital of that country, explain the meaning of that term.

Though there was always fear associated with sitting in rows—am I too different? will I pass the test? does anybody like me?—the desks and chairs and tasks provided an escape from fear by giving me something definite to do. Add the column of figures. Learn the causes of the war.

Now, wandering the world outside of school, having transcended "rows," nothing to do, no place to go, I am terrified. In the huge, dark, unfurnished world without rows, I cower and tremble. Give me back Mrs. Colgan. Let me be in 1B again. Let me learn to add, to subtract, to carry, and to borrow numbers. Give me a problem to do.

I see the light-filled classrooms, rows on rows, desks, chairs, waiting to be filled: let the lesson begin. "Our first assignment will be to learn the periodic table." Let me back in. Please. Let me sit down again, open my notebook to the first blank page, start writing. When is the exam?

7

Goodbye, Ms. Chips

JULIA ALVAREZ

This spring, after twenty-two years of teaching, I decided—a euphemism if ever I heard one for the messy and anguishing process that brought me to this conclusion—to give up tenure. Of those twenty-two years, only the last six have been tenured, the previous eighteen had been spent teaching across America, looking for a tenure-track position. Eventually, I found such a position and earned tenure, and then just a few years later, to the raised eyebrows of friends and acquaintances who had followed my weary migrancy from one teaching job to another, I gave it up.

Please note that I am saying I gave up tenure, not teaching. Even if I don't continue teaching at my current college, I will find a way into a classroom to practice a craft that is, for me, as fascinating and difficult as writing. But after consulting and reconsulting that internal Solomon that helps us decide between impossible choices, I handed the baby over. I gave up tenure because, in fact, I love teaching, and I didn't know how to give it less than my all, now that I wanted to devote more of my time to writing.

A good friend, still in academia, encouraged my choice by quoting Shaw's famous dictum, "He who can, does. He who can't, teaches." She added her own version, "Those who can't write, teach creative writing." But I had to disagree with her. Some great writers have been magnificent teachers: John Gardner, Theodore Roethke, Patricia Hampl, Fred Chappel, Annie Dillard, Wallace Stegner, Lee Smith, Charles Baxter, June Jordan, Gwendolyn Brooks, Sandra Cisneros, Grace Paley, among others. No, my problem is that I have never been able to hold down two full-time passions. Part of being older and wiser is learning to work with the nature you've been given.

So, goodbye, Ms. Chips. Hello, full-time writer.

There is, of course, more of a story behind this plucky decision. I didn't so much "give up" tenure as I had to give up tenure. I teach at a small, liberal-arts institution where years ago the faculty voted in the rule that one could not retain tenure on a part-time arrangement. (A vote that I, even as I fall victim to it, agree with. I keep remembering John Ciardi's famous quip that a "university is what a college becomes when the faculty loses interest in students.") The very spring I earned tenure, my first novel came out. I had been writing and publishing in small magazines for over twenty years. If I belonged to any school of writers, it was to the fringe-school writers who "prided themselves" on never having been published in the *New Yorker*.

That first novel took me over ten years to write. I wrote a chapter here and there, whenever I could, during summers, school vacations, between moves, job searches, eager students. After all, I was a teacher who wrote "on the side," even though I chafed against relegating my writing to this second-class status. Still, I had to earn a living. And the truth was that teaching had also become a passion. I yearned for tenure and tenancy, "a room of my own" in the academy. Serendipitously, I signed the contract for my first novel the very year that I was being reviewed for tenure. I thought of that first novel very much as the book that might earn me tenure rather than the book that might bring me autonomy as a writer.

But the latter happened, and suddenly I found myself with an encouraging readership ("When's your next book coming out?" "What are you working on now?") and with enough money to take time off to do more writing. I'm sure some colleagues felt that I had been waiting in the wings, all along, to earn tenure and start misbehaving. But this was truly a quirk of timing—writing success came at the same time as academic success. The tension that had always been there between these two profoundly gratifying and absorbing vocations suddenly burst to the fore. One vocation was no longer in hock to the other: I no longer *had* to teach to support my habit of writing. So the contest was finally equal and fair, which one would gain the ascendancy. Which one would get to keep the baby?

For years, my emphasis had been on the teaching. Now, fate and luck had put this other possibility before me. I decided to turn the tables and give the writing life the same kind of full-time attention I had given the teaching. I would teach "on the side."

I pulled out a piece of paper and wrote out my letter to the vice president of the college, then read it over, and crossed the first paragraph out, replaced it with a simple, succinct sentence; then reread the revision, which suddenly sounded too clipped and cold and ungrateful; so I elaborated, choosing an alternative word for *regret*, but dissatisfied with the alternative, returned to *regret*, then tried *sorry*, then a few other alternatives, chewing off the cap on my pen, settling finally for *regret;* at which point, I reread the letter, crushed it up, started a new version—a process I repeated several times. It took a whole afternoon to draft my resignation letter.

I was already embarked in my full-time profession of writing.

Like the immigrant who is constantly tempted to cast a lingering backward look to see what it is she has left behind, I keep looking behind me at my twenty-plus years of teaching. Why is it that even though I am happy with my new life, still, when I drive by the college on a brisk autumn day and see the students going up the walk on their way to class, I feel a surge of homesickness, as if I were passing by my old childhood house back on the Island?

I know no other way of explaining it but that the academy has always been my home in the United States. Leaving it is my second big emigration into the blank sheet of paper. Once we arrived in this country, my sisters and I had no guides, no models in the family or among our acquaintances whom we could follow into this new culture. Especially at the beginning, my parents discouraged friendships with classmates and neighbors. These natives were "foreigners" to us. We didn't know what kind of families they came from, Mami said. As for absorbing the culture via the media: the one "good" television was in my parents' bedroom; the black-and-white one was in the basement and unofficially "belonged" to Ada, our live-in Dominican maid. Her only pleasure in her hard and homesick life was keeping up with her *novelas* on the Spanish language channel. No one would think of depriving her of that to watch the Beatles on *Ed Sullivan* or *Patty Duke* or *Father Knows Best* or *Ozzie and Harriet,* shows that might have filled us all in on life in these United States of America.

So my sisters and I had to rely on school to pick up the culture. Not that school was the friendliest place, with kids taunting our clothes and our accents. But from the beginning, I had the good luck of running into some fine teachers, young nuns in parochial schools; a wonderful spitfire biology teacher my first year in high school; Mr. Barstow at a summer school camp; Miss Stevenson and Miss St. Pierre at boarding school; Bill Meredith, and as a brief visitor, June Jordan, at Connecticut College; Bob Pack at Middlebury; Philip Booth and Donald Dike at Syracuse. As I mention each name, I feel a shiver of recognition: each one passed me on to the next and the next until I reached the end of my apprenticeship and became, like them, a teacher.

It happened, of course, like most things in my life, by accident. That is, I followed along, teacher to teacher, high school to college to graduate school. At each juncture my parents questioned whether they should let their daughters continue to educate themselves out of a Dominican future as wives and mothers back on the Island. But by that time, we all knew in the back of our minds that our lives were going to happen in this country. An education was the only true guarantee of a secure future here.

So, education became sacrosanct in our immigrant household. Our otherwise strict old-world parents would allow and even pay for any activity if my sisters and I could put an educational spin on it. We'd ask for permission to go to the 42nd Street Library on a Saturday afternoon, but, in fact, we were headed to the Village to see hippies and maybe even meet a few. In college, on Saturday nights, my parents' preferred calling time, we would leave a message with the dorm receptionist: if our parents call, please tell them we're at the library, studying. And in fact, seven times out of ten, we were actually at the library. It had been drummed into us: our true green card in America was an education: a high school diploma, a college degree, a teaching certificate. My father had a veritable accordion of cards in his wallet, proving that he was a member of one organization or another, the Royal Academy of Medicine, the American College of Surgeons, the American Medical Association; that he held surgical privileges at three New York hospitals; that he had completed any number of courses at association meetings.

Suddenly, it seemed, the whole family was studying. My mother began taking evening courses at the local college for her real estate license. My physician father signed up for more than the required hours of continuing education courses. He also started taking German and Chinese, "just in case," though he never explained what eventuality he was preparing himself for. I, who had been a terrible student back home, a hooky player and a cut-up in class, failing every grade through fifth and having to make up the difference during summer school, suddenly became a serious, but sadly anxious student.

I've tried to understand where such enormous pressure came from. When we first arrived, my mother used to warn us that unless we behaved ourselves in this country, our family would be sent back. Good behavior meant, of course, that my sisters and I had to earn good report cards—for how else could the Americans judge our merits in being allowed to stay? Though I wanted to go back home more than anything in the world, by this time I knew about the horrible dictatorship. Each A I earned was not just a personal accomplishment but a way to save my family and to prove our worth to the Americans. When, a few years later, I started to panic and walk out of exams, the school counselor diagnosed my stress level around tests and papers as so high that I could literally not hear myself think. My teachers, Miss Stevenson and later Miss St. Pierre, found the solution in allowing me to write "creatively" about what I was learning, essays, poems, stories, journals, which I could work on in my room and hand in without the dreaded clock incapacitating me.

I mention this incident because already it was my teachers who were helping me find solutions to the problems and pressures of a home divided by new-world pressures and an old-world style. To the maid, Ada, I confessed my heart every time I came home for vacations, but to my teachers, I divulged my dreams. Being women who had followed their dreams, they presented me with proof that such a translation was possible, maybe even for me.

As the end of college rolled around, my parents began suggesting that my older sister and I come back home to live with them until such time as we would marry. Even better, why didn't we consider going back home where we would meet someone suitable? Of course, the security of the offer was alluring. My Dominican girl cousins were all getting engaged, marrying, establishing themselves in traditional lives of their own. But once back on the Island, I found myself getting into arguments with my aunts, interrupting the men to debate some pronouncement they had made, befriending the maids, scandalizing everyone with my American ways. If I went off on my own to read and write, my family found such self-imposed solitude troubling. (*¿Qué te pasa? ¿Estas triste?*) My American education had spoiled me for life in my native country.

Also, unlike many of my Island cousins, I did not have a private income. We had started over when we came to this country, not that my father had ever had a whole lot of money back home. It was my mother's family who were well-to-do, and though we could benefit from her family's status there, her name and connections meant nothing here. My sisters and I had to earn our livings and make our own way in this country. I already knew I wanted to be a writer, but writing had to be combined with a "real job" to put bread and butter on the table. So, of course, I thought of teaching. There was also the other option: working in a publishing house, which, because it was closer to the wheels of actual publication, sounded much more promising.

Soon after graduation from college, I moved back in with my parents in Queens and landed a "publishing" job in New York City. Every day I took the subway in to an office across the street from the 42nd Street Library. (A touch of poetic justice to have as my daily destination the place I had used as an alibi for so many years!) My job was to put together a weekly newsletter for libraries and businesses on the topic of ecology. Special Reports, Inc., my employer, comprised two men, one of whom I never met, and another one who came in several times a week to see how we were doing. "We" was myself and a talkative, attractive secretary in the main room whose job it was to answer the rare phone call and sort out the mail. I had my own cubicle, and periodically, Lillian would appear at my door or I would come out and sit on the edge of her desk and we'd gab. Eventually, we would arrive at our favorite topic of discussion: whether Special Reports was a front for something else. How could a newsletter with two hundred or so subscribers pay the rent, not to mention our two salaries?

Although I had worried at first about my ignorance, it soon became clear that I didn't have to know anything about ecology. I was to copy news releases from environmental organizations and the E.P.A., rewriting them ever so slightly so as not to plagiarize technically. In that small dark office, without the interaction and community of a classroom, I felt like Bartleby the scrivener, Melville's disaffected clerk, who ends up responding to life by folding his arms and saying, "I would prefer not to."

I decided to apply to an M.F.A. program, not because I wanted to earn a terminal writing degree (the sound of it even scared me), but because I wanted to buy some time to do some writing. I also wanted to be part of a community of learners again. My second year in the creative writing program at Syracuse University, I held a teaching assistantship and taught several "short term" poetry courses to first-year students.

I can't say I really enjoyed this first-time teaching experience: the heavy weight of performance was on me; after all we were the M.F.A.-ers, not the serious Ph.D.-ers, and our capability to teach academic subjects was suspect. It was as if I were back at the exam room, wanting to bolt each time I walked into my classroom. I went in with so many notes and handouts that my students could have said about my class what Peter DeVries said about writing, that he liked it well enough, but the paperwork was killing him.

As the end of graduate school rolled around, I again had to decide how it was that I was going to earn a living. I debated then, and again at several unemployed junctures in my teaching/writing life, whether to go on for a Ph.D. so that I would be taken seriously (that is, hired in a tenured position) by the academy. But every time I decided to go ahead and get my doctorate, a few days sitting in among scholarly academics convinced me that I did not belong among them. I loved living inside a book, but I much preferred creating my own to explicating already existing texts.

So when an opening came up for a poet in a poetry-in-the-schools program in Kentucky, I applied for the job. I could not believe my luck when I got it! My two-year assignment involved ten six-week residencies in different locations. Of course, I assumed these "locations" would all be in high schools, but in fact, they included grammar schools, community colleges, a convent, a correction school for girls, a state prison, an old-age home, ten vastly different communities in all.

During my time in each of these communities, in addition to my daily classes, I gave local readings, adult workshops at night in church basements or town halls, in the rectory of the church, in the nuns' dining room. For each of those six-week residencies, teaching involved total immersion in a community. Though I didn't have as much time to write as I would have liked, I can truly say that I "cut my teeth" as a teacher in Kentucky. At the end of those two years, I felt as if I could be put in front of any group of people, and I could "teach" them something about writing poetry.

In Elkton, Kentucky, one old-timer appeared in my community poetry workshop because he had heard that some lady was here with the government (Kentucky State Arts Commission) to talk about "poultry." Even after I cleared up his misunderstanding, he stayed and "dictated" his poem about growing up on a chicken farm. It turned out that he, like a few others, had never learned to read and write. And so, every evening before the poetry workshop, I taught a small group of locals how to read. I don't know if any of these students ever became fluent readers, but I certainly learned a lot from them about incorporating natural speech rhythms in what I was writing.

This was really the great discovery of why I would want to teach: I could go on learning! I didn't have to be the one who knows. How dreary! What Frost said about writing poetry ("No surprise for the writer, no surprise for the reader") also holds true for teaching. Unless a teacher is making discoveries in the classroom, rediscovering the text with the "beginner's mind" that Zen masters talk about, the class lacks the magical sense of possibility and discovery.

"To teach is to learn twice," as Joseph Joubert once said, and not only did I learn almost everything I needed to know about teaching those first two years out in the field, but I also discovered new authors and texts in my search to find works that might appeal to the different populations I was addressing. And though I learned that I could never predict how a particular class or residency would go, I did discover that the more fun I was having in the classroom, the better I was at teaching.

Sixteen years later when I came up for tenure, all joy would flow from the room the minute some observer dropped in to sit at the back and scribble notes on my performance. The old dread would fill my chest: what if I failed? This time I would not be deported from the country, but from the academy. The upshot would be the same: no place to call home. Once, I went blank with terror and had to excuse myself to use the bathroom. Really, I was headed out the door of the building. I calmed myself down, went into a stall, flushed for appearances and came back out, my heart pounding. I kept thinking of Chaucer, whose "General Prologue" I had just been teaching, of the phrase he used to describe the Parson, "First he wrought, and afterward he taught." I decided that's what I would do if I didn't get tenure. I'd go out and "wrought" for a while, and then come back on some future date and teach again. For some reason, this possibility of another option loosened the stranglehold of terror. I went back in the classroom and finished the hour. A few weeks later, the letter came, announcing that I had been awarded tenure.

I suppose of all the classes I have taught, my favorites have been the writing workshops. Generally, they are the smaller classes and, at least in my estimation, the toughest to teach. Unlike my colleagues in literature courses, writing teachers rarely get a standing ovation at the end of the semester, and evaluations are almost always mixed. After all, you have been dealing with students' creative work, and any serious critique you make, no matter how crucial and helpful it might be to them in the future, takes several years to become meaningful.

The immediate response can be defensive or dismissive. As one student wrote me in a personal letter at the end of the course, "You don't have an appreciation of different kinds of literature. You are really limited even if you are a good teacher." She had been very upset because I had suggested that she cut the endless and abstract rantings on crack of one of her characters, even if the story was "supposed to be surrealistic." Another student, whose female characters I found clichéd and a little flat, wrote in his evaluation that I was too feminine a teacher. I think he meant feminist.

Though I can joke about these critiques now, they trouble me when I receive them. One senior colleague refuses to teach workshops anymore because, as he himself admitted, if you do your job well, they're going to resent you. The final verdict is always the same: "More brilliance!" as my teacher W. D. Snodgrass used to say at the end of each workshop. The last day of the semester when I hear the applause wafting up from my colleagues' literature classrooms, I feel a pang of envy. Creative writing workshops are automatic disappointments to students who sign up, under the false impression that such "touchy-feely" courses are easy, literary therapy groups, where all you have to do is feel deeply to get a good grade.

I try to dispel this notion from the first day by emphasizing the apprenticeship aspect of the workshop. We are here to learn a craft that truly takes all of life to learn! There are models to emulate, skills to be mastered, and mostly, the habit of art to be acquired like any habit, by repetition, that is, revision, revision, revision. Craft is what I can help them with. Talent itself is unpredictable: some writers flower in their youth like Rimbaud with *A Season in Hell* and some come into ripeness when they are older, like Harriet Doerr, who published *Stones for Ibarra,* her first novel, when she was in her late sixties. And talent without skills and discipline is finally useless. So I focus on the latter two "teachable" aspects of writing.

I suppose I am in the writing-teacher tradition of Theodore Roethke, who was known for his daunting assignments, including final examinations in his workshop course that included questions like: *Please write a quatrain of anapestic tetrameter on the theme of spring. Ten stanzas of terza rima with no off-rhymes, please.* Elizabeth Bishop, who taught poetry later at the same university, using Roethke's old classroom, found an inscription scratched out on the underside of one of the desks and signed with a student's name, "Died, June 8, 1952, in an exam of Ted Roethke's."

But though he presented himself as a stern taskmaster, what Roethke most adored about teaching was that it was "one of the few professions that permit love." No matter how rough the students' drafts are, their lives, preoccupations, worries, hopes, dreams, fears are the content. This aspect of a workshop course gives it a special charge. Meg's villanelle is not just a villanelle whose rhyme scheme and repeating lines we can discuss. It also happens to be a poem about her parents' divorce, and a discussion of the poem will inevitably touch on the accuracy of the observations and the rightness of the tone, which inevitably suggest issues of emotional honesty and decorum, which, of course, have everything to do with what is going on in Meg's life right now. Our lives, after all, are the very matter of our art.

As a writing teacher, I find this is the most difficult balance to strike: how much to focus on craft *and* how much to step back and let students discover their own voices and concerns without feeling they will be laughed at or penalized for doing so. And the grade issue is always an issue in academic teaching. Finally, you do have to stick a number on this process that began before they ever sat down in your classrom and will continue long after they leave. My policy here has always been to minimize the grading aspect of the course and emphasize the lifelong process of writing. I've also told some of my workshops what Roethke used to tell his classes, "Those students get the highest grades who take their responsibilities of educating me the most seriously."

Needless to say, my students are constantly challenging me to redefine old insights, to crack open my treasured chestnuts of truth, to learn what I don't know, and to confront my own process of writing in order to help them. This last is perhaps the most educational aspect of my teaching. The best skills become almost automatic, and teaching brings them back again to the surface to be reexamined, sharpened, discarded, or reaffirmed. Some fellow writers claim that this makes them self-conscious as writers, prevents them from writing as spontaneously as when they are not teaching, but I have not found this to be true. In fact, becoming momentarily aware again of what I'd forgotten reinforces that skill in my own writing.

All of this, of course, takes time, not just clock time but imaginative time. It is absorbing work—you are thinking about your students; you are reading and focusing on texts that might provide them with the examples they need to be shown at this stage of their apprenticeship; or you are trying to figure out why a student story isn't working, and then once you think you've pinpointed "the problem," you are wondering how you might help them resolve it technically. You are also reading other texts, searching for models and methods to help them master certain writing skills. Finally, you are just plain thinking about your students a lot—and all of this takes time, energy, imaginative space which you are not giving to your own work.

And so, I am back full circle to why I had to give up full-time teaching to concentrate on my writing.

Now instead of my usual September nightmare, in which I am walking into a classroom, having forgotten my books, or walking into a classroom in which I suddenly find I have to teach postmodern literary theory and I know nothing about it, or walking into a classroom without my clothes on, my bad dream has to do with roaming through my deserted English department building wondering where everyone is.

And then, in one of those sudden dream-state shifts, they file down the corridors, my past students, whose names come back to me like an old roll call, Mike Laba, Lauren Husted, Alan Reeder, Eliza Harding, Ann Mitsakos, Suzanne Schneider, Ofelia Barrios, Abby Manzella—a long line of them.... Not quite Macbeth's line of kings that stretched out "to th'crack of doom," but a substantial enough crowd. Did I really teach that many young people?

It sure seems like it. These days my students are showing up not just in my dreams but in my life! I go on a book tour, and there they are in the audience. I visit a TV station and the producer took my poetry workshop ten years ago. I call for help from a computer software company, and a former student answers. I even got a rejection slip from a magazine with a note at the bottom from a student: *Remember me?* My babies are now out there minding the world or writing their own books or teaching their own students, maybe using one of my stories or poems, maybe saying, *This writer was once my teacher.*

8

But Tell Me, Do You *Like* Teaching?

PATRICIA HAMPL

It started for me with the Wife of Bath. I was twenty-two, and stood, with the assumed nonchalance of a true phony, before a group of college sopho-mores who were only a few years younger than I: my first class. I had not yet heard the word "pedagogy," and I had no wish or will to teach. I had tried to explain this to the kindly professor who told me I was one of the lucky graduate students: I had been given an assistantship and would be teaching Core Lit, which I gathered was a semester-long forced march through the thickets of English literature.

"But I don't *know* anything," I wailed. I wanted to be given a desk job, whatever that might be. I wanted to lick envelopes. Anything. The profes-sor frowned. He delivered a short disquisition on the bounties of a liberal arts education (which, presumably, I now possessed in the form of the B.A. I had earned the year before). He was firm: a person in English should be ready to teach anything.

I didn't think of myself as being "in English." I thought of myself as a writer, though claiming that identity was an act of faith or pure imagination. I was enrolled in an M.F.A. program, which secretly I considered faintly dis-reputable. It was 1968, early days for writing programs, and I retained a Hemingway-didn't-go-to-any-writing-workshop disdain for the academy. I had left my newspaper job, instinctively but confusedly sensing that the Writers' Workshop at the University of Iowa might be a better place for me than the *St. Paul Pioneer Press* copy desk where I had fuddled over headlines forty hours a week since graduating from college. Journalism was okay (Hemingway again), but teaching was, to my arty snobbery, deeply uncool. As an undergraduate, I had successfully avoided the education courses my mother had urged me to take so I would have teaching "to fall back on." After four years reading Romantic poetry and nineteenth-century novels, I left the University of Minnesota unscathed by any skill. I was ready to be the only thing my lack of preparation prepared me to be—a writer.

But here I was, a year later, in spite of everything, standing before the human equivalent of wet cement: a roomful of undergraduates waiting to be formed into a class. I was supposed to teach them the Wife of Bath's Tale. It was the first thing on the syllabus presented to all Core Lit teachers. My terror told me (accurately, I still think) that if I didn't *immediately* captivate these benignly sullen, slouching figures, I would be lost. The wet cement would harden against me. I had no idea what "teaching" was—nobody had told me—but like any cornered animal, I knew what survival was.

I asked a question. I can't remember now what it was. It doesn't matter. The point was that out of the foxhole of my terror, I grabbed a question and lobbed it out there at the massed troops—the enemy. My students. I will never forget the wave of astonishment, of blessed relief, that followed. Half a dozen hands went up, a little explosion of volunteers. I couldn't believe it. *They're doing it! They're being students! They think I'm a teacher!*

I was off to the races. Relief turned swiftly to delight. I discovered I liked teaching—if this was teaching: sitting with elaborate casualness in my Frye boots on the big desk at the front of the room, asking questions that, to my daily astonishment, elicited "discussion." From the Wife of Bath to *The Great Gatsby,* then back to pick up a little Whitman, and finally a lunge forward to a Cheever short story. On and on we went that first thrilling semester.

Core Lit wasn't, after all, a forced march through English literature. It was a romp over the genres; we jumped from century to century like gazelles. Do you think the Wife of Bath is sexy? What? You think she's *pathetic?* Nick Carraway—what kind of person is he? Would you want him for your friend? Would you date him? You think he's a dweeb? What do you mean, a dweeb? And then, getting nervier: What do you think Whitman is talking about when he speaks of "the dear love of comrades"? What is his vision of America? Does it say anything to you about the American presence in Vietnam? I wanted these Iowa undergraduates to hold up the Core Lit syllabus like a lens to the world that was grinding its old idealistic gears, contorting before us, changing forever during those ruinous war years. And my students seemed willing—amazing, improbable!—to do just that, to follow me, to compare and contrast, to discuss, discuss, discuss. I had never been taken so seriously. It was a kind of delirium.

I took hours over their papers. I was a veritable William Shawn of the blue book. I marked and edited, I wrote long thoughtful remarks in the margins. I archly challenged (*oh really? citation? logic?*), I coaxed and praised (*more! v. good! yes! brilliant!*). I indulged in the prissy pleasure of grammatical and stylistic wrist-slapping (*passive voice! paragraphing! awk! awk! awk!*).

And of course I began to see they liked me. There was a performance aspect to my life now that it had never possessed before. For the first time, I had a persona (I even taught my sophomores the word, but I was the one who was learning the meaning of it "on the pulses," as Keats says is the only way to know anything at all). I said things in class I would never say elsewhere—or I said things in a way that was unlike me, more extravagant, with a keen edge. A diva emerged.

This new person spoke with religious fervor about literature; she made the violins come up and the vibrato tremble. An urgency attended all my classes, and nobody missed a session. I had them. A strange authority had sprouted from the cracked earth of my native uncertainty. I made them laugh; I found I could even bring them to tears—those engineering students!—by reading a poem aloud in a ringing sepulchral voice, wholly unlike my own. I nurtured a world of shared meanings; jokes and assumptions grew around us, a lush garden of responses we planted and tended about literature, about language, and finally, about ourselves careening through those tumultuous times.

My teaching was operatic. Or maybe it wasn't an aria with improbable high notes, but a jazz improvisation built of riffs I seemed to maneuver successfully to the delight of my indulgent audience. I remade myself as an unlikely amalgam of the earnest and the hip. I realized with some kind of lateral knowledge that I possessed power over them—where in the world had it come from? It felt like a radiance, not a force, and I never doubted it was benign.

I showboated my way through three years of a performance high, externalizing my (genuine) idolatry of literature for the edification of the children of Iowa who sat before me dazed and probably amused by my urgency, but willing to be led by my lyrical instincts and my literary evangelism. For the first time in my life, I felt like a star. I liked the job description as I understood it: dazzle them.

And then I got my M.F.A. I left the university and spent ten years in a series of dumb and occasionally interesting jobs, writing and hanging out with others as poetry-besotted as I. The teaching, I thought, was over. I turned back into a pumpkin and the mice that I had harnessed scampered away, scattered to their lives.

America has a curious way of rewarding its literary writers (in distinction to its best-seller writers). If you publish a book of poems or a novel (or more recently, a memoir), you become eligible for a teaching job at a university. It's an attractive offer to many people (it was, eventually, to me). This employment pattern has caused much of American writing to be relentlessly workshop-driven even as the proliferation and success of writing programs have, in turn, been part of what has changed forever the English departments that foster them. Far from being the undervalued second-class citizens of English departments (the old version of things), today's university writers tend a growth industry that sometimes makes them appear to be seigneurs, jetting from their day jobs to readings and mini-workshops at other universities, while their scholarly colleagues struggle for scant humanities research funds to support work in arcane fields with small audiences.

But for literary writers it's very strange: you are given, as a sign of your (relative) success, a job that precludes your being the very thing you were hired as: a writer. This is not necessarily a pernicious arrangement, though it can feel absurd—maybe not the worst mental state for a writer. Scholars at research institutions—scientists and humanists—face the same balancing act, of course: the relation of "my work" to "teaching" is always a struggle. It's worth following the personal pronoun: scholars and writers alike speak of "my" work, meaning their writing or research. But when they refer to their teaching, the personal pronoun disappears. It is simply "teaching." This is how things are.

Yet the system is amazingly resilient and enormously successful: hundreds of writers apply for a single university position. The alternatives for most "midlist authors" and virtually all poets apparently are not as attractive, at least not typically, in spite of the examples of doctors and lawyers, insurance executives, daily journalists, and housewives who have been among the great ones in our literature. But it is also true, at least in my random observation, that if a writer hits a publishing jackpot, the teaching ends. Or is greatly reduced. *I'm just taking a leave of absence for a year,* the gleeful writer says. A bit, later, *Make that two.* But eventually, the formal letter of resignation comes: writers want to write.

In the end, many of us teach—a little or a lot. At our best, writers do this work the way work for hire is always done at its best—because we must and because we find we have a passion or at least a minor talent for it after all.

We like the students. Or we like to huddle with others who care about language and its potential. We like the summers off. We like being able to set our own schedules. It's a job, as the greenhouse workers my father worked with used to say with an accepting shrug. That shrug is a natural gesture of decent, ordinary respect for one's livelihood. It's a humble response, and it's a good one for a writer to have when you consider all the pious balderdash people can say about teaching. And having known, once upon a time, how to bring up the violins and make the vibrato tremble, I'd rather keep things simple.

When I came back to teaching, over ten years after my Core Lit performance highs, I was even more hesitant about the classroom than I had been as a graduate student begging to stuff envelopes for the English Department rather than stand in front of a roomful of students. My diva self had stayed back there in the 1960s past. I was no longer a hip older sister figure to my students. I was just older. More than that, I didn't have the will to form them that I had discovered at Iowa. Or perhaps I didn't have the will to perform. I had no pirouettes left in me. I didn't want teaching to be a high. I don't know why I had turned so absolutely against an experience that had been a kick. But I knew I would not—could not—sustain that kind of performance ever again. It was like knowing I'd never do cocaine again.

But this makes it sound drearier than it was. And more of a decision. It wasn't a decision—it was a recognition. I had begun teaching (in 1968) when "the canon" was writ—nay, engraved—in stone. I went through my entire undergraduate and graduate education without taking a single course in "women's literature" or "African American literature" or any other category that is de rigueur today—because there were no such offerings in the course catalogs of my schools.

Like a lot of writers and teachers of my generation, I devised reading lists of unfamiliar authors and prepared syllabuses for courses that had never existed before. I remember, sometime around 1984, filling out a mind-numbing university form to establish a course on "memoir and autobiography." It looked outrageous even to me—giving credit for writing about yourself? Please! Now, of course, there are seminars and conferences on autobiographical writing, and the *New York Times Magazine* has published a cover story entitled "The Age of the Literary Memoir." Being part of this cultural shift, this odd confluence of energies and furies, made it impossible to believe that teaching at a university was a retreat to an ivory tower. The university was part battleground, part salon. It was the Grand Central Station of a living culture going briskly about its business.

I no longer saw the people before me—my students—as wet cement, or as an aggregate of any kind. It seemed less important than it had in Core Lit to whip them into a frenzy of literary idolatry. In fact, that seemed ridiculous as a plan. I was a little in awe of the graduate students in particular: they were often older, they'd been around one tough block or another, and they came to their work with a set look in their eyes: they were going to do this thing—they were going to write. It was impossible not to feel kindred. They weren't my audience anymore. They were something closer to my colleagues. Their passion for the enterprise of words reaffirmed my own. Many of them had given up other careers or risked the scorn (or worse) of family to commit themselves to an M.F.A. program. Their lives were in the balance. I could feel that urgency—it emanated from them, not from a performance I might reel out to them.

Something else: I wanted—I want—great oceans and acres of silence around me—wet or dry, steep or flat, but endless fields of echoing quiet. It's where the writing is for me. I want to stare out a window, hours at a time, to let things coalesce. The oceans and acres, the hours and hours, are few and far between, and maybe that's what makes them sacred and sought after. But this deep hankering for quiet has changed my teaching too. The desire for silence is just about as selfish a desire as one can cherish. It is a desire for the experience of one's own consciousness, not a desire for the experience of others, which is felt as an interruption. This deepening desire for silence would seem to be inimical to teaching, that great hand-holding profession.

But not so. For in slowing down, I see that the students too wish nothing less: they too wish to stare and stare out their windows and into their patch of reality, to coax the sentences to come to them out of the mists of the inarticulate life they too are fleeing, just as I am and always have been. We meet over the word—their word, not mine—and in so doing, we meet as equals, anonymous acolytes before the mystery we are pledged to: the old vocation of wonder, finally written.

But now I see I'm beginning to go mystical, which is a soupy cousin to the balderdash I have promised to avoid. Put it this way: what I first thought, in my terror, must be an exhausting (if exhilarating) performance, has become a relation. I regard with growing awe the faces and manuscripts that pass before me, seeing that they too want to get it right, as I do. I can live with that. In fact, I want to, I must.

Sometime in the course of an interview—when I'm being "the writer," not "the teacher"—the interviewer always asks what I've come to call The Question. It is always placed well into the interview, almost at the end, in fact. And it is always a trick question. "Tell me," the reporter will say with that insinuating gotcha sweetness of journalists stalking their prey, "do you really *like* teaching?" He wants me to kvetch about the time taken away from "my work." Or he wants me, perhaps, to wax rhapsodic about the rapport I have with my students. He wants me to give a performance. And I often do. I kvetch a bit, nattering on as every writer on earth ever has, that I don't have enough time for my work. I sigh a what-can-you-do sigh. I am being The Writer. I am bundled in my black cape and my mystery. I have "my work," and nothing must detain me.

But someday I really should just stop in my tracks. *Tell me, do you really like teaching?* And instead of my doleful sigh, I should give him a pure hundred-watt smile, and offer him the real mystery, the one I don't begin to understand myself: *Yes,* I'll say, *yes, I do.*

9

Me, Myself, Menopause, and I

Dona Lee Davis

I'm fifty. I'm an anthropologist and a college professor. A substantial part of my academic research career has focused on women's experiences of midlife. In my late twenties and early thirties I spent a great deal of time and effort studying and interviewing what I deemed at the time as "menopausal women." While doing interviews and listening to middle-aged Newfoundland fishers' daughters, wives, and mothers talk to each other, I had a keen sense of being a voyeur of other women's aging experiences. I was a transient outsider looking in, and the prospect of ever being menopausal, myself, seemed remote and far away. I did, and do, joke to others, however, about this initial or first phase of my research career as "MY menopause years," and looking back at the books and articles I have written about the topic, I can honestly say that menopause has been good to me.

During my initial periods of research in Newfoundland, I looked on my older informants as somewhat exotic mother figures. These women, individually and collectively, had lived lives shaped by hardship and poverty as heads of families in pursuit of an undependable resource (fish) in a harsh and dangerous environment (the North Atlantic). Compared to my own comfortable middle-class background and relative youth, they seemed old enough to have been shaped by "real-life" experiences. My life as a blooming academic seemed to have no comparable gritty realities.

My mission, during my menopause fieldwork, was to collect data and test hypotheses in order to prove my abilities as a scholar. My goal was to produce academic books and articles. At the time, my menopause interviews, based on those that had been standardized for cross-cultural research, seemed to me to be intrusive and sometimes ridiculous. They contained questions I would never have dared to ask my own mother. Yet in retrospect, I now see at least the more open-ended sections of the interviews, plus my sustained interest in their experiences of midlife, as self-affirming for my research population. While I did ask my informants all the questions specified in menopause interview schedules—questions that placed them in the position of having to describe their lives in ways foreign to their experience (e.g., symptom checklists, attitudes toward aging, life stressor indices, menstrual status assessments, and use of Likert scales), I also presented my informants with an opportunity to reflect on their lives and present themselves on their own terms.

Perhaps it is more truthful to say that these strong and self-assured women took control of the interviews away from me and my silly questionnaires and drew upon their own narrative structures and value systems to represent their lives to an interested, if naive, outsider. By teaching me the lessons learned from their own lives, they helped to make my career and provided me with substantive data that would lead me to inject some common sense into the academic menopause literature over the next twenty years. I remember being at a conference during the middle phase of my menopause research years, where a well-known psychologist was presenting data from a longitudinal, large-sample survey on women's experience of the climacteric. The crux of the presentation was that the menopause was exceptional for being unexceptional. At the end of the presentation, which included lots of graphs and statistics, I overheard a conference participant in back of me say, "They could have saved a lot of time and money if they'd just asked a Newfoundland woman."

What I am now realizing is that these Newfoundland women, who saw me as raw material greatly in need of molding, also provided me with lessons in life that would guide me in the life choices that I have made. These lessons concern the value and meaning of social relationships. They are lessons I took to heart, and they have had positive, long-term effects on the quality of my own life. They taught me to stay focused on what is important to me, to look to friends and family for support, to get through the hard times as best you can, and to enjoy the good times. Perhaps most important of all for my own marital happiness, these women taught me to value gentle men.

I'm fifty. Have I lived a "real" life? I am at the ripe age for a menopause interview, and no dedicated, enthusiastic, naive young scholar has come forward to interview me. My life hardly has the drama of the trials and tribulations that characterized (and continue to characterize) my Newfoundland informants. I do not have their adeptness at storytelling skills. Nor do I have the sense, so acute in them, that my life and lifetime accomplishments have been all that important, or exemplary. At least as they saw it at the time, their self-sacrifice enabled those they cared for to live better lives. In contrast, I am childless by choice and have done pretty much as I have wanted to do.

As of yet, I have no menopausal identity. I have not yet "achieved the Menopause" (as they say in the scientific literature), and I have yet to experience my first symptom, although I am well-versed in what they can be and how they have changed in the research literature over the years. If I took seriously all the symptoms I have seen attributed to menopause, I would probably now be living in a state of perpetual panic. Many of my age mates are beginning to experience symptoms such as hot flashes, but I have yet to feel any sense of commonality with them based on the biology of aging. I continue to be extremely critical of the menopause literature and am anti-estrogen (or whatever drug company hormonal regimen is the current fad) and against the medicalization of menopause, and I find my reactions becoming personal as well as academic. When I was in the midst of writing this essay, the *CBS Evening News* (November 11, 1998) ran a drug company commercial for HRT (hormone replacement therapy), and two minutes later did a feature on women at risk for heart disease followed by an interview with the ex–surgeon general, who came across with nothing less than a shill for HRT. It made my feminist blood boil. I felt personally offended at being the target of manipulative, profit-driven, pharmaceutical industry scare tactics. I guess I would say that my menopause politics, if not my identity, have become more personal. As is true for the majority of women today, I expect to have negligible or minimal problems with menopause.

My own intentionally glib response to the growing number of casual inquiries about my own menopausal years is that "I've taken up polo to see myself through the 'change of life.' " Horses, not hormones, seem to work for me. Even if I do develop symptoms, I am an unlikely candidate for HRT, since I'm at risk for breast cancer. One can certainly accuse me of being insensitive to the sufferings of others at the "change of life." An academic colleague, who suffered terribly from hot flashes (as she informed me when I was finished with my cocktail-party anthropology menopause sermonette), found my cultural relativist approach to menopause—e.g., they don't have flashes in Japan—extremely offensive and wished upon me horrible hot flashes during my own menopause. Each woman, in my opinion, has to make her own decisions about HRT. There is a lot of confusing information and advice out there, and women's experiences are by no means uniform.

This, however, is MY menopause interview, it is about me, the person as well as the academic, and I can stand on my soapbox and say what I damn well please—so there!

From this stance at midlife (my maternal grandmother lived to be over 100), if I were to mark the present and past twenty-five years of my adult life in stages, they would pretty much reflect stages of my adult professional life, not social or biological life cycle transitions related to family cycles, aging process, or reproductive status. These stages I term my Newfoundland years, South Dakota years, and Norway years. This tripartite self-presentation is an artifact of this specific project and the editors' invitation to write about my life as a researcher and teacher. If I were asked to write a self-reflexive piece that emphasized my childhood, or my identities as wife, identical twin, or athlete, the narrative would be decidedly different. Like others in this postmodern world my narratives of identity are multiple and situated. Twenty years from now I may find this essay highly amusing. Certainly twenty years ago I took myself more seriously. I like the change.

The Newfoundland, Dakota, and Norway years do not follow any clear-cut timeline. In reality they feed into each other, overlap, and circle back. They serve as useful starting points for crystallizing my own life history into core themes through which I can explore my challenges, accomplishments, and frustrations as a researcher and a teacher. Periods of participant observation fieldwork, intensive research, and times of high adventure mark the Newfoundland and Norway years. They are times where I seem to take a vacation from my own life and enter the worlds of others. The Dakota years refer to my life at home—a life of everyday teaching. This, rather than the high-flying adventures of strange places, is my real life. It is the daily grind of lectures, grading, committee meetings, overheated offices, and long commutes—all embedded in a financially strapped institution where the professors exist at the bottom of the university pecking order.

THE NEWFOUNDLAND YEARS

Ever since I read my first Margaret Mead book (*Sex and Temperament*) at sixteen, I knew that I wanted to become a cultural anthropologist. My enthusiasm for the discipline has never waned. During the 1960s and early '70s I sailed through undergraduate and graduate school until I came to the point of having to decide on a doctoral research topic and where in the world I wanted to do my fieldwork. I had no clue. All I knew was where I did not want to go and what I did not want to do. I chose to take a few years off from graduate school life and accepted a job teaching anthropology and sociology at a small college, where I worked for three years. I enjoyed teaching and was good at it. Teaching undergraduate anthropology has never been difficult. It is seldom a required course, and students find it inherently interesting. It was at this early stage that I realized that some students had a knack for anthropology and some did not. A rather mediocre student with the knack could be nurtured into a rather exceptional one. Finding students with the knack or giving them the knack was and still is, to me, the most gratifying aspect of teaching.

I probably would have stayed as an M.A.-level instructor but for the fact that college budget cuts meant that the last hired were the first to be let go. I landed on my feet, getting a one-semester job on a university afloat program, where we traveled through southern Europe, North and West Africa, and the Caribbean. It was a marvelous teaching opportunity, and the experience whetted my appetite for fieldwork. I woke up one morning in Trinidad and knew that I wanted to go back to graduate school and do research on some aspect of aging in Newfoundland. Why Newfoundland? It wasn't overrun with anthropologists, it was cold (I get crabby in the tropics), there were no large spiders, and I would not be Bwana. Major decisions in my life have never been a big deal; I think it over and just wake up one day knowing what to do.

I went back to school and began to flourish, finding my niche as I settled into the Newfoundland literature and developed an interest in studying menopause. Fieldwork was still considered the sink-or-swim rite of passage into the discipline. But we had no preparation for it aside from writing proposals and getting them funded (which in actuality was quite a bit of preparation in terms of specific hypothesis to test, methods employed, literature reviews, and explanations of relevance of the study). The notion was to get there and do it. So I did. Fieldwork was a voyage of self-discovery. It was a professional proving ground, and I found that I had the "knack" too.

The first year and a half I spent in Newfoundland was a high point of my life. Doing fieldwork was the hallmark of professional identity in a field that had been the focus of my efforts for ten years. Although I envied my more assertive friends, my natural reticence and shyness were an asset in the small fishing village I chose for research and called "Grey Rock Harbour." I can remember telling friends, before leaving, that I could write the dissertation right now, all I needed was the correct amount of comparative data. Once I got to Grey Rock Harbour, however, I began to understand that it would take some time to establish rapport with local women before I began to ask them pointed questions about their menstrual cycles. For the first nine months of fieldwork, I let my informants educate me. They were excellent teachers. Their knowledge came from shared experiences and an intimate and lifelong knowledge of each other. At this point I began to realize that it was not all about data. Context was everything, and I began to focus my efforts in this area. By the time I actually got around to administering questionnaires, I had a keen sense of how inappropriately they reflected the worlds of meaning and experiences of my informants.

After fieldwork I was able to write up my dissertation, with a sense of confidence that it was going to be good and original. My positive fieldwork experience, enthusiasm for Newfoundland, and respect for and friendship with my informants, combined with an emerging body of literature in women's studies, made the writing easy. I also felt that I was writing something that was meaningful to the women who shared their world with me. This was my coming of age. At this point I also returned to the classroom, armed at last with my very own repertoire of fieldwork stories. I realized that this was where I wanted to be.

I received my Ph.D. in 1980 when the academic job market for anthropologists was coming to a screeching halt. Landing a tenure-track position was a priority for me. Unlike some of my peers, I was not willing to wait, perhaps for years, for a good opening at a graduate-level institution, and I decided to accept a position at the University of South Dakota. For the most part it was a decision that I have not regretted.

THE SOUTH DAKOTA YEARS

The first couple of years at USD were good. It was true joy to finally receive regular paychecks and feel that I could now "settle down." I got married, remodeled a house, and enjoyed my work. I taught large and small courses and developed my own courses in human sexuality, women's studies, medical anthropology, and psychological anthropology. We had a dedicated group of talented and enthusiastic anthropology majors. When I look at the syllabi for those years, I am astounded at the quality of education that our students were getting. My course contents in those days covered over four times the material, and much of it far more difficult, than what I do today. It was also a good time for research. I thrived as the only cultural anthropologist in the state. Research and travel funds were available and there was little competition for them. I was able to attend a number of international conferences that gave a real boost to my career. I taught nine hours a week and worked all the time, including weekends and holidays.

I love teaching anthropology. To me it is hardly like work at all. The environment I teach in, however, has changed dramatically over the last two decades. The tirade that follows covers issues that are certainly not unique to South Dakota. South Dakota is a poor state with no income tax. Our budget cuts predated those of most other state universities. The state board of regents and university administrators became the pawns of conservative state politicians, and a "dumbing down" of education began to take hold. A form of "prof-stitution" set in as faculty positions became dependent on the number of students who took their classes. We were urged to view students as consumers who would dictate their needs to us as faculty and educators. Some faculty responded to this numbers game by lowering their standards as a strategy to keep "warm bodies" in the classroom. I kept my standards high. Why should students suffer, in terms of the quality of their education, just because they have stupid administrators who give in to the agendas of narrow-minded, conservative politicians? Faculty today are up against incredible odds and at my university are demoralized and very negative. Our students want to pass a course with minimal effort. (National surveys show that our students spend less time studying than the national average.) If a syllabus for an introductory-level course states that all tests will be essay tests, half the students will get up and leave on the first day of class. Textbooks are easier now, and their test bank questions are too difficult for most of our students, who refuse to study and expect faculty to grade on a curve. I will not grade on a curve. My standards have dropped as low as they are going to get.

Until recently we were still free to determine our departmental curriculum and course contents. Three years ago, however, our brilliant state board of regents decided that we needed at least ten students in each class. Classes would be dropped from schedules after pre-enrollment; the large majority of students never bother to pre-enroll. Students would show up for the first day of class and find that the class had been canceled. Students could not get the classes that they needed to graduate. This semester, classes that were underenrolled were canceled after six weeks of regular meetings, when it was too late to enroll in another one. Faculty had their pay docked if their classes did not enroll. As one would expect, students voted with their feet, and we had huge enrollment drops. Three years of this system has taught us that ten students is too many for a seminar. Students do not get the individual attention they need and courses have to be taught differently to attract the requisite number of students. The numbers game means that we are pressured to drop difficult courses such as anthropological theory and develop ones with mass appeal like Lost Tribes and Sunken Continents and the Wild West in Film.

Our department has been at the forefront of computerizing our courses. We create assistantships and paid research jobs for our students. We actively recruit and retain minority students. I still feel that my visibility as a professional female role model is extremely important for my students, male and female alike. As a department, we continue to emphasize the development of writing skills among our upper-level students. But because they have fewer skills to begin with, it takes far more faculty time and effort to meet the needs of our individual students. At the same time, we are forced to take on even more students. Students are unable to critically analyze articles I routinely used for class assignments three years ago. We find ourselves spending far more time on the basics. We still have students with a good deal of potential talent willing to work hard. It is still very gratifying to have students who bloom under my tutelage. But our efforts are now supposed to be geared to keeping the most marginal ones in the system. What little professional autonomy we once had is eroding as "experts" from schools of education are now defining the goals of education for us.

This is my life as a teacher. I realize that we are pretty much a part of a trend that is now dominant. I realize that students today come to the university less prepared; many have dependents and work full- or part-time jobs. They have unrealistic expectations of being trained for the high end of the job market. But I also take the wider view that this process of dumbing down is related to the shrinking of the middle class and is designed to create docile, unchallenged workers/technicians for the low-wage service industries that dominate South Dakota's economy. When I first came to USD, I believed that students (at least in anthropology) were getting the same quality of education that was available at the best state universities, and that the best state universities had opportunities equivalent (if the student was ambitious) to the Ivy League. This is no longer true. The upper classes are taking care of themselves, and look at what is happening to mainstream America.

Am I outdated, burned out, behind the times? Do younger professors come into the system with new agendas and strategies to work or fight the present system? Maybe, but my sense of decline is very much rooted in the present and comes from contrasting my teaching experiences at USD with those at the University of Tromsø, a radical and progressive university in Norway. At my time of life I see Norway as the frosting on the cake of my professional career. In contrast to USD, where the new ideal seems to be to train students to be automatons who will sit at a computer all day, and where we are constantly pressured to make anthropology applicable and relevant to the agendas of the state's reactionary politicians, students at UITØ are trained to be critics of the state. The social sciences are highly valued for their ability to produce such critics. The goal of faculty and the administration is to challenge students with a theoretically sophisticated brand of social anthropology.

THE NORWAY YEARS

I returned to Newfoundland for a second period of field research in 1989–90. Quite by chance I met Vigdis Stordahl, a Sami Norwegian anthropologist. Through Vigdis, I was invited to come to Tromsø and deliver a series of lectures on Gender and Fishing. The following year I was offered a five-year visiting professorship in the Department of Social Anthropology and Sami Studies. The position was renewed last year. I fulfill my position by giving lectures and working with graduate students. I travel to Norway for six to eight weeks every year. This is my latest leg in life's journey.

Teaching at USD and UITØ is a study in contrasts. Students at the latter are highly motivated and very serious about their scholarship. They see their professors not as service employees whom they have paid for with taxes, but as highly respected scholars and mentors. Faculty carefully decide on reading lists, choosing what they feel is the best of the anthropology literature. Their standards tend to emphasize the more esoteric dimensions of anthropology as a philosophy of knowledge. Students have a great deal of autonomy, with semester or year end exams and no requirement for attendance at lectures. Lectures are divided in two-hour periods, with forty-five minutes of lecture and then discussion. The students are very adept at intellectual discussions, and I get immediate feedback on what got through and how it was assessed. Students and faculty both actually read the articles I have written (at USD they just count them), and we have an active discussion about them. A number of master's students have and are currently pursuing research in the areas of medical and psychological anthropology, areas introduced and legitimized in the curriculum by me. Although they have no illusions about my standing in the discipline, my Norwegian colleagues and students admire my diligence and productive output. I am surrounded by faculty who are actively engaged in multiple research projects for which there seems to be constant funding. I am hosted graciously and made to feel special and valued. It is, as I said earlier, the frosting on the cake. It does just about double my workload, but has given me a sense of reward in life, from both personal and academic perspectives.

From my Norwegian friends and colleagues I also have learned that there is always time to invite someone to dinner and that no matter how busy one is with work, one must take time to enjoy the natural surroundings. The Tromsø experience has also given me a new appreciation of my students back home. Through new eyes, I now see their creativity, resourcefulness, ability to see their own culture, and writing abilities. At Tromsø, students are told what to read and depend on their faculty to select articles. Our American students find their own articles and rely on their own skills to assess their relevance. They are much better at separating the chaff from the wheat, whereas my Norwegian students tend to get caught up in minutiae. By bridging the two systems, I am positioned to bring the benefits of each system to the other.

I spent last year on my sabbatical in Norway beginning fieldwork in two northern communities. I am living proof that you can learn a new language at fifty, but it does not happen overnight. I am in no rush; my research efforts in Norway will evolve slowly. I also plan to go back to Newfoundland for a final study before I retire. It is interesting that many of my peers are making active plans for retirement. I am content to have my research career slow down but certainly not end.

One of the most rewarding things for me at this stage of life is the realization that I have earned (I am from New England) the right to step back from teaching and research to enjoy myself and to take the time for my own recreational purposes. I now have the resources and make the time to do so. I always had enjoyed riding horses and grew up with them, but could not afford one until the Norway appointment. I started playing polo and then bought my own horse and returned to my earlier interest in eventing. I was once a very successful competitive equestrian; I no longer have the strength, quickness, or talent I once had, but I still have patience and a good bit of nerve. At the stable I'm surrounded by new middle-aged friends who are in the same boat.

Last April I turned fifty. I was in Norway far away from home and husband. If I were home I probably would have gone out for dinner and received black balloons at work. In Norway the fiftieth birthday is very special. You are truly feted as friends and colleagues "celebrate" your life. It was a wonderful experience that lasted for days. I felt validated as a person, a professional, a valued teacher, and a friend. Still, I do not feel transitional, menopausal, or old. I have had my share of visits to the doctors that resulted in the loss of body parts. I took these in stride, but also realize that despite diet and exercise you can still be vulnerable in ways you never anticipate. The lesson learned is to enjoy the present.

I'm fifty. The changes in my life have not really been marked by external events or changes in my own body. They have been marked by stages of my career. I have benefited and will continue to benefit from being part of the baby boom cohort. As a woman I have had opportunities and choices that were far less available to my own mother. As we age, my powerful cohort will not be ignored. Like my peers, I feel less old at fifty than the last generation. I can live with the fact that there are frustrating aspects to my job and that I am no longer attractive to young men (I was recently told I must have been a beautiful woman twenty years ago), that the modest peak of my research career has already been reached, and I have no desire to jump the horse over four-foot fences. I also realize that I have been very privileged. My employment depends on my mind and not my body; I have financial security; my job is inherently interesting, challenging, and multifaceted. My home life is secure and happy. Not all women are as fortunate, nor would all value the life I have lived and that choices that I have made. My husband, a psychologist, has diagnosed me as chronically happy. There is definitely a Pollyanna streak in me. (Do not equate this with being shallow, naive, or dishonest!) But as I said, I'm fifty, this is my midlife statement, and somehow, like my Newfoundland informants, I now find myself "freed up" or entitled to talk about myself and my life. The Newfoundland women told me that "just because life is hard, it does not mean you're sick." I guess I would say, "Life does not have to be hard to be real." Further analysis, reader, is up to you.

10

Reflections on Teaching (and Life in General) Once You've Become a Grandmother

JEAN BETHKE ELSHTAIN

From each of us a CV or resumé of some sort is requested if we have been asked to present a lecture or address a university on some special occasion. I usually send the "short version," which includes a few book titles; a few honors; an approximation of the number of essays, articles, chapters in books, etc., the usual "professional stuff." But I have insisted from the beginning that this "introduction" also include the fact that I am the mother of four children and, as of this writing, the grandmother of three, one of whom, a three-year-old boy, is being raised by my husband and me. Now that final fact I *don't* mention. It raises too many questions in people's minds. What happened to the child's parents? Did Jean and her husband, Errol, adopt the child? The answer to the latter is yes. The answer to the former is that our oldest daughter, Sheri, a person with mental retardation, and her then husband, also a person with mental retardation, could not, even with massive round-the-clock assistance, manage the care of their little boy. He has been with us since he was a month old. In our mid-fifties we are starting all over as parents.

I was always out of sync. I married for the first time very young—eighteen years old, high school sweetheart, five years and three children later—well, the reader can figure out the rest. Remarried within two years of my divorce, I entered a marriage that is now in its thirty-third year, and had a fourth child. And now the cycle begins again. When most of my contemporaries in college were moving into psychedelics or psycho-breakdowns or political action of the relentless and often reckless variety, I wrote letters to editors, went on marches, stood in silent vigils, handed out informational material on sympathy demonstrations with Martin Luther King and the SCLC in Birmingham, but I worried about my little girls, and then their baby brother, a lot. What sort of people did I want them to be around? Folks in the throes of various breakdowns that R. D. Laing had assured everybody would be breakthroughs but mostly resulted in temporary desuetude if not derangement. Children need more than "love." They need predictability and stability and the assurance that certain people will be there for them and won't be so bent out of shape they can't get up in the morning and help with breakfast and getting ready for playschool or so out of it they can't stir in the middle of the night when a tummy aches or a heart breaks over a daytime trauma or a nighttime terror.

Even as many of our friends were exploring without limits, I was writing—even my earliest writing—about the need to pay attention to limits: not just cultural norms and how far one should test or break them, or political rules and how much one should spurn them, but the limits to our own quite mortal and vulnerable bodies. When you are young and full of energy, this isn't the easiest thing to think about. But I had a head start. Having had infantile paralysis at the age of ten; having known what it was like not to be able to wiggle a toe even with the mightiest effort of concentration; having lain for nights wracked with the most extraordinary pain, as if thousands of tiny needles were prickling my entire body; having been kept in "isolation" for ten days, yanked from my family and stuck in solitary confinement in a hospital miles away, for that is what they did to polio "victims" in those days, I pretty much knew life was no protean picnic where you could be anything you wanted to be and never have to pay a price for false starts. I had wanted to be the first woman New York Yankee (of course, when I was a small-town Colorado kid, the Yankees were my team because of No. 7, Mickey Mantle, who hailed from Oklahoma, almost next door, and besides, he was a switch-hitter just like me). I had even figured out elaborate ruses that would enable me to get round the "shower and locker room" problem. Well, that was not to be. Nor did I ever climb Long's Peak with my dear Daddy. In fact, after the age of ten, I could never run again except in my dreams. After a time, the dreams stopped too.

I never did a "why me?" about polio. I figured I had the answer. Better me than my sister, Pat, nearest me in age, because I could "handle it better."

God had picked me for testing. Would I be up to the job? My life has been haunted by that recognition and that question because, you see, on some deep level, constitutive of my very being, I still believe it. So the academy for me was "overdetermined," as we learned to say in the sophisticated 1970s. I couldn't play sports; I couldn't be a war correspondent; I couldn't be a foreign journalist. It wasn't just the physical limits that stood in the way but all those babies. You could combine the academy—and I had been a bookworm all my life—with family better than with nearly anything else given the flexibility of the academic schedule. So: armed with a Ph.D. and four children, I started my "academic career" in 1973 at the University of Massachusetts. Three years later I became an associate professor. Four years after that I "made Full."

But that isn't what made this a resounding success in my eyes. Rather, what gave meaning to it all was the fact that I thought of my life's work as a vocation, not a career. I had been called in some way. This being-called business is inexplicable, I find, to those who weren't raised in the strong Protestant tradition of the meaning of a call. To be called is to be infused with a sturdy sense that *this* task has been given one to do; that there is some design and purpose at work that one might not fully understand but to which one must respond. Think about how often we say, "Somehow this seems meant to happen." Or: This "just feels right." These latter are diminutives, so to speak, of the claim that, to the believer, is a call from God that emerges after prayerful reflection and to which one must give prayerful attention. It isn't some silly idea of the deity whispering in your ear but of some clear sense of your purpose.

Given the backdrop of the call, the word "career" always stuck in my craw as, well, too "careerist" sounding. So I never used it. When I started teaching, although I was a multimom, I was also quite young, in my early thirties, not much older than many of my students. We seemed part of the same cohort in many ways. We had gone through, or remembered, the same tumultuous events. In the 1970s, professors could "hang out" with students at the local pub and drink beer and talk for hours and nobody "thought anything about it." We all knew of some liaisons that would now fall under a cloud of suspicion. But no one really cared. It was a different time and place. Many lines were blurred, including the "professional" and "private" or "social" divide.

But times change. Subtle, then major, alterations in the zeitgeist, especially about faculty-student relations—some for the good; some, I am convinced, quite ill-conceived—have frozen the surface of much sociality. But one starts to think, as you move well into your forties and your teenage children, especially your daughters, don't like to see mothers who still dance to rock and roll and who still catch the eyes of men, that something's got to give. Some women resent this mightily. I resented it but understood it, and besides, the crush of professional responsibilities and growing public duties and recognition effectively quashed the remnants of my late-1960s persona—that and the decline of my parents.

Fortunately, I come from a large, closely knit, and quite wonderful family. My sisters and brothers and I all played a role in tending to our parents, although my sister Bonnie and her husband, John, who lived just a half mile from "the folks," bore the brunt of their unhappy deterioration: with Dad, Alzheimer's; with Mom, Parkinson's disease accompanied by depression. There were many trips to Colorado, each sadder than the next. But life was being renewed as well. My dad died with our daughter Heidi (who was in Colorado with her husband to help care for her grandparents) holding his hand. She was seven months pregnant with the first great-grandchild for my parents; a first grandchild for us. My mom lived to see this child, JoAnn Paulette Welch, another "Bethke woman" with all the traits already attributed: willfulness, energy, smarts, don't-tread-on-me-ness. A damn fine heritage, I'd say.

And my energy? It goes into work and into family and into travel. I "hit the road" around 1981 and have never gotten off, though the onset of some postpolio symptoms and the jolt of new parenthood promise to force me to ease up some.

The thing is: I love what I do. I like most of the people I meet and find that even some of those I may have jousted with most vociferously in print are real human beings with things to say that can't simply be wrong, any more than what I say can simply be right. For me, "midlife" women's stuff was a nuisance because I had all sorts of "troubles" that culminated (my choice) in a complete hysterectomy in January 1992. But I was back on the road and in the classroom in three weeks. And I have never "missed" my excised parts: they had done ample duty and I just felt relief. One of the things I learned during polio was that excessive focus on one's body can be debilitating, paralyzing, if you will. One gets up in the morning and does what it is given one to do. I am so grateful that the academy has given me this space and that I have wound up at an institution—the University of Chicago and its divinity school—with such an extraordinary tradition of intellectual accomplishment, scholarly inquiry, and collegial decency.

I feel blessed. Too damn busy. But blessed. The rest of my life will be spent sorting out the nature of this blessing. I described myself recently as halfway between Wittenberg and Rome on the pilgrim's progress of my life. I have found that thinking "with God" rather than without God is far more challenging intellectually. But I also know that these are not, certainly in the Christian tradition, primarily matters settled by reason but, rather, by love. Yet it is a love laced through and through with thought. As Robert Bolt has Sir Thomas More proclaim in his play *A Man for All Seasons*, God made human beings to "serve Him wittily in the tangle of their minds." Serving wittily isn't bad. I hope I have many more years of service ahead. There are more books in mind and there are those grandchildren to marvel at: what will their vocations be?

II

Mud Ponies

DIANE GLANCY

WHEN THE WALL IS FALLEN, SHALL IT NOT BE SAID UNTO YOU,
WHERE IS THE DAUBING WITH WHICH YOU DAUBED IT?

Ezekiel 13:12

MUD DAUBER *N:* ANY OF VARIOUS WASPS (ESP. FAMILY SPHECIDAE)
THAT CONSTRUCT MUD CELLS IN WHICH THE FEMALE PLACES AN
EGG WITH SPIDERS OR INSECTS PARALYZED BY A STING TO SERVE AS
FOOD FOR THE LARVA.

Webster's New Collegiate Dictionary *(1981)*

Actually, I've arrived from the passage of midlife pas-sage.

My students are younger than my children.

Midlife is grown children, tenure, publications.

What do I have left? More publications? Fellow-ships so I don't have to teach for a semester or two? Full professor, though I only have a M.F.A. and no one without a Ph.D. is a full professor at the college where I teach? Retirement? Grandchildren?

In Exodus 2:3, Moses' ark of bulrushes was daubed with slime and pitch. In Genesis 6:14, Noah's ark was pitched. I guess I could say midlife is having the cracks (some of them) filled with work (some of it anyway). Chances are the vessel will float.

There's a Pawnee story called "The Boy and the Mud Ponies."

A long time ago there were no horses. A boy had a dream about ponies. He knew their shape and how their tails and manes looked. He made two ponies from mud. He took the ponies to the creek and pretended they were drinking. He took the mud ponies to the good grass to eat. One night, the boy had another dream. He dreamed he heard singing and he remembered the song. When he woke, he sang the song. In his singing, the mud ponies came alive. That's how the horse came to the Pawnee. (Astrov 1946)

For years I wrote without publication, but I kept daubing. Kept wanting publication. I kept singing my work a song to live.

Now these are some of the mud ponies I saw. Writing that is daubing, that is significant as the vessel (the life) it daubs, though one meaning of daub is crude, unskillful. To reflect the broken context. The contra-dictory. To walk in two worlds. To walk in none. To straddle a mixed-blood heritage. To write about faith/tradition. To break up paragraphs. Sentences. To work with the cohesiveness of dis-cohesiveness. To remake a mud nest into various genres instead of rooms (after the children are gone). Because it takes a mix of genres to reflect the fragmentation. (There actually was a mud room in an old house we had—just inside the back door, to hang coats and leave boots.)

In *Firesticks,* for instance, my second collection of short stories, I use creative nonfiction with the short story and a novella, the sections of which are divided between the stories and creative nonfiction. *Firesticks* are words. Which make campfires. Which are stories. And the relationship of the stories to one another.

It is the song, the voice, the breath, the words in the story, the force and determination of them.

I recently asked for two new courses at my college: environmental writing and writings on faith. I will teach nature writing in the spring. Faith has to wait at my school. But I had an e-mail from a student I had had before. She wanted to take nature writing, but asked if she could take it as an independent project, which means no class attendance, no reading of the material, no critical input on the work of her peers during workshop, and more importantly, no critical comments from them on her work. She just writes and I read it and make comments.

It may have been she who asked if it were possible to speed-read in my Native American literature course. I said that I didn't think so. The literature is usually convoluted with many narrators and not a straight narrative, with a lot going on in the subtext. It is hard enough to read slowly. Something like the Bible, which I read when I'm searching for more faith.

The word that came to mind about her is *shortcut.*

Maybe I could speed-read the Bible to get over those long and uncomfortable passages more quickly. To save time—so I can go on to other things. Maybe I could shortcut grading student papers. Maybe I could shortcut a lot of responsibilities.

As a Christian, I have found there's something slow about the way God works that is sometimes irritating. But more irritating is the shortcut or shortcutter. Maybe it is the untempered daubing (whitewash) warned against in Ezekiel 13:14–15.

Maybe midlife passage is an acceptance of the work it takes. A recognition of how much is involved in getting where you want to go, and how long it takes to get there, especially if it has the significance (in my opinion) of grown and responsible children, of teaching and writing. Especially when you come from nowhere and have a long way to go, and have no one but yourself to get you there.

My second novel, *The Only Piece of Furniture in the House,* published in 1996, was written when my children were small and playing beside the table as I wrote. My son is now thirty-four, my daughter thirty-one, and the book was just published three years ago.

But years ago I didn't have an outlet. I sent the manuscript out and it was rejected, and I put it in my files for twenty-five years.

My first novel to be published, *Pushing the Bear,* about the 1838 Trail of Tears, took eighteen years to write. It seems like it took longer to find an agent and a publisher.

I had so much written before I was ever published. I still have so much written which is not yet published. I work on several projects at once. Two novels, more essays, some poetry. In the summer of 1998 I received a fellowship to the Sundance Native American Screenwriting workshop at UCLA. Now I also am working on a script for my third novel, *Flutie.* During the same summer, I also gave workshops at conferences in poetry and fiction in Utah, New Orleans, Colorado, and the Arts Guild in Chicago. I drove to see my brother in Missouri. I drove to see friends in Michigan. I also separated from a companion of seven years. We didn't have the same vision. I'm not willing anymore to make adjustments, to accommodate.

But then I had to deal with the loneliness. Well, after three months, I called my companion. We had dinner. I don't know what will happen.

I want to say that *Flutie,* my third novel, came out as soon as I finished it, and I wrote it quickly. Two research trips back to Oklahoma. But *Flutie* was a com-posite of the students I had while I worked as artist in residence for the State Arts Council of Oklahoma. She was partly me, and it had taken my whole life to deal with the subject of shyness. Of not being able to speak.

I don't know why it took so long, but it did.

There has been a long obedience to writing. I didn't have as much trouble with that as I did the obedience to a Christian walk.

But how should I interpret obedience (which faith takes)? Especially as a writer. There is obedience to the tenets of Christianity that can be different than the obedience to a vision. What do I do with the stuff that comes that Christians frown at? In my new collec-tion of short stories, *The Voice That Was in Travel,* there is a story called "She," about incest between a mother and daughter. It was in church I heard that story. Years ago, women with various hurts in their lives met once a week at the church I attended. One of the women's stories was about her mother's abuse. The minister sat there and listened and prayed with us. It was a story that stayed with me, and I finally decided to write about it. There also is obedience to one's artis-tic vision, even if it has the feel of transgression.

I was sitting in my office in January over interim two years ago, when I stopped what I was doing and wrote, "I only wanted to have my hands in the threads. I only wanted to sew." As I continued writing, I decided it was the voice of the New Testament Dorcas, the seamstress, also in midlife passage—well, past it. Whenever I had a chance, I continued to write about her life, death, and return to life. I had the same sense of transgression as I put words into the mouth of a woman who had lived. Who probably didn't particularly want me writing about her. I called the manuscript *Dorcas,* which my daughter said was a dorky title, and now it's called *The Closets of Heaven.*

I finished the manuscript and sent it to my agent. Six or eight months later she called and said she couldn't sell it, and furthermore, she was moving to Israel. Anyway, it's back to the beginning without an agent or publisher for this manuscript. But I've sent it out again. By midlife, I know it's a matter of time until it is published. Christ's sufficiency is the waves where I don't always want to float. But I've received grace for obedience to the faith (Romans 1:5).

Though he were a son, he learned obedience by the things he suffered; and was made author of eternal salvation (Hebrews 5:8–9). For the Christian, anyway.

I've always liked the story of Job in the Old Testament. He lost all his animals, his servants and children. His three friends came and offered advice. Finally, in chapter 38, God asks the friends, Eiphaz, Bildad, and

Zophar, *Where were you when I laid the foundations of the earth? Where were you when I shut up the sea with doors?* After they closed their mouths, the conclusion to the whole story comes in chapter 42 when Job says, *I have heard of God by the hearing of the ear, but now I see him with my eyes.*

Cynthia Ozick writes about Job in an article, "The Impious Impatience of Job" (1998). "The ways of the true God cannot be penetrated," she says. "The false comforters cannot decipher them. Job cannot uncover them." In other words, we can make mud ponies, but the dream and the song from which the horses come do not originate with us. All our daubing, however necessary, is only a part. There always is something other than what we are.

The writing of words takes obedience and patience also. When I'm writing, I go over and over the words. Sometimes I have to shut my ears to the discouragement around me. I think I am more than I would be without obedience. It has been for my benefit.

I think I've already said midlife feels solid and grounded. I have learned to be patient with slowness.

My daughter, when she graduated from high school, wanted to become a lawyer, after I was divorced and on my own, traveling for the Arts Council of Oklahoma, knowing there was no way around the hard economic wall we faced. But we borrowed money for the seven years she was at the University of Kansas. She was (we were) $30,000 in debt when she finished. The student loans were called Sallie Maes. Bit by bit we returned the money. The loans were paid off in January of 1998. She is a lawyer in Kansas City, Missouri. In the summer of 1997 she married Scott Brouillette. I am going to be a grandmother in October 1999.

I called to the Lord and my cry came before him, even into his ears. The earth shook and trembled; the foundations of the hills moved. There went up a smoke out of his nostrils and a fire from his mouth devoured; coals were kindled by it. He bowed the heavens and came down, and darkness was under his feet. He rode upon a cherub and did fly upon the wings of the wind (from Psalm 18).

I think, too, of the years it took for my son to settle in his teaching career.

But Daniel prayed three months for an answer.

Israel was in Egypt four hundred years.

Noah waited a week closed up in the ark with the animals, the neighbors taunting him until it began to rain. Rain no one had ever seen.

I still have spaces between the boards of the house that I'll always have to daub. A Native American and Christian aesthetic. Writing and teaching. Mother and self. It is why I have two feet, one for each world. Or I have four more feet by riding a mud pony. Then (actually) I have six feet. For mud ponies, arks, mud-daubers' nests, mixed genres, mixed metaphors, heritages and mixed messages.

I keep a small mud-dauber's nest in my collection of natural objects. I don't remember the house it came from. Probably it was in Oklahoma. But I think of the pieces of mud the mud-dauber carried over and over, bit by bit, until the nest was shaped. Then the work of catching and stunning insects, packing them into the chambers. I could transfer that image to my own writing. I'm working on *The Library,* a novel in which I'm trying to write a creation myth for the written word. It's the spoken word that's magic in Native American belief. The voice creates from the sound it makes. But written words kill the voice. Leave it in a coffin on the page.

I'm also working on *An American Language,* which is about words and their loss through Alzheimer's.

Daubing has affected my life as a teacher also. I started with various fractures (*fictures* is the word I first wrote). Working which is writing the structure of courses, teaching, reading, and making comments on students' papers. All the other details of teaching. Going over them and over them. Sometimes I'd rather be reading a book I want to read, or writing, or working with critical theory for the Native American literature I teach. The multiplicity of its subtexts. The fragmentary decenteredness of its texts.

Gerald Vizenor has a term, timberline, he uses in his book *Fugitive Poses,* which I use in my Native American literature course. The term describes our two-sided language. I struggle along his timberline of word and silence. Of language as meaning and no meaning. All that floats between. Equine language. The stories behind the words behind the voices of the stories. Language as a living being like the earth that depends upon a variability of variables and layers of recipro-city. A wobbliness I worked with in my essays, *The Cold-and-Hunger Dance.* Pulling the abstraction of contemporary poetry into the essay (parts of it anyway).

What lasts after all of this is over? The chambered nest when the wasps move out? I have walls that still need to be daubed with faith and work. I'm into a new semester and the travels that come each year. The Poetry Society of America's What's American about American Poetry? conference in New York. My play *The Woman Who Was a Red Deer Dressed for the Deer Dance,* presented at Raw Space by Sage Theater also in New York City. Another conference called Women of the Book: the Changing Face of Feminism in Judaism, Christianity, and Islam, at the University of Texas at Austin. The professional conferences: American Studies Association in Seattle, Wordcraft

Circle of Native Writers in Albuquerque, MLA in San Francisco, Associated Writing Programs in Albany.

But what will stand when it is over? That's my concern of (past) midlife. Especially on a rough flight back from Austin, Texas, in a windstorm. If my life stopped, what mud wall would stand? Maybe death is the ability to face the same uncertainty that life is. You get into it (like birth) not by choice but circumstance. Probably what lasts (I hope) is the understanding, the discovery of voice, thought, the spirit that is more than life.

Why do I do this? Because I choose to. Because I have an inclination for it. The words keep coming. The act of daubing. Wall after wall. It is what I found to do. It's what I made room for to do. It's what I had to do or else be open to the ravages. I imagined walls that make a habitat for imagination. Things disappear as life moves on. Even though the walls are daubed. Other things stay. I know the real horses come from mud ponies. I know a song that makes them live.

I remember walking to my car, looking at it from behind, when I was loading it for the trip to Missouri or Michigan. Its doors open on both sides, held out to me like arms. A biplane, if I opened all four doors. Ready for takeoff.

In my patience I possess my soul (Luke 21:19).

12

Unsettled Weather

GAIL B. GRIFFIN

August 1998

Dear Ramona,

I got your letter just before I left for two weeks. I have been writing back in my head ever since.

Today is a day exactly like the one on which you wrote, as you describe it so beautifully: "unsettled but heavy and still. Plotting something."[1] Oh, yes: the hardening of the arteries of a midwestern summer. That collection of repressed atmospheric gunk heaped over a Michigan July. Stifled and stifling; irritable, potentially murderous weather. Just like being around a really angry but silent woman.

When I spoke to Emily by phone, she said you kept referring to the letter as "crazy" after you sent it. After I finished it I smiled, remembering that assessment. Pure Ramona. What you deem crazy attests to how controlled, organized, and focused you think you ought to be. "I am as unsettled as the summer," you say. Working for the college food service while flailing around in search of God, passion, calling? Shoot, girl, I wanted to have it bronzed as an eternal testament of what it means to be a college senior at millennium's end.

But you don't want or need to hear that, I know. The last thing anyone wants is to hear that her struggle is typical, especially of her age. Believe me, I keep trying the term "midlife crisis" on for size, and every time, I come up with a stockbroker buying a Miata and having an affair with his secretary.

The longer I teach, the more students I usher in the door at eighteen, out at twenty-two, the more I am convinced that your particular moment in life—the moment before the exit—is one in need of voice. Since the days when people left college with a B.A. and entered a career, virtually everything has changed but the language with which we talk about this awful boundary.

In your case, maybe in most cases, the "job issue"—the question of what you will actually be doing to earn a living a year from now—masks a much deeper question, one I hope we have indeed wrestled with productively in the classes we've asked you to take: the question of meaning itself. Oddly, it's our most significant questions that can be reduced to clichés: "the meaning of life" is what all college students have the solipsistic luxury of worrying about, right? But in your historical moment, it seems to me that this issue has reincarnated itself in monstrous form. The question of meaning is *the* postmodern question, isn't it? The problem of transcendent meanings casts its shadow over this bloody century and its works, from Woolf and Hemingway to Toni Morrison and Tim O'Brien; from the Great War through the Holocaust, Vietnam to the horrendous slaughters in Africa and Eastern Europe. So now, at century's end, how could someone of your intelligence not wonder about the capacity of an English major and a music minor—the English language and the language of music—to see you through, to keel your voyage, to provide a linguistic framework that will make sense of the world? Here at the millennium, twenty-one signifies more than a legal beer.

Nor can forty-eight, I find, be explained in terms of menopause and empty nests, the two traditional tropes that are supposed to make sense of a half-lived female life. I've helped to raise thousands of other women's children, and frankly, I'm thrilled that they're not waiting for me when I stagger home at night. And the main change menopause will make in my life will be that I won't have to worry about whether my Super Plus will make it through a two-hour committee meeting. Yet I do find myself intensely conscious of my time of life. It seems to have brought me to new vistas. Above all, it seems very contradictory: to play on your word for the weather, so much seems settled—determined, established—that even more seems unsettled, unsettling.

I wonder if your letter has accompanied me in my travels and back to Michigan because I see some commonality between the critical moments at which we stand, looking at each other—you entering adulthood, I entering the second half of my life. Women were not supposed to be adults; innocence was always a woman's prime virtue, youth her prime attraction. Her legal status has often paralleled that of children. Women who grew old got, and get, poor, desexualized, despised, ridiculed, burned and hanged as witches. You and I stand at the boundaries of territory charted mostly by cartographers who knew nothing of us and did not wish us well. As I think about it, it seems to me that one of the fundamental projects of women's studies in its first generation has been to "write a woman's life,"[2] a whole life, livable and meaningful unto its end. For second-wave feminists crossing fifty, that project is urgently personal.

In your letter, your term for the source of meaning that informs and directs a life is *passion*. Already you've located yourself in a tiny minority, the lunatics who think life can or should be defined by some kind of passion. You look at your parents: "I don't know what either of them is passionate about, or if they even are passionate about anything. I do not know if they understand passion—I don't think that figures in." Not wanting that, you turn to yourself, in "an attempt to determine, or at least truly think about, what it is that I love, want, am, and what I have always simply done, either because I'm good at it or out of some obligation. . . . I know I must be passionate about something, but this realization leads me back to an uncertainty as to what I am passionate about, and the luxury and frivolity of what I am passionate about."

Reading your letter across a twenty-seven-year divide, I find myself in dizzying motion. I am most obviously situated with your parents in this drama, remembering a time when I thought life would be lived passionately, every minute (or at least every other day). I want to tell you life's not like that; I want you to know how much of it is dailiness, drudgery, obligation. I want to ask how well you think you know your parents, how much of their lives, before and after your birth, is obscured from you. I want to tell you how the passion of fifty is different from that of twenty, how it burns lower because it must burn longer, steadier, without burning down the house.

And then suddenly I'm no longer your parents; I'm you. I'm forty-eight, but asking the same question, trying to winnow "what it is that I love, want, am" from "what I have always simply done, either because I'm good at it or out of some obligation." My horrible midlife recognition is what a good girl I have been. Despite departing from every model, every stereotype of the middle-aged woman, despite never marrying and never having kids, never even changing jobs, I have been such a good girl. I have lived more of my life than I can bear to think about for very long out of obligation of one flavor or another—obligation to parents, to teachers, to students (overwhelmingly to students), to institutions, to some ingrained notion of responsibility that is, I know, profoundly gendered.

I am trying to remember if, between twenty-two and forty-eight, there was a moment when it all came clear to me. I think there was. I think it came on a bright morning perhaps four or five years after I started teaching at Kalamazoo—that would put it around 1982 or '83. I would have been facing tenure. And tenure suddenly became problematic: a lame-duck president established the first tenure quotas in the college's history, and my department was otherwise tenured up. Around me, colleagues were anxious, zealous, lobbying and worrying on my behalf. But I moved in a calm that I now recognize as ludicrous if not insane. I don't think it was arrogance. I remember it as a strange kind of deep-seated knowledge that I would not be leaving Kalamazoo, that something would intervene to prevent it, because I was where I was supposed to be, doing the work I was supposed to be doing. It was *settled,* as was I.

This ridiculous faith rested on a triangular base, a delta, the three points of which were language, feminism, and teaching. This was my pyramid of power, my holy trinity. And, as in the hymn I used to love, they were "one in three persons," part and parcel of each other, forming and informing one another. I came to feminism through teaching; I came to teaching through language; I returned to language from feminism and became a writer. On my office door was a brown-and-white sticker, ubiquitous in the 1980s, that read, FEMINISM SPOKEN HERE. It went up originally for the same reason there is now a "Safe Harbor" sticker on the door to reassure gay, lesbian, and bisexual students: I wanted terrified proto-feminists to know that inside my office they could try out the language and be understood. It took me a while to realize that "language" was not metaphorical here—that quite literally feminism formulated itself as a language for me, that its project was fundamentally linguistic: to provide alternative terms in which to construct reality. It was during those heady, dangerous, intense days, struggling to establish women's studies as legitimate not only on campus but also in my own head, that I began thinking about my first book. So there came that bright fall morning, as the Reagan Eighties settled down over the country and I settled into Kalamazoo, when I looked up into the burnishing leaves and saw that I stood on a triangular patch of ground between three tall trees. My mother tongue, my native land, my life, to echo Adrienne Rich. After a youth spent feeling dispossessed and alien, finally I was home.

And wasn't I right? Hasn't that been my home, in the sense of a home base from which all my good work has been done? Certainly. But midlife is a weird passage. The essence of the eponymous *crisis* assigned to this time is, I think, the desire to run away from home. The settled (the *resolved* as well as the *ensconced*) becomes unsettled. Maybe another way of putting it: *estrangement.* One day the house you've been living in doesn't seem to be yours. The familiar faces are frightening. The work you have been doing for-ever seems unnatural and unendurable; the choices and accidents that brought you here, which you once saw as destiny's minions, have become the horses of the chariot of doom. And the face in the mirror? Lined, baggy, furred with the soft down of age. Who is she, this crone?

I realize my students must be asking this. I realize that on some level I have sustained the illusion that the Cool Young Prof, the Defiant Young Feminist I used to be, is still visible to them. I fear I am as laughable as the matron with a ponytail, the grandma in the miniskirt. So now, who am I in their eyes? That rare specimen I myself never witnessed: an *older woman* in the classroom. And I thought it was hard to avoid being cast as Mommy back in 1978! The only time I've heard the word "cool" applied to me recently was when a student discovered that I was in a long-term, long-distance rela-tionship and was driving to Colorado to spend the summer with a man. The fact that I am heterosexually partnered but unmarried—that's apparently "cool." That's romantic. That lifts me out of the trash bin of useless role mod-els for a generation of women seemingly consumed with whether they will find love and the magic pill for "balancing work and family."

Yes, part of the estrangement is that the students have changed too. In accordance with the suspension of certain laws of physics in the academic Twilight Zone, they're the same age as they were twenty years ago. But they're not the same people. Their passivity, like a black hole, saps me, sucks me dry. Their helplessness without supplied structures drains me. They can't seem to figure out how to do anything on their own. I assign an essay with a full single-spaced page of description and guidelines, and I have to spend a full class period brainstorming it until they even see it as do-able. No instruction, no guideline fails to bring a rain of questions and confusion. Their personal lives seem so chaotic that I feel myself drawing back from the old eager involvement in their lives as from quicksand. Their attention span seems to be exactly the length of the average sitcom, with serious implications for structuring a class period, not to mention for selecting texts: will I ever teach *Middlemarch* again?

And maybe the worst of it is that these children born in the year Rea-gan took office see feminism not as deviant or rebellious, but as Authority, as entrenched Political Correctness against which their natural response, at eighteen, is resentment, resistance, and ridicule. Even the junior feminists see me as Second Wave, already broken on the beach. I wonder if maybe they're right.

When I ask first-year students to write or talk about what makes a good teacher, a good number of them always come up with that word that haunts your letter, Ramona: passion. On one level I'm always gratified to be reassured that in the middle of the "Whatever" generation, I get students who think education has anything to do with passion. But I also feel a little finger of fear down my spine. I ask questions that sound like a women's magazine article on midlife: *Have I still got it? Am I drying up? How often am I faking it?*

A couple of years ago I had an especially cold season in the classroom. I don't think the classes suffered much, actually, but I did. My students seemed pretty consistently to bore or annoy me. It seemed ages since I had felt that jubilation after a class, or that sharp tenderness for a student in crisis or in the throes of discovery. One day I heard myself voice to my best friend the thought that was chilling my innards: "I don't think I love them anymore." The cry of the fortysomething wifemother on the verge of an affair, a Thelma-and-Louise road trip, a good old nervous breakdown.

And then there's feminism, that fraught, freighted word I insist on continuing to say, as if it were the luminous beacon of my thirties. At the women's studies conferences where we labored to frame this new perspective whose vista seemed endless, we used to speak of the time when women's studies would have established itself in the academy as a sort of millennial age. How, after all, could something this radical establish itself without transforming everything around it? We would all walk in the light. The darkness would fall away around us. Well, here we are, Tenured Radicals. The college or university without some measure of a women's studies program is a dinosaur. Critical theory rests solidly on assumptions we spoke with trepidation twenty years ago. We are the establishment, we who railed about not being taken seriously, not having power, being marginal, not being included in theory-making or policy-making processes. "You Are Here!" as the mall maps assure me. Last spring at a TGIF for women faculty at Marigene's house, I was wondering when the senior faculty would show up. Then I realized we already were there.

Frankly, the millennial trumpet sounds like a plastic kazoo. The feminist scholarship industry is thriving, and most of its products are unreadable by the uninitiated. Much of it owes its life to the Holy Male Trinity of Derrida, Foucault, and Lacan (or Benjamin, Bhabha, and Bahktin, if you prefer). Commitment to anything is suddenly dicey. Identity is merely performance, so the fundamental stories that launched the second wave of feminism are ringed with irony, tacked to the wall with quotation marks. Pornography is equated with choice or speech or affirmed as a liberation of women's sexuality, and women are driven snarling into opposing corners.

Meanwhile, back at Kamp Kalamazoo, having finally reached the point where we have barely enough women's studies faculty to get around a table, I can't gather them for a quarterly meeting without the internecine politics and personal resentments playing such a disturbing continuo beneath the official agenda that the meeting disintegrates. The Women's Resource Center seems to be constantly in internal disarray and dysfunction. On both fronts, the kind of nastiness between women of which stereotypes are made. And I'm still running a program on $1,500 a year, unable to find either more funds or someone to take it over.

And the third point on the delta, the anchor-point of language, the primum mobile and ground of being? A passage in your letter repeats like a tape loop in my head:

> I used to believe poetry and books to be my religion, my communion with what I wanted my god to be. But it is not complete that way. Frederick Strong, a religious scholar, wrote in *Emptiness, a Study in Religious Meaning,* that "words themselves are regarded as inadequate conveyers of the reality perceived in the religious awareness." Lately words have been so inadequate that this rings very true with me. And this is all I know—words, voice.

This is all I have ever known too. Is it the destiny of English majors to come to a point where the whole premise of the discipline—the worthiness of language as a field of study—collapses, or at least begins to shudder? My own moment came later than yours—in graduate school, about the time I turned in a master's thesis entitled "The Raid on the Inarticulate," a study of the inadequacy of language in T. S. Eliot's poetry. The title was taken from *The Four Quartets,* "East Coker," to be exact, where, in the final section, Eliot takes stock of himself as a poet:

> *So here I am, in the middle way, having had twenty years—*
> *Twenty years largely wasted, the years of l'entre deux guerres—*
> *Trying to learn to use words, and every attempt*

Is a wholly new start, and a different kind of failure
Because one has only learnt to get the better of words
For the thing one no longer has to say, or the way in which
One is no longer disposed to say it. And so each venture
Is a new beginning, a raid on the inarticulate
With shabby equipment always deteriorating....
(V. 1–9)

How often I return to that reactionary old fart, another erudite, effete husband of another mad wife. How those lines have haunted me, from that day to this, growing truer and truer. Has there ever been a better description of writing, of the maddening repetitive futility of writing? Of the papers you write and the essays I write and the poems we both write? And, beyond this, of all formulations, all constructs, all principles, which, the moment you've got them right, reveal themselves to be transparently *wrong* and proceed to dissolve in air? Of all teaching, every course from which I walk away muttering, "I've failed, failed again. They didn't get it"?

... That is not what I meant at all.
That is not it, at all.
(T. S. Eliot, "The Love Song of J. Alfred Prufrock")

Eliot's "inarticulate" is, of course, God, as well as all the things poetry fails to say. Or rather, God, for Eliot *is* all the things poetry fails to say, the unsayable at which poems are thrown like flares into a dark night. God is the Word, as St. John put it, beyond all words. So is it any wonder that, in your advanced-English-major disillusionment with language, your Senior Project, planned as a collection of short lyrics, is turning into long meditations on God? "I do not know who or what my god is," you say, "or why even it is important. But I do know that I need to find out, and that for a long time I will be lost.... Somewhere, there must be some truth. Or there isn't. Either way, I'm looking." But, conversely, is it any wonder that in your looking, as you write not *about* but *toward* God, you become progressively more frustrated and disillusioned with language? Or that I, in my twenty-fourth year of teaching, become progressively more frustrated and disillusioned with pedagogy, classrooms, students, texts, my own professorial self?

Your letter concludes by asserting that the truth "is, as they say on The *X-Files*, out there." And finally, I guess, my message back to you, across the generation between us, is that it isn't. I described midlife mostly in terms of loss, without mentioning the fundamental loss: the loss of belief in truth, in ultimate, stable meaning. The terror of midlife is the knowledge that you're really working without a net. For some—mostly men, I think—this loss spells despair or nihilism, or at least a new, younger wife. For me, it hasn't made itself felt as a loss, but rather as a clearing of space, a falling away of old structures to make room for something new but ancient-seeming: a deep sense of process and cycle, a certain stillness at the heart of constant motion. Maybe that doesn't sound like much. But it has felt very rich but very… *inarticulate,* silent and profound as trees. It has seemed deeply *true* without seeming like "truth." This acceptance of ultimate instability happens to underlie most of postmodern/poststructuralist thought, conveniently enough, so I find myself oddly in sync with my times, which otherwise I find almost completely estranging. But somehow when I read it in the language of critical theory it is about intellectual gamesmanship; it lacks the emotional content, the psychic dimension, the tangible quality it has for me.

Put very bluntly, my sense of life is that we are bound to seek and never to find, and that wisdom lies precisely in our ability to live in that tension, to tread that water, to balance in that wind, to remain radically *unsettled.* Specifically, as a feminist this means speaking of women, as a woman, all the while knowing how tenuous that category is. It means finding, after the collapse of historical progress as a paradigm, another reason to struggle for justice for women—because not to struggle is death. As a teacher, it means representing truth while not believing in it, returning each term to begin two new courses I know will fall far short—the art of faithful failure, as I once called it elsewhere (1995). And as a writer, it means another "raid on the inarticulate / With shabby equipment always deteriorating." In Anne Sexton's wonderful words, it means the "Awful Rowing Toward God"—shore of our meaning, site of our passion, receding eternally in the distance—in the knowledge that our being lies in the rowing, our motion through the motion of the waves surrounding us.

I titled my first book *Calling* (1992) because I liked the double entendre. The title is both noun and verb: calling as vocation, and calling as an activity, a process. In that last sense, to write, as to teach, is *to call* into the silence, and to keep on calling whether any voice answers or not, and to do so neither in faith nor in despair but in sufficiency, in contentment that to call is in itself sufficient, is good. I also agreed to the title change because the metaphor of voice was, indeed, what the book was really about. "Voice," the word where your two worlds, your major and minor, collide: it too is both noun and verb. Once I thought of voice as *expressive*—that is, as conveying truth, identity, being. I have come to see voice as *constructive*—as making meaning and selfhood. And maybe that is where I have arrived in my relationship to language—a place where my faith in language, the faith you are just losing, is not in its expressive capacity—its ability to convey truth—but in its constructive potential—its ability to make, shape, form, create, embody. Frankenstein's poor Creature recalls watching human beings use language: "This was indeed a godlike science," says he, himself the product of a godlike scientist. In other words, he (representing his "creator," Mary Shelley) sees language not as expressing some absolute reality but as creating its own universe.

I wonder if "truth" is not a verb too, and if the truth that is "out there" is your own awful rowing, your long poems thrown out like fishing lines into the dark water where your god is lurking, your deep contralto notes cast across Stetson Chapel. If the measure of the significance or the "success" of your medium is whether it hooks you a god that can be reeled in, landed, stuffed, and hung over the fireplace, I fear you will always be frustrated. After the poem, after the song, will come the silence again. But if the measure is the spirit with which you write or sing; the beauty with which the words and notes arch into the dark like fireworks, expressing all your yearning after the inexpressible; the responding movement within your readers or listeners; then you've found your god-in-hiding. Stillness in motion: the journey is always beginning and always already complete. "Every phrase and every sentence is an end and a beginning, / Every poem an epitaph." (Tom Eliot again; "Little Gidding," *The Four Quartets*). The truth, as they don't say on *The X-Files,* is *in here.*

It is no less a Feminist Moment than it was twenty years ago for a woman to understand this. As women, settled, transcendent meanings have not served us. More: they have sought our erasure, enforced our silence. They have endangered us, sometimes killed us. What feminist movement (as bell hooks calls it) has been about, most importantly, is the making of meaning: we have had to make our meanings, relying on ourselves and each other, intellect and intuition, experience and theory, inheritance and imagination. Nothing is more radical than women's meaning-making; it is precisely the conjuring work for which they burned and hanged us, and still do. We persist in casting our spells, casting them out and out. What I am currently conjuring, with very little to go on, is the meaning of a woman's middle life.

Okay, maybe the raving loony feminist of twenty years ago is still alive and kicking. Another midlife insight has been that human development turns us into matryoshka dolls, with all our previous selves nested inside us. Sometimes I become sharply aware of their presence. For instance, a young male colleague recently wrote me a hate letter in which he acknowledged being forced to come to the conclusion (widespread, to hear him tell it) that I am a "superficial and dangerous ideologue." I must be doing something right.

As are you. Keep writing, keep singing. These will lead you to a worthy life. I'm not sure you're right that "for a long time [you] will be lost." You'll be in the dark, but you won't be lost, just unsettled. It will not always feel passionate, but there will be moments. Moments will come in which the rest of your dispassionate time is illumined. "For most of us," says Tom, "there is only the unattended / Moment, the moment in and out of time,"

> *The distraction fit, lost, in a shaft of sunlight,*
> *The wild thyme unseen, or the winter lightning*
> *Or the waterfall, or music heard so deeply*
> *That it is not heard at all, but you are the music*
> *While the music lasts.*
> (Eliot, "The Dry Salvages," *The Four Quartets*)

When I watched you sing the week before the regional competition, your eyes had the look that great singers' eyes get, not blind but unseeing, fathomless. All your vision was inward; you were the music. There are times when I am teaching or writing that this happens to me—I become the music. I don't know if I have the "passion" I had twenty years ago, but I think that as I get older and, blessedly, less concerned with whether the students love me or not, these moments get deeper, simply because *I* am deeper. Like your voice, you will deepen.

In other words, Ramona, your passion is worthy because it is yours. Should we follow all our passions out to their end, the place where they met would probably be the god you're looking for. I keep doing what I do not because it brings me closer to truth but because it seems to be mine; its rhythms are my outlines. I make it as it makes me—that oscillation at the heart of things. It's the boat I row. I don't know where it takes me, and here at the middle of an invented and unconventional woman's life my direction gets clearer in many ways, in other ways more obscure and treacherous. It certainly does not get easier. Most of the clarity I find is in what returns like the seasons: There are memories I come to recognize as my "life-tropes." There are epiphanies that echo each other. There are books whose resonance deepens with each reading, each teaching, so that the first line uncurls like a hand:

> *There was no possibility of taking a walk that day....*
> *Quiet as it's kept, there were no marigolds in the fall of 1941....* [3]

And there are students appearing on the shore, always different, always the same. Stepping out from the rest come women like you, moving toward me, full of beauty, pain, hunger. So I am always in that double-consciousness I mentioned earlier, locating myself simultaneously with your parents and with you. To teach is to be both, I guess, forever in two places at once, moving across time. In your eyes I return to myself, encountering again the questions that have driven me this far.

Later on the day I began this letter, the lurking, oppressive weather broke. The storm rolled in over Lake Michigan; I watched it from upstairs, in the dark: the low rumbling in the west, the silent lightning ripping down the sky, illuminating the field across from my house; then the rain starting, with the dusty smell of hot, wet blacktop, then getting heavier, until a steady tropical downpour settled in and sang me to sleep.

The next day I checked the five-day forecast on the back page of the paper, the five little squares with meteorological icons and one- or two-word predictions. Tomorrow: "Unsettled."

Love,
Gail

III

Feisty ❦ Girls

I AM MORE MYSELF THAN I HAVE EVER BEEN. THERE IS LESS CONFLICT. I AM HAPPIER, MORE BALANCED, AND (I HEARD MYSELF SAY RATHER AGGRESSIVELY) "MORE POWERFUL." I FELT IT WAS RATHER AN ODD WORD, "POWERFUL," BUT I THINK IT IS TRUE. IT MIGHT HAVE BEEN MORE ACCURATE TO SAY, "I AM BETTER ABLE TO USE MY POWERS." I AM SURER OF WHAT LIFE IS ALL ABOUT, HAVE LESS SELF-DOUBTS TO CONQUER.

May Sarton

ONCE WOMEN PASS FIFTY, IF THEY CAN AVOID THE TEMPTATIONS OF THE ETERNAL YOUTH PURVEYORS, THE SELLERS OF UNNATURAL THINNESS AND COSMETIC SURGERY, THEY MAY BE ABLE TO TAP INTO THE FEISTY GIRLS THEY ONCE WERE. AND IF, AT ADOLESCENCE, THE IMPORTANCE OF THEIR OWN CONVICTIONS HAS BEEN REINFORCED, THEY MIGHT, AT FIFTY, BE READY TO TAKE ON RISK, DISPLAY A NEW-FOUND VITALITY, AND BID GOODBYE TO CONVENTIONAL LIMITATIONS.

Carolyn Heilbrun

AFTER FIFTY MOST OF THE BULLSHIT IS GONE.

Isabel Allende

13

Academic Witchery
Snakes and Snails and Scholarly Tales

Dean Falk

TOBIAS AND THE BANK MAN WORE THE SUITS OF THEIR TRADE, DARK CONFIDENCE BUILDERS WITH GRAVITAS. MARGARET HAD COME IN FLOWERY PRINTED WOOL, SOFT AND ROSE-RED AND DISARMING, HIDING THE STEEL-HARD BRAIN. HOW RIDICULOUS, I THOUGHT, THAT THE MALE MIND COULD OFTEN ACCEPT A FEMALE AS EQUAL ONLY IF SHE PRETENDED TO BE IN NEED OF HELP. MARGARET AMUSED ME. SHE CAUGHT ME LOOKING AT HER, READ MY THOUGHT AND WINKED. MEN WERE RIGHT TO BE AFRAID OF WOMEN, I CONCLUDED: THE WITCH LIVED NEAR THE SURFACE IN ALL OF THEM.

"THEY BURNED WITCHES . . . GOD HELP THEM."

Dick Francis, To the Hilt

Looking back, I am amazed that it took so long for me to realize that there are, indeed, such things as academic witches. But then, most female academics with "steel-hard" brains fail to grasp how they are regarded by many of their colleagues. To acknowledge the whispers that one is a witch would be too hurtful. A little repression, a little self-blame, is therefore adaptive—especially if one chooses to spend one's energies lighting fires under students and pursuing intellectual interests. But I bumbled into the secret during a job search at one of the six colleges and universities where I have worked. I attended the talks of all three candidates who were brought in for interviews and was particularly struck by the presentation of a young energetic woman who had many high-quality publications and a good deal of grant money. Her talk was wonderful. She exuded enthusiasm about her subject matter and was fun to watch because, rather than being wooden as some candidates are (giving interview talks is one of the more stressful activities in life), she appeared spontaneously to think on her feet. After detailing the results of several experiments, she said something to the effect of "and now I'll tell you why these results are important." By then, I was sitting on the edge of my seat, and I remember thinking, "Yes, yes, tell us." She did; and I, for one, found her reasoning persuasive. While the other two interviewees were very good, they did not strike me as stars in the making, as this candidate clearly seemed to be.

I knew something was wrong with this interview after the talk, when the candidate had been whisked away to meet some dean, and everyone began turning to everyone else and saying, "Well, what do you think?" (Anyone who has been in academia very long knows that this informal, gossipy spin-assessment is a crucial part of the interview process.) One male colleague remarked something to the extent of "she can't possibly know all of those techniques, nobody does." Another replied, "Yeah, and did you hear her say that her work was important? Can you believe anybody would stand up there and do that?" My initial reaction to the after-talk spin was bewilderment—why was my impression of the candidate so different from theirs? Then the real character assassination began: "Her vitae looks suspicious. Why has she moved around so much?" I replied something like, "Well now, having had numerous jobs myself, maybe I can help with that. I moved to get timely promotions and pay raises." Another person said, "Why would anyone who is supposed to be so good want to come to a dump like this? Her recommendations are probably exaggerated." "Yeah," said another colleague, "if she's as good as they say, why didn't they do something to keep her?" "Well now," chimes in Mr. Too-Many-Jobs, "I thought she was a little uptight and I've gotten some information about her through the grapevine—I hear she's a difficult person." I remember saying something like, "Well if she seemed a little uptight to you, I'm surprised, but perhaps it was the stress of going on an interview. Anyway, from what I've heard her credentials are the best. If that's true, offer her the job. If you don't like her once you get to know her, don't have coffee with her."

By then it was crystal clear that those people bad-mouthing the candidate felt threatened by her and were rationalizing their resistance to hiring her. I am pleased to say that the initial job offer was extended to this candidate. Although this whole thing was potentially awful for her (on a number of levels), I believe that she remains in sweet ignorance about what transpired at that particular job interview. For me, however, it was an epiphany. Branded as "difficult," asked about my numerous career moves, and (I might add) repeatedly lowballed on salary (only to find out later), I had been there, done that. What I had just witnessed was gossip-spin kindling being laid at this woman's future stake. I realized that she was an academic witch—and so was I!

Furthermore, I realized that I knew what was in store for this young innocent, although she herself hadn't a clue. And it was not a pretty picture. She would continue to be highly productive and, as she did so, would be perceived as a greater threat by many of those she surpassed in the traditional, scholarly, male-oriented publish-or-perish arena. Would all of this be out in the open where she could see the writing on the wall and defend herself? You've got to be kidding! Academic witches are whispered about by less competitive men and women, not dealt with in an up-front manner (that would be much too scary, as Dick Francis so beautifully suggests in the beginning quotation). And petty gossip wins all too often with administrators who allocate resources. I knew that behind-the-scenes backstabbing would cause resources, including appropriate salary increments, to be withheld from this scholar. And, unless she took time out from being an avid teacher and scientist to do some deep probing, she wouldn't even know when, let alone why, it happened.

But how many of us were there? Upon reflection, I realized that I knew of a number of other academic witches at assistant, associate, and full professor levels. For example, one federally funded scientist published in the most visible journals in the world; e.g., she had multiple publications in *Nature*—no easy task. Furthermore, before she came up for tenure, she received an incredibly prestigious national award (not quite at the level of a MacArthur "genius" award, but not far behind). Although she was eventually tenured (it would have been a travesty if she were not), I gather that the proceedings through the various levels of her institution were stormy. This was especially disturbing because her university routinely granted tenure in the vast majority of cases (regardless of merit). It was clear to me from speaking to some of her less visible colleagues that their competitive hackles were up. For example, although she had formed and headed a productive laboratory team and her publication record was just fine, one man said, "How come when she has all of this grant money, she doesn't have more publications?" My explanations about what constitutes reasonable numbers of publications for laboratory teams working on multiyear projects were lost on this less productive and jealous colleague.

Another woman scientist, in another field: This person is very senior and very renowned. She is simply the world's leading authority on her subject matter. She has served as an elected president of a large, prestigious professional organization and has received multiple, well-deserved international honors. I telephone this great woman periodically to ask for advice about how to handle certain difficulties. Her advice is always the same: "Dean, what you are experiencing is nothing compared to what I have endured. Just let it roll off your back like the proverbial water. Write your books. Publish your papers. That'll get 'em." However, my dear friend pays a price for her laid-back strategy. Although she established a research center and brought in the outside funds to hire a pivotal faculty member, her voice on the search committee was ignored by her less successful and less visible colleagues. My friend loses sleep over this, as would I. Shame on her university for letting this happen! Unfortunately, this is not uncommon. Being denied opportunities to serve on meaningful committees, or to chair departments, is a common complaint among highly accomplished female faculty. Toadies may serve; academic witches need not apply.

To the arts: This may be the most outlandish case I know of. A female associate professor in one of the studio arts was coming up for promotion to full professor at an institution that will remain unidentified. Talk about dazzling credentials! Her publications and exhibits were not only voluminous, but in incredible places. Her internationally known work had appeared in the *New York Times,* the *New Yorker,* and the best museums in the world. She had also taught a larger number of students (and with rave evaluations) than anyone else in her department. And guess what? Reports have it that her promotion case was as stormy as that described above for the scientist. What, you may ask, were the reasons for this? I asked some of her less visible colleagues, and here is what some of them said: She was "opportunistic," and only went "where the money was." Her work was "popular," so it couldn't be that real, that good. She was eventually promoted. But I can't help wondering how much stomach lining she lost in the process.

Many institutions put a great deal of emphasis on their faculty bringing in extramural funds. This is because most universities and colleges tax those grants by adding additional charges to the budgets to pay for overhead expenses, e.g., the costs of administering the projects, and related expenses (paying for electricity to run labs, etc.). Most scholars who bring in high-dollar grants are esteemed and richly rewarded by university administrators, at least if they are men. For example, I know of a social scientist who heads his own center and brings in around a cool million dollars annually. The perks he receives include repeated salary increments and release time from teaching *for his wife*, who is tenured in another department. In contrast, a female professor at the same institution who also brings in big grant bucks (in a different field) received a cold shoulder from the administration when she asked for modest support for her academic spouse. Another highly funded colleague at this institution, a well-published senior woman in the humanities, has one of the lowest salaries of any full professor in her college!

Upon reflection, it is clear that these women have certain things in common. They are all highly competitive and successful in areas that have traditionally been dominated by men. They are all treated as if they are threats by some colleagues who have branded them as "difficult," "demanding," "assertive," or "unpleasant." Paradoxically, despite this harsh characterization, these women are generally regarded as dedicated, nurturing teachers who altruistically further the careers of their students. Highly productive female academics pride themselves on their independence, and are appalled at the thought of asking for special considerations based on their gender. Most do not join women's groups. Instead, they go into their labs, offices, or studios and hunker down to work, sometimes obsessively. As they grow older, however, they come to realize that something is terribly wrong. Why, when their credentials are among the very best in their entire colleges or universities, are their salaries *way* below average? The answer is that they are academic witches, and they are being burned alive at the stake. Are highly accomplished men ever treated like this? Not that I've seen. Rather than being condemned as witches, they are regarded and rewarded as wizards.

WITCHES' STRATEGIES: CHARMS, CHAMBERS, CRAFTS, COVENS, AND SIGNS

So what's a poor academic witch to do? I have given a good deal of thought to this question and have some suggestions. The first is, if the pointed hat fits, wear it—acknowledge your witchery ("Hi. My name is Dean Falk and I am an academic witch"). Next, resist the impulse to accept the torment of your colleagues with the easy-way-out rationalization that "what is important is my work, I'll just focus on that and keep my head down." If you don't deal with the situation, your colleagues' whispers over the years will translate into greater relative reductions in resources for you, and that's *just not fair*. Finally, give that cauldron one last stir, and choose from the following menu of strategies. Whatever you cook up, it'll be more savory than the "eye of newt and toe of frog" (William Shakespeare, *Macbeth*, act 4, scene 1) that most academic witches are expected to subsist on.

1. Charms:

> *What are little girls made of? What are little girls made of?*
> *Sugar and spice, and everything nice.*
> *That's what little girls are made of.*
> *(Anonymous)*

This is the strategy used by Margaret in the opening quotation. If you can bear to wear soft-colored printed dresses and defer to less productive colleagues, this approach can be highly successful. I've seen it work. What is required is that you spend a lot of time being self-effacing while stroking the egos of your more insecure colleagues. Twisting your pointed little toe in the dirt, while using submissive language ("Ah shucks, I'm such a dufus") and deferential body language (glance down a lot) adds to the power of being charming. Basically, what this is all about is asking forgiveness for being a highly competent woman. The downside is that your charms might be so powerful that you risk being categorized as a bimbo. However, if they like you rather than regard you as a witch, you will probably benefit in the goodies department. Personally, I can't bring myself to use this particular strategy. However, I will be happy to give blessings (can witches do that?) to any witch who wants to.

2. Chambers:
Otherwise known as getting legal, this strategy is, unfortunately, a long shot for academic witches, even though there is no doubt that they are discriminated against, both personally and economically. The problem is that, although women are a protected class, not all female academics are academic witches. I have seen male colleagues whose hackles appear continuously erect (how's that for imagery?) when it comes to academic witches break their arms patting themselves on their backs for promoting women who are totally unthreatening. This strategy, of course, insulates them from claims of discrimination against women generally. Sad to say, academic witches have not yet been recognized as a legally protected class. However, my daughter the lawyer thinks there could be a cutting-edge lawsuit here, so please go ahead if your little witch shoes are well-heeled and you are so inclined. (Be forewarned, however—a lawsuit is likely to take years, leaving you little time for other witchly pursuits.)

3. Craft: Now we're getting somewhere. Craft a salary study at your institution. I've done this at one of the schools where I've been employed, and it worked! You can either go it alone or bring other women into it. But it's not easy. In my study, I collected data on salaries, numbers of publications, numbers of grants, numbers of grant dollars, and numbers of citations in the literature—covering a period of five years. I analyzed the data by sex and by department, and developed a formula for ranking scholarly merit. Finally, I compared the merit scores with the rank of each person's salary. The differential between witches and wizards was so stark that it was almost comical. Even so, it was an entire year before the administration agreed to raise my salary and that of one other witch whom I had identified in the process. Further, this was done only after I finally, in great frustration, took preparatory steps to get legal and go public. After they gave me every penny that I requested, I wrote personal thank-you notes to the institution's president and vice president (see strategy 1). I recently had a conversation with one of the nation's leading attorneys in sexual harassment cases, pertaining to strategy 2. "What," I asked, "are women supposed to do if it's so hard to prove sexual discrimination in universities?" "I'll tell you what to do," she said. "Go back to what they did in the seventies. Do salary studies."

4. Covens: As in form them. Academic witches tend to internalize some of the nastiness that is directed their way. Don't go into your lab, office, or studio and brood. Get together with other witches on your campus and compare notes (scrawls). I recently invited all of the witches I could identify on my present campus to a cauldron-luck dinner at my house. I provided the bubbles; they brought other concoctions. And it was exhilarating. At one point, one near-retirement woman looked across the room at another and said, "How long have you been at this school? I've never seen you before." Both had been here forever—working unobtrusively in their own highly circumscribed worlds. At your coven, why not plan how to implement strategy 3 ("double, double, toil and trouble; fire burn and cauldron bubble" [*Macbeth,* act 4, scene 7])?

5. Signs: Don't keep academic witchery a secret. It's time we witches came out of the dark and enjoyed a little sunshine. Let your colleagues and administrators know about us. The civilized world eventually outlawed persecution of witches and so too should our erudite centers of higher learning. (This essay is an application of this strategy.)

I am certain that this essay will be viewed as whiny by some readers. So why have I written it? Let me answer that. Recently, my five-year-old granddaughter, Helen Dean, asked me, "Grandma, is there anything bigger than the earth?" I interpret her repeated asking of such big-picture questions as a sure sign that she was born to be an academic witch. However, unless things change, Helen Dean will grow up to be branded as "difficult," "demanding," "assertive," and (my favorite) "worse than a man." Little Helen is a good child. She deserves to be better regarded. She also deserves a fair opportunity to be rewarded for her future accomplishments. Don't we all?

> *O, well done! I commend your pains,*
> *And everyone shall share i' the gains.*
> *And now about the cauldron sing,*
> *Like elves and fairies in a ring,*
> *Enchanting all that you put in.*
> (Macbeth, act 4, scene 1)

14

Choice Points and Courage

DIANE F. HALPERN

I am deeply honored to be included in this anthology of reflections at midlife. In preparing this chapter, I suffered a real identity crisis. What could or should I say about myself that would help to explain how I came to this place—both psychologically and physically—where I would be asked to stop a while and share my reflections? It did not take long for me to notice that my life is quite ordinary, a realization that made me feel even more uneasy about this task. I became particularly concerned about the message that I would be conveying in telling the story of my professional life. I am afraid that I am not a good enough feminist model, especially for younger men and women who are at choice points in their own lives and may be looking to others who have been there before them to act as guides through life's middle years.

But as I thought more about the choices that I have made, both professional and personal, I came to rethink my own definition of feminism. It is strange that it took so long for me to come to grips with what I mean by this term. When I taught at Moscow State University in Russia, I had students write and then compare their own definitions of feminism as a way of starting what was probably the first-ever Russian class on the psychology of sex and gender. To me, feminism is about having choices to make and rejecting the idea that there is a single best choice for all women. I believe that the choices that I pondered are similar to those that face many Western women at this time in history. I am at the time of life euphemistically called "middle age," even though at fifty, I would have to ignore the basic principles of probability to believe that I still have half my life ahead of me. The choices that I made decades ago set me on the path to the present, yet they were made with no thought about their long-term consequences.

Like many other women who are currently at midlife, I married my first husband at a very young age, during the summer between my sophomore and junior years in college. He was only a year and a half older, and just about to begin the grueling ordeal of law school. But, unlike most of the other stories that start this way, we are still married. I am often asked how we have managed a two-career family for over three decades at a time when the divorce rate is astronomically high. This question has the same answer as other seemingly unrelated questions that I am frequently asked: how did I end up in the psychology department at California State University, San Bernardino, or why did I decide to get my doctorate at the University of Cincinnati? Although these may seem like different questions, they all have the same answer: I followed my husband's career, attending graduate school where his job took us and later finding an academic job where his next job took us. It is with some embarrassment that I admit to this. But it is important to keep in mind that each one of us is more than a professor, and that, thanks to feminism, we have the opportunity to make decisions about all aspects of our lives, including the way we want to balance family and work life. I am not sorry about the choices that I have made, but I do need to find a way to stop apologizing for them.

It is difficult to understand how any of us select the paths that we travel to get to midlife and beyond. My early years were not happy ones. I prefer to believe that the adage "The child is the father of the man" is sex-specific and that women can remake themselves many times throughout their adult years. I think that the myth of the "happy childhood" belongs only in storybooks or television sitcoms. While growing up, I was clearly given the message that education was not an appropriate priority for girls. My father often reminded me that "career women" were a detestable lot—hard, cold, and lonely—and that college was only for rich males. To place this in context, I might add that he never believed that women should have been allowed to vote because they would be swayed by the more handsome candidate and ignore the important qualifications for public office. I realize that he was as much a product of his own culture and historical background as I am of mine, so it makes no more sense to blame him for these attitudes than it makes to blame me for mine. School was one of the few places where I was successful, and several teachers throughout my years in Philadelphia's much maligned public schools encouraged me to study and to keep the possibility of college in sight. These unsung heroes were an important part in shaping my own thinking about who I am—a lesson that I remember every day in my interactions with students. I hope that I have helped to shape the decisions that they will make about their own lives.

My two children are an important part of my identity and how I view the world. I never made a conscious decision to be a mother. I had always known that I would be. I would no more have questioned that assumption than I would question the value of breathing or the laws of gravity. My children are both adopted and both biracial (African American/white). My experiences in a mixed-race family have colored my perception of the world and have influenced countless aspects of my work and my away-from-work life. My life has been deeply enriched because of my close relationships with people from many different racial and ethnic groups.

I stayed at home for several years when my children were babies. As I recall, I spent much time pushing a baby carriage around the circle in the apartment complex where we lived at the time. There must have been other activities, but for some reason that one stands out most vividly in my memory. I don't think there is any psychological significance to the memory of walking in circles—it reflects the shape of the road and not, I hope, my feelings about that period in my life. I am very glad that I had the option of being a stay-at-home mom during my children's first few years of life. At the time, I didn't appreciate this luxury, which is not a real choice for many parents. Children require a great deal of time, work, and money. I know that there appear to be superwomen who can do it all, but like all superhuman feats, doing it all has high costs. Although I have strong opinions about almost every topic and no difficulty doling out all sorts of advice, everyone must decide for herself and himself what makes sense when considering questions about parenting. I am angered at the media gurus who attempt to shame mothers who decide to return to work when their children are young.

There are some lessons that I have learned after five decades of life. When I decided to return to graduate school for a doctorate, my son was five years old and my daughter was two. My husband and I were deeply in debt, having borrowed a huge sum of money to get through our education thus far. When I told friends and family that I planned to start graduate school, there was no rush of support. First, I would be putting my young children into day care. Second, I was already deeply in debt, so getting a paying job made far more sense than getting more education. Third, the job market was bleak for prospective professors, the profession that I really wanted to enter. I was repeatedly labeled with the pejorative "perpetual student," a derogatory term for someone who was afraid to leave academia for the real world. Fortunately, I did not listen to the many voices of reason, and I urge you to do the same. For life's really big decisions, only follow advice that you can accept with both your heart and your head. (Except, of course, this advice that I am giving you. I have made it exempt from this proclamation.) My husband was fully supportive of my decision, probably the real reason why we are both still working on our first spouse.

Whenever I meet new people, the discussion soon gets around to the topic of work, and I have come to realize how central work is to one's self-identity. Select your life's work as carefully as you select a spouse. Although we all play many different roles in life, I respond to questions about what I do with the word "psychologist." My dissertation was in an area of visual perception known as "subjective contours." I enjoyed the intellectual pursuit of studying how and why people see these elusive contours when they do not exist on paper, but I soon learned that only a handful of other people in the world cared about the questions I was researching. I went into psychology because a few charismatic professors made me believe that it was a vital field that asked the most interesting questions about human and animal nature and because psychology offered the hope that we could make the world better—cure or alleviate some medical and some psychological illnesses, eliminate or reduce war and poverty, solve the problems of loneliness and alienation, stop drug abuse, end prejudice, encourage world peace, and more if we were smart enough in figuring out the underlying causes and if we tried hard enough. These "big" questions seemed far removed from my study of subjective contours, and gradually I returned to the more intrinsically interesting questions that attracted me to the discipline in the first place.

I gave up most of my research in visual perception when I took my present job. Research in visual perception requires expensive equipment, most notably a good light meter and long hours in a laboratory. There was no way I was going to get a good light meter at my present university (light meters are very expensive), so after some frustrating attempts to borrow one, I decided to change the topics that would be the focus of my research. I didn't have far to look to find others.

The students in my classes were raising enough interesting questions to keep any research psychologist busy for several lifetimes. During my first years after graduate school, I was teaching classes in the psychology of women and cognitive psychology, and the same question came up in both of them. It was the question of the similarities and differences in female and male cognitive abilities. This seemingly simple question led to several decades of research and reflection. I wanted to create a meaningful context for the study of social and physiological factors and their joint actions, while also understanding the political ramifications of studying such a controversial topic. Good thing that I didn't pick a complex question.

The question of sex differences and similarities in cognitive abilities is highly volatile. There are many psychologists whom I admire who don't believe that we should even be asking questions about sex differences and similarities. I understand their concern. I have also been involved in other, what I have come to call "follow my nose" research to describe the practice of following interesting findings with more questions wherever they may lead.

I don't want to squander this marvelous opportunity to say something meaningful about life and careers and the perspective that one has on these topics from the vantage point of midlife. I could talk about something that I know well, but it would be hard to keep anyone reading while I explain the intricacies of data analysis or give you the details for a favorite recipe. I considered and then rejected a large number of possible topics. I could write about the value of education, the real joy that comes from teaching and learning, or the way my own knowledge of psychology has changed since I opened my first psychology textbook, but I rejected each of these topics in turn. Instead I opted for a more personal and painful theme. It concerns the need for courage—not the sort of courage that is required to face an enemy on the battlefield, or the courage needed to fight a dread disease, or the courage needed to protest a violation of civil rights. In these examples, we know the right thing to do: the enemy must be stopped; the cancer treatments must be endured; the wrong must be made right. We know that these are important battles worth fighting and that if we can win, the world will be better, and if we lose, it was for a good cause.

The kind of courage that I want to focus on is academic courage—a kind of courage that you never learn about in graduate school, colleagues are unlikely to discuss, and you may never have to face. Unlike the other examples, the situations that call for academic courage are more ambiguous; you cannot be certain that you are on the "right" side or that the issue you are fighting for is worth all of your pain and effort. It's the kind of courage needed when responsible psychologists engage in research on politically and emotionally charged topics. I never expected to need or even to think about this sort of courage.

In understanding why I feel so passionate about academic courage, it is important to know that I began to make some unpopular conclusions. In my text on sex differences in cognitive abilities, I concluded that there are some sex differences that are large in size and important in many practical settings. I became increasingly convinced that psychological explanations of a whole host of behaviors and traits need to also consider the various interactions and predispositions that intersect the domains of biology, sociology, and psychology. This is not a particularly radical idea if you are a biologist, but the prevailing zeitgeist in psychology, especially among feminists, has been strictly environmental until most recently. I found that my work was being staunchly criticized not only because of my conclusions that the biological bases for femaleness and maleness are important, but for the very fact that I chose to study sex differences and my use of the word "sex" when most feminists believe that the correct term is "gender" to signify the social influences that are also involved in shaping who we are. Thus, the nature of what I chose to study, the words that I used, and the conclusions that I reached were all treated as though I had turned my back on feminism. To my surprise, I found that I had landed on the hit list for almost everyone. I began to receive angry, sometimes threatening, letters from individuals on every part of the political spectrum, accusing me of obvious bias. Interestingly, I am accused of being biased toward both the biological and environmental explanations, depending on who is writing the letter. In case there was anyone whom I had not managed to offend with my conclusions, I also expanded my work to include laterality effects and sexual orientation. I am certain that many sex-typical behaviors and traits including cognitive patterns on selected tests, extent of cerebral lateralization, and sexual orientation have common origins and can best be understood with an encompassing theory that includes the reciprocal influences of biological and environmental variables. The number of critics I managed to anger increased dramatically when I engaged in a heated and vociferous debate on *The Bell Curve* with an anthropologist who enjoys the nickname "the Raging Bull of Berkeley." It is an act of courage to face a raging bull armed only with theory and data. Instead of the quiet life of an academic in midlife, my penchant for being outspoken has thrust me into the eye of many storms.

There are also personal costs to unpopular conclusions about social science research. Even some close friends have told me that they don't like my work. When pressed to explain this statement, what they mean is they don't like my results. Undaunted, or you may conclude, dumbly, I have continued working on controversial and potentially explosive issues. I never planned to generate so much attention or so much disagreement. I do not enjoy it, although I am sure that there are some people who do. I cannot be sure that I am right or that the end justifies all of the aggravation. Many of the encounters that I am describing have all the warmth and pleasantness of an exchange between Mark Fuhrman and F. Lee Bailey. It would have been far easier for me to return to the study of subjective contours, where disagreements were more civil and far more private. There is no obvious compelling need to fight these fights. In every case, I stayed close to the data, read as extensively as I found humanly possible, and made conclusions that were responsible and—most importantly for me—were my honest assessments of what science has told us. I do not believe that I can say the same for some of my detractors. It is a case of "let's shoot the messenger." Some people have clung to their preferred beliefs unfettered by data.

Overall, the entire process has been very negative. Similarly, people with no knowledge of the research literature or the extent to which my conclusions are supported by studies conducted all over the world have no difficulty claiming that I must be wrong. When there was no basis to criticize the studies, critics have engaged in ad hominem attacks. So why do it? I firmly believe that we all have an obligation to seek and speak the truth as we best know it, an action that will require courage when the truth that you see is in conflict with some cherished belief or someone else's truth.

I have come to learn that modern psychology consists of many courageous acts committed, sometimes unwillingly, by individuals who have bucked the crowd. There are many psychologists who have found that the costs of conducting unpopular research can include social ostracism, ridicule, threats, infamy, defamation, and even loss of employment and threats of imprisonment. I have come to learn that I am not alone in suffering from the unanticipated consequences of studying phenomena and reporting data that caused an explosive reaction in the general public and among some of our colleagues.

What is the moral to this message from midlife? I urge readers to have the courage to ask the tough questions and conduct the tough research. This means that sometimes you will get answers that you may not like. In deciding about controversial issues, adhere to one rule: be as honest as you can be, with yourself and with others. When others present opposing points of view or data that you have trouble believing for any reason, remember that errors will get corrected and that good hypotheses will be supported with additional independent research. Personal attacks, name-calling, and innuendo do not advance the field, and they say far more about the initiator than they do about the target. If you have a colleague who finds himself or herself in a media maelstrom, a kind word or other indication that you believe in his or her ability to get through it can mean a great deal.

From my perspective, a feminist is first and foremost a good scientist—one who bases her conclusions on reliable, valid data and sound reasoning, even when the conclusions don't fit well into the prevailing zeitgeist. It does not advance any ideology to shrink from difficult questions or to ignore findings that some may find personally distasteful. The conclusion that the biological underpinnings of femaleness and maleness are an important part of who we are is not a sexist statement. Feminism must be broad enough to encompass a variety of perspectives and strong enough to encourage debate and dissent. An understanding that differences are not deficiencies needs to be coupled with investigations into the ways in which we differ and the ways in which we are the same.

If there is a study that you believe is wrong, you have an obligation to respond in an ethical manner. You could write a letter to the editor explaining why you believe there is an error, you could conduct your own research that will test the hypothesis that is being disputed, you could write to the author and ask questions or ask to reanalyze the data. These are reasonable and honest responses. But we must not create conditions in which only certain outcomes are acceptable and only some topics can be studied. Censorship is always dangerous, far worse than the truth. If we all follow basic rules of science and civility for handling disputes and encouraging creative and new ways of thinking, then future psychologists may not need to be quite as brave and can spend their time more productively with their students and studies instead of defending their right to "follow their noses" and their thoughts into new areas of study.

15

I Can't Hear...I Can't See...I Can't Remember Anything

Lynne Taetzsch

I teach in an English department where literature professors are always spouting lines of poetry or referring to some character in a Great Book. Everyone is supposed to get the reference instantaneously, but I'm usually out in the foggy pasture without a clue. When one of my students brought up the name Jane Eyre in class one day, I asked, "Is that the name of the author or the book?"

The only way I get through the academic day is by carrying lists in my pocket of things I'm supposed to do and places I'm supposed to be:

post office: mail manuscript
pick up manilla folders in supply room
9:15 Sharon Z, office, discuss grade from 293
10:30 Eng 202, room 207—bring extra syllabi
12:50 Eng 396, room 206
    READ FRANNIE'S STORY FIRST!
3:10 University Grad Meeting, Ginger Hall 201
    REMEMBER PROPOSAL FOR 587
Bring home 396 text, papers from 202

The trouble is, I don't always remember to look at the list.

A student comes up to me after class: "Can I see you tomorrow during your office hours?"

"Sure. Let me write that down. What's your name?"

I never had a great memory to start with, but since menopause there's nothing left.[1] I can recite the opening lines to "The Love Song of J. Alfred Prufrock," which I learned in high school, but I can't remember a movie I saw last week.

At first the memory loss frightened and embarrassed me. I would try to hide it by pretending to know what people were talking about when I didn't. If I ran into a colleague whose name I couldn't remember, I'd greet her with a generic "Hi, how are you?" As for students, I'd avoid making eye contact as I walked across campus. In my classes, I'd blush every time I called a student by the wrong name.

Memory loss is a serious handicap for an English professor. I teach mostly creative writing and some literature classes. In either case, I have to read and discuss written texts with my students—either published ones or their own. The only way I can be ready for class is by reading the texts for that day immediately before I teach them.

It would appear, then, that my students are being shortchanged by having me as a teacher. After all, if they bring up a book I read last year or even last month, I may not remember it well enough to talk about it. And when they turn in a revision of a story they've written, I won't be able to tell what they've revised unless I go back and reread the original.

No wonder employers would prefer to hire a thirty-five- than a fifty-five-year-old!

Facing the losses of aging has not been easy, but it has been valuable. For one thing, I've become kinder to myself. After all, if I were missing a leg I would not berate myself for failing to run up a flight of stairs. I'm learning to accept my limitations and to laugh with my students about them.

"Look, I can't see, I can't hear, and I can't remember anything. So speak up when you talk, type or print when you write, and remind me about everything. If you screw up, I'll forget."

Should all professors retire at fifty? If so, I'd never have had the chance to enter this profession. I was forty-four when I started a master's program in creative writing at San Diego State University. It seemed very strange at first, especially sitting in an undergraduate class I took to meet a prerequisite for the graduate program. There was one other *older woman* in that class, and she was a severe embarrassment to me. Alva talked too much, presumed to know everything, and treated the younger students condescendingly. She would walk into the classroom ten minutes late and barge into an ongoing discussion as if we were all just sitting around waiting for her to arrive.

The other students quickly began to avoid Alva and gave each other knowing looks whenever she opened her mouth. On days when we had to divide into small groups for special projects, no one wanted to be in Alva's group.

My big fear was that the other students would lump me in the same category as Alva and shun me as well. This fear was intensified because Alva assumed that I would be her ally and friend. She called me all the time to complain about her grade or to ask my advice (which she never took) about how she could improve her papers. We were about the same age, so of course we should both have the same worldview, right?

Wrong!

I see now that I have been working very hard over the last ten or fifteen years to differentiate myself from the group named *older women*. Having dismissed them as irrelevant for most of my life, I was certainly not about to become one.

In the first year I taught at Morehead State University, I had a mixed graduate/undergraduate class in fiction writing made up of mostly young people under thirty. One week a young male undergraduate brought in a short story which was filled with expletives. His story had been assigned to Marian, the one *older woman* in the class, to critique. Marian was an experienced writer and teacher, and most times she and I were on the same wavelength.

After pointing out a few positive qualities in the young man's story, Marian finally admitted that she simply did not like it, period.

"I'm sorry," she said, "but I can't get past this foul language. It's a generational thing."

"No, I don't think so," I said. "The language doesn't bother me."

"Well, you're not as old as I am," insisted Marian.

"Yes I am. In fact, I'm a year older than you are."

Instead of focusing on the young man's story and what this language might do or not do successfully in that context, I had turned the discussion toward my need to differentiate myself from this other *older woman*. I had to prove to my students that some of us could still be outrageous and cool, and thus worthy of their interest and respect.

Most of my life I've thought of myself as the rebel or outsider. When I was a student, I challenged the professor and tried to shake up the class, either performing as an exhibitionist or a leader of the avant-garde. Going back to graduate school at midlife, I didn't have the typical respect for the professor or the reticence a younger student might have had. I didn't worry about making a fool of myself and just blurted out whatever I thought. When I was introduced to a new idea, I attempted to connect it to the rest of my life experience and knowledge, testing it against what I already knew. This made the classroom exciting for me, although it might have irritated some of my professors.

When I took my preliminary exams for a Ph.D. at Florida State University, one of my committee members noted, "These are the most opinionated exam responses I have ever seen." This professor seemed appalled that instead of respectfully summarizing Plato and Foucault, I ruthlessly dismissed any of their theories that didn't work for me. This difference in approach to learning is one thing I've noted about nontraditional students in general. They don't separate academic learning from life.

That's what I love about them. Give me a class full of nontraditional students (barring Alva) any day over a group of eighteen-year-olds fresh out of high school. The nontraditional student has had a life outside of school that helps her put what she hears in the classroom into a larger context. That's what I would like all my students to be able to do, and I encourage them as far as possible in that direction.

"How can you connect what we're reading to your life?"

Some of my younger students would probably prefer that the nontraditionals shut up and that we focus on getting the information necessary to pass an exam or write the assigned paper. Why are we recounting stories of our mothers, our sisters, our children, or what happened to us in third grade? It is true that sometimes I do have to rein them in, but for me this kind of exploration is where the education really takes place.

At Morehead State, almost all of our temporary full-time (non-tenure-track) and part-time English professors are older women who went back to school at midlife to get graduate degrees (as I did) and then looked for some way to put those degrees to use. These professors are treated like third-class citizens in terms of pay, benefits, workload, and respect. Perhaps that's why they are shunned by the tenure-track faculty, who don't want to admit to themselves, "There but for the grace of God go I."

Having been in a temp position myself at George Washington University before I came here, I made a token effort to befriend the women in these positions when I arrived. But I know that my efforts were out of guilt, not desire. These women are somehow tainted by their inferior status here, whereas a young man who holds the same position is not. He is simply taking whatever work he can find until he decides what to do with his life. I have no problem being the young man's friend. But then again, he doesn't have "that look."

What look do I mean? The tenured older women on the faculty at George Washington commanded respect from me, not pity. They exuded a sense of confidence and belonging in their world, with clothes, hair, posture, and speech that said, "I am a graduate of Princeton or Yale, as were my parents before me." Here at Morehead, I'm always horrified by the versions of *older woman* I see before me. Sticking out most visibly is the aging southern belle whose makeup, jewelry, and clothing suggest a garden party. Another version is the frumpy housewife attempting to dress up for an important occasion, but failing to do it right. Scariest is the stiff-suited matron who might pass for a jailer in a women's prison.

The one thing I hang on to is my young looks. When I walk into a room in my jeans and turtleneck, no one thinks of me as their grandmother. If you don't look closely, maybe you'll think I'm in my late thirties. Certainly I can pass for forty-five.

I look in the mirror and do not like to see the signs of aging. When I first noticed the red blotches on my neck, I tried to figure out what I could wear to cover them up. Turn my collars up, perhaps? But eventually there will be things about my aging body that I can't hide. I suppose if I were dedicated, I could get them lasered off at a dermatologist's, but that will simply mean postponement. The trick is to learn to live with my aging body, to find a way to present myself to the world that doesn't depend on youth.

When I began teaching at GW, fresh out of graduate school, I tried to dress like the tenured women faculty I admired. But the fact that I held a lowly non-tenure-track, temporary position meant I might as well have been wearing a scarlet letter proclaiming my inferior status.

Perhaps if I had been twenty-five or thirty, taking a temporary position until I could find a permanent one might not have been so mortifying. I've had lots of low-level jobs in my life, especially since my pattern has been to change whatever I am doing and wherever I am living as often as possible, never sticking to one job or place for more than a few years.

Perhaps it was that I had to "settle" for that position at GW that made me feel so uncomfortable. I'm not used to being turned down for jobs. In fact, I've been able to talk my way into positions I'm not even qualified for. I beat out candidates with experience and degrees in education to get a job teaching disadvantaged women in Newark, New Jersey, when I had never taught anything and had no college degree. I was hired to teach small business management as an adjunct at three different colleges without ever having taken a business course in my life, and having failed at running a small business myself. I did a good job in these positions, too, because I worked very hard and believed in what I was doing.

When I graduated from Florida State in 1992, for the first time in my life, I actually had credentials: a Ph.D. And what was it good for? I couldn't even get to the interview stage to talk anyone into hiring me.

Of course, I don't think of my Ph.D. as a "real" one. I've spent so much of my life as an outsider, a rebel, a passer-through, that there's no way I can identify with any established institution or profession. The way I relate to my students is by showing them that I am even more antiestablishment than they are.

The other day I played tennis with a nontraditional male student and his teenage son. "This is Dr. Taetzsch," my student said to his son, "and she's got a fouler mouth than I have, can you believe it?" This little episode pleased me. I must be doing something right if they identify me as foulmouthed.

My appearance and approach immediately signal to students what my class will be like: informal and interactive. We sit in a circle and talk to each other. When I ask students to do a writing exercise in class, I do it with them, and share mine just as I ask them to share theirs. In fact, I always share a particularly bad example early in the semester to show that there are off-days or hours for every writer, no matter how experienced she is.

But another way I use my own writing to communicate with my students is by sharing the outrageous stuff I write—my desire for revenge against my enemies; a scathing critique of the university; tales of sex, drugs, and rock and roll from the days of my youth; whatever personal muck I might dredge up in that day's exercise. I don't want students to know me as an older female college professor—wife, mother, and grandmother. I want them to think of me as "one of the guys."

This is how I've always loved to see myself since I was a little girl trying to hang out with my three older brothers and ditch my little sisters. I like it best when I'm the only female in a group of males, and they don't even notice that I'm not one of them. I was taught to be "male identified" early in life, and so far, the knowledge of how this works has not helped me shake it. My natural inclinations are always to choose the "guy group" to hang out with, so I counter this inclination by deliberately sitting next to a woman colleague at a meeting, approaching a faculty wife at a party, or asking to hold a new baby.

Yet occasionally I find myself thrown accidentally into the company of men. A search committee I chaired last semester met at our local Mexican restaurant to have dinner with a male candidate. The only other woman on the committee was unable to join us. As I lifted a bottle of Dos Equis to my lips, I had a sudden jolt of joy—joy in the company of men. It was an eerily familiar feeling reminiscent of my days at Cooper Union Art School when I would drive around New York City with a carful of guys. I wasn't dating any of these guys, or interested in them romantically. I just wanted to *be* one of them.

At the beginning of each semester I would ask my students to introduce themselves, and I would begin by introducing myself. In an effort to counter my natural inclination to emphasize my identity as an artist and as a writer (which fits a male "achievement" image), I would talk about being a wife, a mother, and a grandmother as well. But students followed my lead and soon would be talking about their families, too. At some point I realized that this introduction wasn't working because I didn't want the focus of our discussion to be on family life. I wanted them to think instead about their beliefs and values, their political positions, and their place in the world. Ironically, what was radical for me (identifying myself as a wife, mother, and grandmother) was too cozy for them.

Because I came to university life later than most new professors, and because I had a variety of careers and occupations before I got here, I don't see academic achievement as the only path to success in life. I often talk to my students about other kinds of knowledge being just as, if not more important, than the kind you can get in college. I respect what they have already achieved, and the knowledge-bases *they* have which I do not. When we read Flannery O'Connor's "Everything That Rises Must Converge," we note that Julian's college education has not helped him to understand himself or his mother, or to have any real compassion for others.

I try to help my students succeed in class and to overcome whatever obstacles might keep them from completing their degrees. But if one of my students has no alternative but to drop out of school for a semester, I reassure her that it will probably not be a big deal in the long scheme of things.

"It took me twelve years to get my B.A.," I say, and she feels comforted. The nontraditional students especially appreciate my tales of going back to school later in life.

Perhaps this is why I fit in better here at Morehead State than I did at George Washington University, where most students were hell-bent on fast-track careerism: take a heavy courseload; maintain a 3.5-plus (A-) grade point average; line up prestigious summer internships; end up with an early acceptance at a top grad school in political science, law, business, or medicine, and keep networking throughout the process. GW students were firmly fixed on their goal and would do whatever it took to get there on schedule.

Here in eastern Kentucky, most students put people ahead of their educations. Absenteeism is high because they are expected to go to every funeral and wedding of even their most distant kin. They leave school to visit friends and relatives in the hospital, to keep someone company at a doctor's visit or in traffic court, or to help out on the family farm or business. These students make me realize what I have missed over the years by not taking an interest in my extended family. (We are scattered all over the country and I have cousins I haven't seen since childhood.)

Because of family demands and other pressures on students here, I find myself relaxing some of the rules. I still have an attendance policy in order to motivate students to come, but I don't enforce it as strictly as I used to. Doing what is best for a particular student at a particular time in his or her life is more important to me than upholding academic standards. The course students are taking with me is one small piece of a large complicated life full of all kinds of stresses and demands, so I don't worry too much about them *getting away with something.* Sure, I know students sometimes lie about their situations, but I would rather err on the side of believing a student who was lying than the other way around.

When I began my university teaching career, I thought of teaching as *transforming lives.* I forced my students to think about the BIG questions: What does it mean to live a *good* life, a *meaningful* life? And how are you preparing to face your own death? I wanted them to question all of their assumptions; to confront themselves and the imperfect world we live in; and to make commitments to change. These are the themes I dealt with when I taught first- and second-year composition as a teaching assistant, then as a part-timer, and then as a full-time temporary instructor. I approached composition classes as if writing could change your life.

I think my expectations are much lower now, or perhaps different. I teach writing, not life. Actually, I don't even do that, since you can't teach writing directly. All I do is suggest some strategies, model some behaviors, provide experiential exercises in a hands-on workshop. We meet only two and a half hours a week for fifteen weeks. I'm not a miracle worker.

Overall, then, my expectations are much more modest about what can be accomplished in one class in one semester. But in other ways they are much higher. I have great respect for the capacity of students to find their own way and surprise me. I try to listen more, to be receptive to what is happening with students, to help them find their own path. It is this, after all, which will provide them with a process they can use the rest of their lives.

What most of my writing students need is the confidence that they have something worth saying to the world. Otherwise, why write? Part of my job is helping them tap into that inner reservoir of material that only they possess. It is hard to go very deep if everyone is uptight about revealing stupidity or weakness, so one of the things I do is to provide a *safe* environment for dialogue and sharing. Part of that process is revealing my own weaknesses, and not being afraid to make a mistake in front of my students.

Another part is acknowledging that we are bodies as well as minds in the classroom. If we've been up all night throwing up, worried sick about our grandma in the hospital, or hungry because we didn't get our financial aid check on time, we will not be able to concentrate very well. When the classroom becomes stiflingly hot in early spring because maintenance has not yet switched from heat to air-conditioning, my propensity for the hot flash is intensified, and I can hardly think. I take off whatever clothing I can without offending the laws of decency. I fan myself with my notebook. I endure. But I may end class five or ten minutes early that day.

So when a student falls asleep in my class, I don't take it personally. He might have the flu. She might be pregnant. I remember being pregnant myself when I was a student at UCLA in 1966. I had an 8 A.M. history class that I would tend to fall asleep in, so I sat in the front row, immediately in front of the professor, in the attempt to keep myself awake. It did not work.

The most valuable thing I've learned in my short career as a professor is to trust myself. I cannot be all things to all students or necessarily follow another instructor's successful method, even if it is the newest pedagogical thinking. Fads come and go. I've seen them myself as a student beginning college in the late 1950s, completing my undergraduate degree in 1971, and then going to grad school in the late 1980s and early '90s. I have witnessed tremendous learning take place with unsound methods, and little learning take place with enlightened methods. The desire of the student and commitment of the teacher had much more to do with the results than the particular methods used.

I am always reevaluating what goes on in my classroom, and what I might do to make it more fruitful for more students. At the same time, I know that I am only one little piece in the puzzle, and that this course will be a very small part of most students' lives. Yet, rather than shortchanging my students, the perspective I bring to the classroom because of my age and experience allows me to give them a broader, fuller, and more varied space in which to grow.

16

Memories of a "First Woman"

Tikva Simone Frymer

This fall I fell victim to one of the typical academic snafus that seem to bedevil us all. I sent in the description and days of my course, but the secretary entered my colleague's schedule. As a result, I taught a three-hour class Wednesday morning, attended community lecture, and then taught another ninety minutes. The congruence of teaching these two classes together illuminated many of the issues of my teaching at this time of my life.

The first revelation was utter exhaustion. There was a time when I could easily handle two classes a day. Many years ago, in a situation typical for married women, I had no real university job, but my husband was not ready to leave Ann Arbor. I was underemployed, not free to pursue my own career because of family commitments, and adjuncting all over the place. When there was money, I taught Women and Religion at the university. I also taught at the Midrashah, an institute for Jewish learning. I drove an hour, taught two two-hour classes, and drove back. One semester I flew from Detroit to Toronto and took an hour-long van ride to Hamilton, where I taught two graduate courses at McMaster University, flew back, and taught in Ann Arbor the next morning. I won't say I loved the regimen, and I hated not having a real academic job. But I seemed to have limitless stamina, and the sheer exhilaration of teaching carried me through. No more. This year I could feel the exhaustion during my second class. Marathon teaching is for the young.

The other revelation had to do with types of teaching. The morning was an exegesis class. Six students sitting around the table, reading the ancestor stories in Genesis, translating, commenting on the issues, relating their extra research. My role in such a seminar is as a "coach," spotting their weaknesses and helping them improve their skills; and as a "virtuoso," a star musician in a master class, demonstrating how I read the text and bringing my own insights to add to what they acquire by reading the literature. The afternoon class was an introduction to reading the Hebrew Bible, in which I lectured to around forty students, whom I did not know, and my teaching assistants led discussion groups. My role is part performer, part informant. It is the serious equivalent of a stand-up routine. I entertain, I impart facts, I seduce and entice them (I hope) into fascination with the Bible. Teaching the two courses back to back and the invitation to contribute to this volume have led me to reflect on the nature of my teaching career and on my personal odyssey to this place.

I always knew that I wanted to teach college. When I first decided—at age ten—that I wanted to be a nuclear engineer, I always added that it didn't really matter what I studied, because in any event, I planned to teach college. I do not know where this desire for academe came from. The only academic I knew was a cousin, and my father had a political activist's disdain for the "ivory tower." Yet somehow I knew my destiny. When I found that my "hobby" of scripture and religion compelled me to spend ever more time with it, I switched over to study to be an Assyriologist and biblicist. But always as a college teacher. During my junior year, I began to teach in Jewish supplementary schools, going out to Queens two afternoons a week and Sunday morning to teach fifth-graders elementary Hebrew and equally elementary Jewish studies. I have been teaching ever since.

In graduate school I taught Hebrew high school, confirmation classes (for thirteen- and fourteen-year-olds), first-grade day school, and graduate school. Once a week I would finish my daily three-hour stint as the first-grade Jewish studies teacher at Ezra Academy and drive down to Yale to teach my graduate course in first-year Sumerian. It is hard to imagine two teaching experiences farther apart on the educational spectrum.

I was better at teaching graduate school than I was at teaching first grade, better at teaching Hebrew high school than I was at teaching confirmation classes. The high school students were reading the biblical text, the confirmation classes were discussing issues of ethics, morality, social action. In one class we really did have some interesting sessions. But one confirmation group was often an exercise in disaster. The class was mostly boys who had turned thirteen that year. Each boy wanted the other boys in the class to know that he didn't want to be there, and each session was a competition between my desire to teach and the students' requirement to be cool. I didn't know how to win. I wanted to impart information, and viewed obstreperous interruptions as the great enemy. I had no talent as a disciplinarian. I kept getting waylaid by discipline in my first-grade teaching too. I could keep students interested and motivated, but when a student rebelled I became distracted, giving too much attention to the misbehaving student. Some teachers can handle discipline issues without losing their spontaneity or the atmosphere of enthusiasm in their classroom. I am not one of them.

But I was (I am) a very good lecturer. Public speaking is as natural to me as breathing, easier than private conversation. Like a lot of performers and actors, I feel at home in the spotlight. Partly, this talent is genetic. My father was famed as an orator who could keep an audience enthralled and happy. My parents delighted in telling anecdotes about my father's speaking ability. In one, he was still a young schoolboy. When a famous essayist visited his school, he was called upon to read his own assigned paper before the famous author. Rather than admit that he hadn't prepared, he "read" his essay before the class from blank pages. But he was too good: the visiting author asked for the essay, and my father had to hand over the blank pages. Another story took place at university. My father's friends wagered that he could not deliver an interesting talk, unprepared, on a topic that they would select. When he accepted, they directed him to talk about the armoire in the room. My father knew absolutely nothing about armoires, nothing about furniture, nothing about wood. But he won the bet.

One of my parents' stories rose above the level of anecdote. My father was the head of the Zionist youth organizations in western Europe. Because of his fame as an orator, the Polish government in exile sent my father to America to make friends and raise money for the Polish cause. It was January 1940. France was at war, and my father brought my mother and infant sister along. When Paris fell, they were allowed to stay in America. My father's prowess as a speaker had saved us from the Holocaust.

These stories made a deep impression on me, giving me a deep appreciation for the power of the spoken word. But I had no patience for my father's kind of speech, the spellbinding talk that is sound and fire with only a grain of content. People can still be affected by such speeches, but I wanted to give denser talks. I was eager to use my lecturing ability to convey the knowledge that I was pursuing. In other words, I wanted to teach.

I was somewhat frustrated in my graduate school teaching. I certainly worked a lot of hours, but I was eager to teach what I was learning. In particular, I longed to be the teaching assistant to teach first-year Akkadian or to be a discussion leader for the large undergraduate Bible class. I was never asked. A male graduate student became the Akkadian teacher. I could swallow that, flavored with a little envy. But the teaching assistants for Bible were not even knowledgeable. They were plucked out of literature courses and learned the lessons the day before class, while I, with an undergraduate major in Bible, was never asked. I knew it was because I was a woman. My femaleness made me absolutely invisible to the men looking for teaching assistants. When I was the only one who knew enough Sumerian to teach when the professor of Sumerian went on leave, I taught. When a man was available to do the job, I was never asked.

There was yet another reason I did not become a teaching assistant: I never asked. This, too, probably had to do with my being a woman. Raised in the 1950s, I was simply more diffident than the men. Compared to the stereotype of femininity, I was assertive, even aggressive. But compared to the real-life men around me, I was very timid. I could argue points of fact and theory without fear or self-consciousness. But when it came to asking for something for myself, I couldn't do it.

As soon as I finished my exams I received an offer from a now defunct women's college to teach an introductory religion class and an intro to philosophy. I probably should have stayed at Yale, but I was carried off by the romance of teaching, and so for the next two years I spent my fall at Mount Vernon College and my spring at Yale. Mount Vernon was an all-girls school, and the dynamics of the classroom were quite different from that in the Hebrew schools, which at that time became more male at each advance in grade. There were, of course, no discipline problems. No one acted up or spoke out of turn. The girls were not overeager students, and silence in a classroom can indicate a lack of interest as well as noise can. However, silence gives you a chance, an opportunity to talk, to perform, to bring humor and enthusiasm, knowledge and discussion into the room, and sometimes to generate interest where before there had been only passivity.

I was very good at this type of teaching, and I could see the students come alive during the semester. But nothing I was teaching had any bearing on what I was learning. Not even remotely. Not even in the same field. I had a few philosophy courses in college, but I knew exactly what I had been taught. No more. So I taught what I had learned. And frequently sat the night before class and crammed into my head the material I was going to teach. TAs often have this experience, but at least they are working under the supervision of a professor who—we assume—knows something about the subject. I was working without a net, the only person on campus even remotely qualified to teach religion.

It didn't seem to matter. Maybe my lack of knowledge helped: I was full of enthusiasm, and I knew from immediate experience the difficulties in learning the material. I could hold a class's attention; I could explain complex ideas in a way that made them easy to learn. I had a glimpse of the special potential of teaching, when the sparks I sent out would catch fire in a student. Suddenly, long-resented lessons, sermons, and stories would come alive, and the student would float above the normal "will this be on the final?" level of concern and begin to ask questions and wrestle with answers. The rarity of these interactions makes them memorable.

My successful teaching experience at Mount Vernon sent me back to Yale on a high that sustained me through the often tedious rigors of scholarship. But there is a downside to being a successful lecturer. The fact that I could keep the students' attention and interest while knowing so very little had a boomerang effect on my self-confidence. I knew that I was a good speaker, but for years whenever people were enthusiastic about one of my lectures, I attributed any success I might have to my abilities as a speaker. Not to what I had said. My father's armoire story haunted me. He had held his audience spellbound while he spouted inanities about a piece of furniture. Maybe I was doing the same. Maybe what I was saying—the fruits of my learning—was not really all that interesting. Maybe I was wowing the audiences with my timing, my arch wit, my subtle body language and facial expressions.

This doubt had enormous impact on my writing. Or rather, on the paucity of my writing. My success in speaking about matters of which I knew little paralyzed my writing. I couldn't quite believe that I had anything to say that could survive without the force of my personality. I would deliver talks in classes, at professional meetings, even in synagogues, but I wouldn't write them down. When I wrote conference papers, I didn't send them out for publication. When women began to write about women in Judaism, I never published my thoughts. Two articles, published twenty years apart, have come from my thirty years of investigating and teaching the Book of Genesis. And my dissertation, which took me twelve years to complete, is still not published.

I had no one to talk to about this. I had no mentor in graduate school. My professors were never quite comfortable enough with a woman student to take a personal interest in me. I had a woman classics professor as an undergraduate, but the very few women biblicists or Assyriologists I knew were not interested in nurturing a female graduate student. As far as anyone could see, I was a brilliant graduate student, and even if my term papers were always late, they were always As. My verbal abilities successfully masked my insecurities. These came out in perfectionism and procrastination, but not even I was totally attuned to the clues.

My first full-time job did not help. When I came back to Mount Vernon, the job panic had begun. Students were advising each other to find jobs before they all disappeared. So I went on the job market. The plum job that year, the one involving Assyriology, I didn't even have a chance to try for. My own adviser suggested someone else, someone not his student. He apologized later: he "hadn't even thought of me" (the old invisibility of the professional woman, again), but it was a fait accompli.

I went to Wayne State University, the younger stepsister of the University of Michigan and Michigan State University. The saving grace of that job was my one Bible course, for I had a few students in whose life I made a difference. In undergraduate teaching you can have a real impact on students' lives, broadening their horizons, stretching their ceiling, and giving them new concepts to think with. Teaching Bible or religious studies gives you a chance to give students new adult insight into worlds that they had left behind as children.

I was no good at other aspects of academic teaching, academic politics, and the career path. One day, as I was preparing some class worksheets, an old hand saw me. "You have to get your priorities straight," he said. "Spend more time thinking about yourself and less about your students!" The comment made me mad. I was sure that he, not I, had his priorities backwards. But ultimately I discovered that, from the point of view of the administration of a large public university, the excellence of teachers doesn't count for much. One year the dean presented me as one of their best young faculty. The next year I didn't get tenure. My chairman sent two people up for tenure from a four-person department. The university committed to one position. They promoted me to associate professor, denied me tenure, and offered me a part-time position, all at the same time. I heard rumors that they had reasoned that the single male would move away, but the married woman would be likely to stay on their terms. They were right. Ironically, I didn't take maternity leave because my chairman said that if I did, the tenure committee would not think I was serious. I should have left. But I needed the money and couldn't move. So I stayed and accepted part-time work.

The strange part is that I had stayed in that job so long. But my husband didn't want to leave. During my second year at Wayne State I was offered a job teaching Bible at Hebrew Union College in New York. But my husband wanted to stay in Ann Arbor. Perhaps I should have insisted. After all, it was 1975 I had devoted years training for my career. But I acted in the age-old pattern of families staying and moving according to the husband's career. Once I made that choice, I no longer looked at other jobs. Unless something were to open at the University of Michigan, I was at Wayne State for the duration. I even told myself that part-time work was better for a mother with a small child, that I was forging what would later be called a "mommy track."

Three years later, my position closed entirely as Wayne State eliminated all exotica to become an "urban university." By this time I was also teaching Women and Religion at the University of Michigan. Eighty-five students took the course, and the programs on religious studies and on women's studies tried to create a regular position, but the university was not interested. For seven years I continued to live in Ann Arbor, in the classic position of an academic "Mrs."—underemployed, adjuncting all over the place. I was never without work. It is almost axiomatic that part-timers work more than part time, and some years I juggled five courses at once. But I felt undervalued and frustrated. When people complimented me on my lectures, their compliments fueled my hidden resentment: if I was so good, why didn't I have a job?

I did not hunt for jobs in those years. Occasionally, when someone called me about a job, I would talk to my husband about applying. He always had the same answer. He had never intended to come to Ann Arbor or to be a rabbi; he went to see the president of the Ann Arbor synagogue only because he was curious to see the first woman to be a synagogue president in centuries. As he listened, he felt called, and he knew he would become the rabbi in Ann Arbor. He "knew when to come," he said, and he "would know when to leave." I didn't quite believe it. "Sure," I thought, "he's waiting for a 'call'! He doesn't want to go!"

After a while I began to feel that I was no longer marketable, that I had been out of the academic path for so long that I could no longer be hired. I became immersed in the study that led to *In the Wake of the Goddesses* and to *Motherprayer*. I had fascinating research, a book contract, and two children. More and more I defined myself as a writer rather than a teacher. Even though writing remained difficult for me, and the years of adjuncting had certainly not helped to lessen my underlying insecurity, I began to lose my frustration at not having a "real job."

Of course, as soon as I became content, things began to change. I taught at Ben Gurion University of the Negev in BeerSheba and considered accepting a position there. And then Art Green came to Ann Arbor as part of a lecture series. He told me that the Reconstructionist Rabbinical College, which he headed, had a search on for a Bible professor. That night, as I related this news to my husband, he stood stock-still and said, "This is it! Apply for the job! You're going to get it and we're moving to Philadelphia."

I was stunned. I had never really believed that he would suddenly "know" when it was time to leave. But there I was, applying for the job, invited to come "give a talk." Wanting to make a good impression, I decided to speak on a chapter in *In the Wake of the Goddesses* for which I already had a preliminary draft. As I sat in front of the student body with my manuscript in front of me, they brought me a glass of water. I began to say hello, and I knocked my glass of water all over the manuscript. I will never know whether it was an act of Providence, but it was certainly providential: since I couldn't read my soaked manuscript, I just talked the topic through. Years later they told me that I had the job the moment that I did that. So we moved to Philadelphia. I finally had a real job again. The teacher had come home, I thought.

Not quite! I loved the RRC, my colleagues, and my students. There was no academic friction, no politics to which I had to pay attention. The school was dedicated to ethical values that I shared, and if it was a bit in a time warp from the countercultural 1960s, so was I. But I was not yet a master teacher. In adult education the teacher is there to impart information; in college teaching she has to impart the information, stimulate the students, and teach them how to react as independent thinkers. In graduate education the teacher has to train the student to do without her, to impart skills and methodologies as well as information, to show students how to be creative, and how to balance that creativity with discipline and discretion. When the graduate education is for a rabbinic career, the student also has to learn how to internalize information and integrate it into a spiritual worldview.

How do you teach such things? Knowing that frontal learning has its limits, and using the Socratic method, I asked questions and reacted to their responses. I was careful to be encouraging in my answers, agreeing first with what I could support, and only afterwards rebutting with a counterargument or a fact. But the students rebelled: how could I put them on the spot that way? How dare I ask questions to which I already knew the answers? "Even when you agree," they said, "we are waiting for the 'but.'" They wanted to feel validated. I worried that if I agreed with everything they said, I wouldn't be helping them develop skills. Through our negotiations, I learned to encourage other students to speak to the issue. If error was still in the air, I could always speak up. I also became aware of power. As a student, not understanding power was a blessing. I was never intimidated in the process of learning. Shy as I might be at small talk, if there was actually a topic under discussion, I focused my attention on the topic. I "took risks" in what I said, for I was never aware that I was risking anything. I "took risks" in my scholarship (so others pointed out), following the path of my ideas without worrying that someone with power might have a vested interest in a different opinion. Sometimes I have suffered consequences from this, but I realize that my blithe disregard for the power of authorities has been a gift to my learning.

Not everyone is so blessed. My students at the RRC taught me to realize that others, most specifically students, might be conscious of power and intimidated by my authority. I had always prided myself on encouraging the interchange of different opinions. But I began to learn that my very knowledge could block students. Few students would volunteer answers. I had, after all, a lot of power over the life and death of their careers. I thought of myself as nurturing and supportive; they saw me first and foremost as the person who would sit in judgment over them. In some way they were aware that they had a lot of power over the future of an untenured teacher. But in their mind, the powers didn't balance out. If I stayed mindful of the systemic power imbalance, I could work to create an atmosphere of trust. But if I just blithely disregarded it, they could not feel free.

The students were also likely to be intimidated by the more knowledgeable of their classmates, to feel inadequate in the presence of students who had greater background, more Hebrew, or verbal virtuosity. I began to spend time "going around the room," requiring each student to speak, but in a predictable order so that they would not sit and "wait for the axe to fall." I interspersed questions of fact (for which I knew the answers) with questions of opinion. I was very conscious that each student in the class needed to develop a personal relationship with the material we were learning, so I allowed time for them to "vent" their reactions to the stories in the Bible.

This type of teaching requires a juggling act. The more frontal lecturing you include in your lesson, the more information they learn, and the less opportunity they have to become comfortable with it. The more you apply the techniques of the open classroom, the less hard information is transmitted, and the more they have to learn on their own. How much of each ingredient you include is a matter of trial and error, and I often thought that I began each September as an expert in teaching the group that I had taught the year before.

I stayed at the RRC for seven years. My students taught me to always consider the impact of a biblical text on contemporary readers, to always allow for a "vector to the present" to make the material come alive. The environment was conducive to developing a mode of scholarship that was engaged (or as we now say, engagé) rather than removed, that demonstrated commitment to the importance of the material while being aware of its flaws. Seminarians need to learn enormous amounts so thoroughly that it becomes second nature, they need to integrate what they learn into their worldview, and they need to maintain their sanity. Newly minted Ph.D.s are notorious for having put their own emotional and spiritual development on hold till after they have finished their dissertations. Rabbinical students cannot afford to do that, for nobody would hire a basket case for a rabbi. Seminary teachers have to be aware of this issue; they have to allow the students time and space to internalize and to maintain their equilibrium. And they often have to invest time in personal discussion and mentoring. I found these responsibilities spiritually rewarding and so stimulating that, despite the time-consuming aspect of the job, I managed to finish both *In the Wake of the Goddesses* and *Motherprayer* while I taught there, and I did much of the preliminary work for the book on women in the Bible that I am now completing.

One day I picked up the phone and Clark Gilpin, dean of the University of Chicago Divinity School, asked me to come to Chicago to discuss becoming professor of Hebrew Bible. I had not known that they were looking, and I hadn't applied. But it is a Chicago tradition not to look only at applicants. I was intrigued enough to come for a visit. On a lark, I offered to give a lecture. I had nothing to lose. I chose a chapter for which I had not even completed the research, and I began to cram. This is a kind of academic brinkmanship: under the pressure of this deadline, my work would start to flow more quickly than in less frantic times. The time pressure helped my ideas to gel, but, of course, I ran out of time. I was still writing on the plane (which gave me another hour by being delayed). I was still scribbling in the taxicab, which took a long time in traffic. I ran in from the cab to find the audience waiting, and began to speak.

Coming to Chicago was a hard decision to make. Professionally, I really liked the RRC. Personally, the decision was even harder. My husband was associate dean of the rabbinical school at the Jewish Theological Seminary in New York. I couldn't ask him to move to Chicago. We had a daughter who was a junior in high school, and a son still in elementary school. To my husband, there was no decision to be made: we would simply continue as we were. But, I argued, "It is your decision not to go to Chicago; it is my decision whether *I* go." Nineteen years earlier I didn't go to New York. I was nineteen years older, and I went to Chicago.

I don't suppose that my story is typical. Quite the contrary, I have spent my life being the "first woman": the first woman in the Talmud major seminar at the Jewish Theological Seminary; the first woman to come lecture at various institutes and retreats; the first woman Bible teacher at a rabbinical seminary; the first (or maybe the second) woman tenured at a rabbinical seminary. I have felt like somewhat of a pioneer, which is exciting. I have also felt somewhat like the lead goose, breaking the wind for others and feeling the brunt of it. I no longer feel alone. There are many women now studying Bible, Judaica, and the ancient Near East. There are also many people—women and men—informed by feminism and using its insights and methods to illuminate their own work. There are also other people—still depressingly few—seeking to combine their learning with religious insight and a commitment to tradition and community. There are more people along "the Oregon Trail," and that makes the path different.

I was eager to share my story because I have learned a lesson that I would like to share. The world has changed—or maybe the old verities were never true at all. It used to be thought that if you didn't get tenure, you were finished. And yet here I am, and as I look around the major professorships in my own field, I see other leading professors, holding chairs at major universities, who—for one reason or other—didn't get tenure and just kept going. It also used to be thought that if you dropped off the academic ladder, you could never get back on. Women were advised never to take time off to have babies, never to take a few years off to raise children or follow a husband's career move. And yet here I am, and once again, I look around me and see other scholars who have come back from part-time work, or who came out of nonacademic jobs to take serious and prestigious positions in academe. I was also taught that if you went to work at a seminary you would never be able to transfer to the universities. But once again, here I am, and I know several former JTS and RRC faculty now teaching at Brandeis,

Brown, Columbia, and Yale. It turned out that it was not absolutely essential that people follow a uniform career path.

It is nice to go into a tenure-track job, be awarded tenure, and then get promoted to full professor. But it is not necessary. If you stay committed to a field even while it is ignoring you, if you are stubborn and keep studying, "they" may let you back in. It is nice to know that as long as you keep studying, you do not have to perish, and that even if you perish, it may not be forever.

Rant for Old Teachers

PAULA GUNN ALLEN

In this my thirty-first year as a university instructor, battle-scarred veteran of more internal wars than I can count, I find that the first week of my final year is all but unendurable. I am discouraged, disengaged, and (for which perhaps I should be very grateful) disenchanted. I have been discouraged for many years—since graduate school. But I thought that working, publishing, getting literature by the literarily dispossessed published and recognized, attending conferences, giving and hearing papers, publishing, teaching, developing curriculum, and speaking would together eventually result in a nourishing intellectual environment. I hoped for a climate where the intricate and fascinating matters of literary and broader cultural studies in the United States could flourish, and, most of all, where the literature and lives of American Indian people would form a visible portion of America's store of common knowledge. After thirty-plus years on the lines I realize how naive my notions were and how bitter the struggle has been. In short, I am beyond discouraged; I am over it, big time.

Why is that?

Oh, how I wish I knew.

For some time I paid a psychotherapist weekly in order to stay on the job. By the mid-1980s I was aware that the only way I could continue to function in an unremittingly hostile environment was via a weekly stress blow-off session. "The price of keeping my job," I called it, and considered it money I had to spend, like it or not. Ditto acupuncture, and a variety of other measures, including two bouts of major surgery, a horrible auto accident that left me damaged permanently and even more discouraged, and continual flare-ups of Epstein-Barr syndrome, fibromyalgia, and the chronic fatigue symptoms that accompany it.

The discouragement of the latter case can serve as an example of the trials of the past thirty years. Two events occurred as a consequence of the wreck, which itself occurred in April of 1994. In the first incident, one of my colleagues, who, I think, has a personal grudge against me (why, I don't know—except that he opposed my hiring at UCLA), insisted that I return to campus for a part-two exam for a Ph.D. student although I was barely able to move. I could have refused, of course, but then the student would have paid a price in missing deadlines, screwed up job-seeking needs, and the like. Had it been another chair, other than the one who was then in charge of graduate studies in our department, I could have gotten a competent colleague to take my place. There were two or three I spoke to who agreed to take over in my stead. Or we could have done the exam over telephone conferencing. But that particular director of graduate studies was adamant, so I returned to campus to hold the exam, and also to meet with the two classes I was teaching that quarter. To do so I had to fly from Albuquerque, New Mexico, where I lived, to Los Angeles. I had to drive and walk when I was all but incapable of doing either. My colleague's insistence meant I had to terminate some crucial therapy. I am still suffering from his resolve.

The second consequence was that during the following fall I applied for accelerated merit-increase on the basis of the publication of a book, several articles, and several poems, along with some national awards and a number of keynote addresses at universities nationwide. Not only was my application turned down, but also among other insults the committee (composed of faculty who have little idea of what constitutes American Indian literary studies or my international standing as a major scholar/critic and writer in that field) attacked not only my competence as a writer and scholar but as a teacher, citing angry comments from several students. Those students, enrolled in classes that I taught that dreadful spring quarter, were especially angry that I missed two weeks of classes. They were distressed at my reader—a Ph.D. candidate in English—who took over while I was gone. In their letter, the committee accused me of being a racist. The specific comments were, it turned out, directed at my graduate student, but the committee chose to ignore the part of the comment that specified the party being accused, and put, in writing, the damning charge. They cited an "African-American student" as its source, although the student remarks I read contained no racial identification. I could hardly move the blame onto my assistant, who is also a Native American. After trashing my teaching pretty thoroughly, the committee did admit that for the most part my evaluations were consistently in the 7.0 range (quite high), with many at "outstanding" ratings, but they said I had trouble in courses for more "mixed" attendance. By "mixed" they were referring to lecture courses cross-listed in American Indian studies and women's studies. That student racism and gender bias were major factors in each of those situations was, of course, blithely ignored, perhaps because none of the members of the committee had ever taught racially loaded or women's studies courses.

I was going to protest the report, but my chair assured me that should the matter go before the English faculty (in my case, full professors only), I would lose the struggle. It seems that my esteemed colleagues were upset at me because I wasn't a "good citizen." Which was something I discovered quite by accident when a formalist member of the full professor group informed me that "we" didn't support me because I "haven't done committee work for the department."

Never mind that, with the recent exception of Greg Sarris, another American Indian writer, of all the members of our faculty my name is the best known; never mind that my publication list outweighs those of the particular committee members and most of the full professors; never mind that I work for and with students all over this country—American Indian and all categories of women (particularly lesbian women); and, as I realized on painful rumination over the preceding years at UCLA, never mind that the three men who had chaired the department since the second year of my tenure (1991–92) were "formalists," white men committed to erasure of the study of "ethnic" and "multicultural" varieties of American literature. None appointed me to any committee work. Never mind that I had been assured, before taking the position at UCLA, that committee work would not be a major part of my commitment because of my extensive publishing, public speaking, and university service in the broader American and foreign university communities. It was a kind of "you forgot to say 'Mother may I' " snobbish elitism that I for the life of me can't understand. I thought we all did what we were good at, and thus the university prospered. I thought that my off-campus contributions were the equal of or superior to any contributions I might make serving on committees, playing university power politics, or advancing my status by kissing the right arses. Oh dear. What a foolish woman I have been. And the worst of it is that I had *no* idea how my disrepute with my colleagues would negatively impact on my graduate students! Those unfortunates who had me as their dissertation chair or on their committees could be sure that they would receive *no* departmental financial support, would be told they "should never have been accepted" into graduate studies, or would be turned down with no defensible reason for acceptance into the program. Am I discouraged? Disengaged is a more accurate descriptive of my present orientation toward the fabled groves.

On Monday, October 5, 1998, I formally submitted a letter to the department chair, informing him of my intention to retire effective June or September 1999. I will be sixty in the fall of that year: thirty-two years on the battlefield, in the trenches, on the front lines. Post-traumatic stress syndrome can become my diagnosis. I don't know what it's called while, however traumatized and stressed one might be, one is still on active duty. Perhaps Stockholm syndrome, the name given to the lasting psychological symptoms suffered by people held hostage.

It's not only myself whose treatment troubles and dismays me. My chair, the one I spoke to about protesting the personnel committee's action, said that the letter I found so outrageous, filled as it was with deceit, innuendo, and profession-bashing, was not the only such missive. He'd read the files, he assured me, and what was in them wasn't a pretty sight. I was aware of the truth of his assertion: I had had occasion to read two such professional trashings, one against a colleague whose major sins seemed to be his penchant for teaching courses on American Indian literature and backing the appointments of Native academics such as myself. This professor, a white male specializing in British literature, had gone up for accelerated promotion shortly after I began work at UCLA, and the vicious tone and slanderous comments his colleagues had found themselves compelled to put on paper and sign their names to appalled me. Reading the letter I felt as though I had been poisoned. I felt a sense of something ugly and dreadful, like a shadowy manifestation from English Gothic novels, lurking about the floors of Rolfe Hall.

In another case a young professor, up for tenure, was very nearly denied. His major sin seemed to be his sexual preference and occasional course offerings that employed, in a scholarly and pedagogically sound manner, materials about the subject that were also part of his "lifestyle." I'm sure his race had more than a little to do with the slamming he took in faculty meetings and in written commentaries on his professional accomplishments. Unlike me, he didn't go down without a fight; his protest was heard, and he was promoted. Then there was the case of another of my colleagues, another nontraditional, nonformalist specialist in one of the various categories of American literature. She suffered not only the sort of belittlement that only those skilled in rhetoric can inscribe in a committee report/letter, but, like me, suffered indignity upon indignity from those colleagues who crusaded to protect "the Tradition" from all who were in any way deemed, by them, to be a threat to it—and them. I learned the truth about their motives during one heated discussion around hiring a stunningly qualified candidate for a position. This candidate was a white gay man, and most of his publishing was in queer studies. Brilliantly conceived and soundly realized, his work had been published in prestigious journals and by prestigious presses; his earlier career in academe was exemplary. So qualified was he, so glowing the letters of reference, that even I began to wonder if any mere mortal could possess the sterling qualities his recommenders ascribed to him. Notwithstanding his prestigious academic background, his glowing references, his superb work, his excellent teaching and "good citizen" record, my formalist colleagues fought hard to prevent the applicant's appointment on the grounds that "if the department continues in that direction, we will lose control of the tradition," as one of their most powerful members said.

I hear of one colleague who, mugged and sexually assaulted, caught in the dreadful trial of a beloved partner dying young (of a disease), when requesting extra time for a promotion preparation, is denied and humiliated; I hear of another who, seriously disabled with circulatory/heart problems in one quarter (classes are covered by other faculty during the hospitalization and recovery of the professor), is scheduled with a double courseload upon return. This colleague is also suffering severe stress for familial reasons. At one campus where I taught, two faculty members, both in third-world studies, wound up hospitalized for nervous breakdowns, and that outcome is no stranger to other campuses and faculty of my acquaintance.

When I was a graduate student at the University of Oregon in Eugene in the late 1960s, the Graduate Student Union did a study of the income, health, family, and allied dimensions of graduate experience. The results were so appalling that the state legislature intervened. The number of deaths from suicide, the outbreak of alcoholism and drug addiction (not "fun" drugs), the number of divorces and early deaths from "natural causes" like heart attacks, were frightening. As major causative factors we identified outrageous workloads, particularly in the sciences and the law school. We discovered severe poverty, and teaching assistantships in some fields—I remember music, but there were others—where pay for graduate instructors (TAs in my day) was disgraceful. Many of these people had families, and we all lived in conditions that made many low-income neighborhoods seem classy by comparison. You'd think I'd have learned then that the barbed wire fences of academe were shrouded in granite wall and ivy for good reason, but I was always a slow learner. Or maybe the alternatives were even uglier. Or maybe I kept hoping that that elusive goddess, "the life of the mind," would grace me with her splendid presence if I were a sufficiently devoted acolyte. Whatever, I don't think things have improved much in thirtysome years. I have learned that the "uglies" long ago took over most of Western civilization and that they thrive in university settings, from whence we loftily scorn the grubby world beyond our hallowed halls.

The most recent case of academic iniquity I want to mention concerns a spate of anti-Semitism that I had thought long banished from the hallowed halls of academe—in the United States, at least. I can't imagine why I thought Jews would be exempt from the academy's otherwise general exclusion of most kinds of American writing. I suppose, had I given it any thought, I would have realized that "Jew" and "colored" and "woman" and "queer" were interchangeable terms; where one failed, another would do, so long as "we don't lose control of the tradition." This case was again about an appointment, but it entailed only transfer between departments. Suffice it to say that the intense efforts to prevent the transfer by way of humiliation of the professor were only stopped when our present chair courageously insisted that he would only transmit the faculty's insulting request if the faculty demanded he do so. In the face of his challenge the opposition dropped back, and the offer was made and, I think, accepted.

All of which leads me to my present: where have I been these thirty-plus years? Where's my head? How could I have so long supported and been supported by, at least financially, more or less, such a vicious institution? Is it the institution, or is it some people within it? For a long time I believed that every workplace is plagued by office politics, and I have long been all too conscious of elite-white-male-hetero standards within the university. But for some reason I thought that teaching was a good idea because one could turn the situation around—slowly, to be sure, but solidly. Boy, was I wrong. The philistines thrive and at present dominate not only the academy but also much of the Western and non-Western world. Perhaps my formalist colleagues in English do not realize that this is the United States, we don't have a royal court, and England was defeated long ago. They seem oblivious to the astonishing accomplishments of American writers, artists, musicians, performers—the lot that has made this century the American Century in ways beyond commerce and warfare. And while those who subscribe to the idea that English studies include American literature only at the peril of the discipline are relatively few, they are not confined to the older ranks. Worse, they tend to be those who most anxiously serve the department—and themselves—gaining over the years enormous power. By dint of unremitting effort within the halls and over lunch, handball, tennis, whatever, they build a power base that allows them to make or break most who oppose them. The concept of academic freedom—which, I have learned, is an oxymoron comparable to "army intelligence"—is unknown. We are indeed free to think what the academy dictates, to serve the tradition of the Elite Tribe. To do proper service we must take our nourishment, our energy, from a heavy diet of jealousy, envy, disharmony, rage, isolation, discouragement.

It is a dreary story, one lived by many before me, such as the Pequot writer and clergyman William Apess. He figured it out more quickly than I, though, serving on the lines for around twenty years before he abandoned his public career and disappeared into the forests with his people. A divine, lecturer, and political activist, most visible to the general public between 1829 and 1836, Apess was a controversial figure in his native New England, drawing national attention for a short time. Eventually numbered among that class Americans love to mourn—"the vanishing Indian"—and reframed as abolitionist by American scholars, Apess was de-Indianized and swallowed up the great American Liberal Tradition. But Apess's writings fared far beyond the boundaries of abolitionism. An early and articulate spokesman for Indian political rights, Apess incisively examined the underlying system of thought and belief that underlay both slavery and the dispossession of Native nations, identifying racism and "only the right of conquest" as the fundamental conditions upon which American society dwelt.

As Anne Marie Dannenberg expresses it, "Apess refuses the normalization of extinction by pointing out the ideological nature of American jurisprudence, by contending that institutionalized racism—rather than so-called natural processes—threatened the Indian, and by urging political intervention to alter the supposed destiny of indigenous peoples in America."[1] She notes that Apess, "Speaking of contemporaries who might be deluded by rhetoric sympathetic to Indians," comments, "Although in words they deny it, yet in the works they approve of the iniquities of their fathers. And as the seed of iniquity and prejudice was sown in that day, so it still remains.' "[2] A bit shocking: 163 years after those words were written, they still apply, though greatly multiplied.

God help us. Were it only me, Paula Gunn Allen, and only the University of California, Los Angeles, Department of English, the matters I'm discussing here would not merit one small note to a valued friend, much less a prolonged rant to strangers. But it is not just me, not just this department or this campus, that is helplessly entangled in the system of the invidious: it is the United States; it is the idea of freedom and justice; it is the life of the mind that is ensnared in the centuries-long grip of white male supremacy on this continent. Given the example of William Apess and the thousands who follow the trail he blazed, I am aware that I am saying little that is new. But it must still be said: I must after thirty-odd years, *we* must, after centuries, say the obvious to and about the engines of power, knowledge, and politics that our great universities represent in this nation and in the world: This is dreadful.

Right now, I'm tired. I say, "Get me out of here."
I quit.

Teaching in Time

EVERY GOOD TEACHER KNOWS THAT ON HER LOVE FOR THE SUBJECT SHE IS TEACHING DEPENDS HER ABILITY TO PASS IT ON TO OTHERS. RESPONDING TO HER LOVE WITH HEART AND MIND TOGETHER, SHE SO RECREATES THE SUBJECT THAT OTHERS IN THEIR TURN MAY RESPOND.

Helen M. Luke

AS THE MIDWIFE/TEACHER IMAGE DRAMATICALLY CONVEYS, EDUCATION IS RELATIONAL——A RELATIONSHIP THAT INVOLVES KNOWLEDGE, ATTENTIVENESS, AND CARE; CARE DIRECTED NOT ONLY AT DISCIPLINARY MATERIAL BUT TO WHO STUDENTS ARE AND WHAT THEY CAN BECOME. IT INVOLVES RESPONSIVENESS AND A STANCE OF HOPEFULNESS.

Ann Stanton

THE CLASSROOM REMAINS THE MOST RADICAL SPACE OF POSSIBILITY IN THE ACADEMY.

bell hooks

18

A Teaching Life

CHRISTA L. WALCK

I have been thinking about teaching, not as a task or a job or even a vocation but as a life, a way of being and doing that constructs who I am.[1] I was led here by an extraordinary book, *The Writing Life* (1989), by Annie Dillard. Although Dillard, a writer, describes her life and we learn what her life is like as a writer, it is not the writer at which she aims her pen—it is the writing and how writing creates her life. It started me thinking about how, or whether, teaching creates a life for me and whether such a life could be the artistic and creative life I desire.

When I first read *The Writing Life* I was struggling with my life as a teacher. Ironically, I was on sabbatical, engaged in writing, not teaching, yet I found myself thinking about teaching as much as writing. A life dedicated to teaching was a life I felt edgy about. Teaching seemed to be separating me from the person I wanted to be, the life I wanted to live. By the time I left for sabbatical, the teacher that stood in my classroom seemed not to be me but someone else I had constructed to do the teaching. She set up experiences for others, manipulated the action, provided information, and in doing so, set her self aside despite the guise of interaction.

What I found myself trying to discover was this: Is there more to teaching than content and delivery, technique—didactic or experiential—and evaluation? Is there a space to bring myself into the teaching, to release the artist in me, and can I risk it? It seemed to me that a teaching life should be, as the blurb on the book jacket of *The Writing Life* suggests, a "life of dedication, absurdity and daring—[a] life at the edge."

What follows is a meditation on teaching as an art—on the teaching life as an artist's life—inspired by Dillard's text.[2] She is a good guide, for she is courageously direct about the realities of an artist's life. As Dillard aimed her pen at the writing, I will aim my chalk at the teaching. I begin with an inquiry into the ideals and realities of the teaching life and invite you to bring your chalk to the board and write your teaching life along with me.

IDEALS AND REALITIES

"The youth gets together his materials to build a bridge to the moon, Thoreau noted mournfully, or perchance a palace or temple on the earth, and at length the middle-aged man concludes to build a woodshed with them" (Dillard 1989, 5).[3] When I was young(er) and not teaching, I fantasized the teaching life. If only I were teaching, I thought, I would have a whole life. What I read and what I wrote would become what I taught and what I taught would become what I read and wrote. All these words, all these ideas, would not dead-end with me—stopped, stuck—but would flow through me into a temple of living words, of conversations and dialogues with students and colleagues. What a life! I thought. If only I could live it. This ecological fantasy of the teaching life—no waste, no end, a fecund, ceaseless cycling of thought in which all things are interconnected—still sustains me, despite its distance from my reality. Fantasy, imagination, and dreams about what a teaching life could be like are as necessary to me as air. They keep the artist in me alive.

Unfortunately, these fantasies have not yet made me whole. Instead of shimmering temples, I discover I have been building Thoreau's woodsheds. One woodshed I have built is this: teaching as if I had the keys to the temple. Purveyor of truth, master of rigor, critic in the classroom, I urge disciplined, principled thought. As keeper of the keys, I feel powerful. I have answers to mysteries! I live to build bridges from the abyss of ignorance to the temple of knowledge. Alas, I have discovered that where there is power there are also prisons. Directing my gaze at students, taking them to the woodshed to discipline and punish them for transgressions of temple rules, I act out the internalized gaze that disciplines and punishes me: Guarding the temple has not taken me to the moon of my dreams.

This is partly an intellectual matter. I increasingly see what glimmers in the temple as fool's gold. Nagging questions nibble at my resolve to deliver management wisdom: Is not management really a euphemism for control and domination? What happens to people who are constructed as resources to be made more productive? Why are societal and environmental issues marginalized in managerial decision making? Why is diversity something to be counted or managed instead of celebrated?

But it is also a pedagogical matter. The more I jingle the keys to the temple in my pocket, the more I expend myself on catching people out—examining (literally!) people, assessing their ignorance instead of clearing a space for learning to take place, subtracting from some hypothetical "right answer" that I duplicitously tell students does not exist instead of adding to or multiplying their knowledge. I build ever more intricate evaluation schemes and waste time quibbling over allocations of points instead of exercising the judgment I have been educated to have. I am caught in my own management trap.

The second woodshed I have built is this: teaching as if I am selling shoes. Dillard (1989) muses that a writer is free, whereas a shoe salesman is not, for he must answer to several bosses, do his job their way, and be at their place during their hours to do their business (11). Am I free? I show up for work at designated places at designated times and attend to multiple bosses—peers, deans, accreditors, students. I sell the ideas of others, and occasionally my own, packaged in (text)boxes. I worry about covering a proliferating list of theories and developing a growing list of skills with which our graduates must be shod. I try a shoe on: Is the plain tennis shoe sufficient or do I need Reeboks that light up in the dark and propel me onto the stage? I look to see whether the shoe I offer fits the student or whether he or she needs a larger or smaller size or a completely different style. I am not consoled by Dillard's judgment that the shoe salesman is useful, that everyone needs shoes. Yes, selling the ideas of others is useful work; it is a life of service and responsibility. If I failed to appear, what would students learn? How would they learn it? Even so, constructing teaching in this way, I feel boxed in, a conveyor of commodities. This is not the teaching life for me.

If I am not guarding the temple of received wisdom or selling textbooks, what am I to do with a teaching life? What kind of life will put me back on that bridge I was building to the moon? It is time to climb atop the woodsheds I have built and dream on.

TEACHING AS AN ART

"Your freedom as a writer is not freedom of expression in the sense of wild blurting; you may not let rip. It is life at its most free . . . because you select your materials, invent your task, and pace yourself" (Dillard 1989, 11). I am learning to think of teaching as an art and to construct my teaching life as an artist's life. It is often said that teaching is an art, not a science, but what does that mean? Opposing science to art somehow lends to the production of art the notion of whimsy, of fun, of ease—of quick and spirited inspiration over plodding, tedious, and disciplined labor. Is this true? Dillard suggests it is not.

Art requires creation and invention from the materials, the possibilities, that present themselves. As an artist, I create what can be taught, and how, and when, with the materials at hand. The canvas is only so big, the class only so long. There is the space of the class, the topic of the course, the lives and aspirations of the students, my talents and skills, a wealth of knowledge captured in many forms. These are my materials. Some I select, some I am dealt. I try them in different ways, in different combinations. I set a pace, seek a rhythm. There is no one way, no best way. I must be open to discovering what is right for this time, this place, this set of students. An example: Only ten students showed up for a course designed for thirty. I groused, for my design would fail; the canvas was too small for the painting I had planned. I stopped, took a deep breath, took a risk, and dared to invent myself and the students into one team working together. What emerged was a unique piece of work, an original, not a copy, and nonreplicable. When I gave myself the freedom to write something new in the space of that class, I felt a teaching life stirring.

Art requires acceptance of failure. When you risk invention, when you put yourself out there beyond the lesson plan, you must quietly accept that failure is part of the process and the process takes time. As Dillard says, on plenty of days a writer can write three, even four pages, but on plenty of other days a writer concludes she must throw them away (14). On plenty of days I feel competent, even inspired. The stars are properly aligned, my head is clear. I have read or thought something that gives me energy or enthusiasm—I have something important to say, something that will change lives. Or I have thought of something interesting to do; I have discovered a great story or activity or film that will open eyes and ears and suppress yawns. If I put myself in the way of good materials—read interesting books, watch interesting films, go interesting places, talk with interesting people—the materials select themselves like magic. But on plenty of other days I am tired; my head is somewhere else; I wonder what I am doing here. I have spent hours thinking about a class, but I have nothing inspiring to impart. I drag myself into class, tail between my legs. On those days, I must remind myself that failure is part of the process.

Still, I want more of those inspired days, inspired classes. Unlike Dillard's solitary writing life, the teaching life requires interaction and engagement with others. A lot depends on me, but I also know a lot depends on the students. Bring on the students! The questioning, alert, critical, engaged, lively students! These are the students I want to teach, students eager to learn. Instead, I find before me, for the most part, cats and dogs who, if they are not already sleeping (mentally and sometimes physically), challenge me silently to make this worth their while (cats) or woof for a treat for small tricks performed in class (dogs).

Dillard is not daunted by such disengaged companions—she realizes her job as an artist is to crank herself up (49). If teaching is an art, how do I crank myself up to do it? How do I prepare myself to make the two hours of today's class the best part of a student's day—the time that they wake up—and the best part of my day? Dillard claims that writing requires "a peculiar internal state which ordinary life does not induce" (46), "an extraordinary state on an ordinary morning" (47). So too, teaching. I wonder how I can cross the border from ordinary life, ordinary class—teacher here, students there, text there—into an extraordinary place where learning occurs.

Sometimes I have donned the actor's mask, worn a costume into which I extend myself, growing into something more than myself, something other, "the teacher," something grander than my own small self, my own small life. I have written myself good lines and practiced them, donned the words with the mask until I felt the part was mine. With these props, I have entered an extraordinary state. After a while, though, the mask began to feel heavy and false, the script wooden. Perhaps because I knew the script so well—I had been teaching for years!—teaching and life seemed incompatible. I was not sure I could teach anymore.

I had forgotten that art depends on destruction as much as creation. I had so much invested in this and that way of teaching—in these syllabi, in these readings, in these exercises, in these cases. Hey, I was getting good at it! I had published articles on my methods, my tools. But it began to feel wrong, like a beautiful but ill-fitting suit, carefully tailored but outgrown. I loved it, loved the fine threads and classic detailing, and cringed at the thought of pulling it off, ripping it up, tossing it out. Perhaps I could change just this case or that exercise. How could I abandon that classic reading? And then I heard Dillard's clear voice demanding the courage to demolish anything that weakens the work: "The path is not the work. . . . I hope you will toss it all and not look back" (4). I realized that clinging to these artifacts cloistered me and weakened the work, weakened the teaching. They had been part of the process that brought me to this place in my teaching life and for that I thanked them. But they were not the work itself. So I tossed them, every one, and started over. I have not looked back.

I now seek an extraordinary state inside myself. Like a yogi, I try to find the trance state within myself, that calm place that is open to the world. I try to come to class in that state of openness to all that can and will happen. I try to come as myself, ready to hear the words that come from my mouth and the mouths of students, to watch closely what is happening and use it like paint, like thread, to create something that we can all see and learn from.

Becoming a yogi, becoming an artist, becoming a teacher, takes years—a lifetime. But it is not because it takes years to master poses and techniques or find the right brushes and paints. It takes years because it is a process of building a frame of mind. It takes time to imagine life in a classroom.

IMAGINING THE CLASS(ROOM)

"The written word is weak. Many people prefer life to it. Life gets your blood going, and it smells good" (Dillard 1989, 17). The classroom is an artifice. I tell my class we are an organization: I pretend to be a manager, they pretend to be employees. But we know it is not true. They cannot wait to get out of here. They tell me this in no uncertain terms. They want to be in the "real world," where real things are happening. I am manager only of this weak and pallid imitation, this simulacrum, conjured in yesterday's words and pictures. It is hard to imagine it otherwise.

I remember what it was like to work in business. Things had to get done. Quickly. Relationships with people were intense. You talked to other people a lot. You were on the road, moving around. Everything was always changing. You got to look important in your suit and cropped hair and gold jewelry. You got pumped for the big meeting. By comparison, the teaching life is sedentary. I move from home to office to classroom and back. I read and read and read and write and read. I slip into comfort clothes, durable clothes that resist weather. Things change slowly, even students. Repetition wears me down until I have all the liveliness of a smoothly weathered stone.

I complain about the physical space of my classroom. The ceiling is low, the chairs small and childish. Dusty chalkboards line the walls. An ancient wooden podium is forcibly chained to the Formica table. It depresses my spirit. I rearrange the chairs, the table, breaking the static rows into dynamic circles, but the whitewashed cement-block walls still weigh me down. I think I need a better stage, better props, to be a better teacher. I go to a local bank and marvel at the ergonomic furniture in cheerful colors, the multilevel training centers with screens that appear with the touch of a button, the good-looking stuff that excites the eye. I want these things, to bring me back to life. I resist Dillard's warning to avoid appealing workplaces: A room with no view invites imagination to enter (26).

I start to worry: Am I so addicted to the physical world that I have forgotten how to imagine the class(room)? Is teaching—is learning—in the shiny books, the four-color overheads, the Powerpoint presentations, the five-minute video clips, the interactive teaching lab, the on-line connection to World Wide Web? I stick a toe in the water of educational technology and the current sucks me in. I am soon swimming furiously to catch the next wave. I am becoming a teaching tool master. I am uneasy with this. In a world demanding more and more with less and less, I am doing less and less with more and more. Hours are gobbled up creating prettier handouts or overheads, setting up e-mail lists and Web pages, at the expense of reading an article or a student paper or simply sitting and pondering whether this or that might be a more effective strategy for exploring a case. Students too seem to be attending to image—the look of the Powerpoint slide and not its content.

What am I teaching, I wonder? What are students learning? And then I dream: Can I imagine a space where we can pause, think out loud about what we are doing? Listen to our desires? Hear our souls talk? Can I open a door to the life of the spirit—in a management class? Can I think of the stark room as a blank stage on which to conduct our own play, the students and I? Or is management so material it cannot imagine such a class(room)?

THE ART OF TEACHING

> I said I hated to write. I said I would rather do anything else.... Why did I do it? I had never inquired.... Why wasn't I running a ferryboat, like sane people? ... But I rallied and mustered and said that the idea was to learn things; that you learn a thing and then as a matter of course you learn the next thing, and the next thing. (Dillard 1989, 53–54)

I confess it. Sometimes I hate teaching. I hate it when the factory whistle blows and off I go into the classroom, my mind still spinning with the debate in the faculty meeting or the paper I was writing or the conversation I was having with a colleague. It feels insane, this responsibility to trick students into learning. Lately, I have abandoned teaching when possible, and opted to captain the ferryboat across the lake—I have angled for administrative jobs that transport me into the "real life" of the university where "things get done"—committees are convened, reports get written, policy is made. My blood indeed gets moving. But after a while I get bored. I feel like I am not really learning anything. And that is the point of life, for me; to learn. So I head back to the classroom, where I can be excused for concentrating on the activity of learning. Perhaps this is how teaching can be a life, my life.

I am good at learning. I excel at it. My students, it often seems, do not. They present themselves not as eager empty vessels to be filled but as doubtful, bored, suspicious, restless bodies with heads loosely attached. What, I wonder, is the difference between them and me? Why do they write on my teaching evaluations that I am too excited about all this dull stuff I try to teach them? It is more than age that separates us. It is, I fear, love of learning. I love it as the goal of life; they are often indifferent to it as a mere means to something else. To reach them, I think, I must not rely on will and power—park it in the woodshed! I must turn to art, be artful as a writer writing the text of student. I have to imagine that my class is like a good book, which will linger in memory until the reader needs it again and will turn back to a given passage for sustenance, insight, and reassurance.

Great artists, suggests Dillard, *love* the range of materials they use. This love, this caring, suggests the tasks, and the tasks suggest the schedule (71). For each class I have thirty or forty scheduled hours in which to create my art. If I have thirty hours and the knowledge of a thousand pages, a hundred lifetimes, to impart, this is impossible. So I must ask, What do I care enough about to share with thirty students for thirty hours? What is the true task of this class? I am preparing, again, to teach a class called Cultural and Behavioral Aspects of International Management. A real mouthful. My true task is to help students understand the fragility and resilience of culture, its underground currents, the way it bubbles up when we encounter another and informs our behavior. My true task is to reveal the complexity and ambiguity and uncertainty of interaction as we cross borders and attempt to accomplish work. My true task is to reveal what has been done to people conceptualized as "other" when hegemonic management practice crosses borders. So I interrogate the textbooks that thump into my mailbox: Can you do this? Can you do that? If not, goodbye. I hunt for other words, less homogenized and pasteurized than those that pour from textbooks. I turn again to Dillard (1984) encountering a frustrated foreigner doing business in China; to Robert Olen Butler (1992) imagining the life of a Vietnamese expatriate building a business and a life in Louisiana; to Brian Fawcett (1986) skewering what passes for work in a small committee. I try to work, respectfully, from my love of the task, from my love of learning.

From this range of words, written and spoken, and exercises, mental and physical, I will try to sculpt a memorable experience that tones the mind and heart. Of course, these are not my only materials. The students are material too.

Dillard (1989) counsels that if you want to chop wood, aim for the chopping block, not the wood (59). It is true. If you aim straight for the students, you will have nothing. If you aim for their answers on the test, their answers to questions asked, their demonstration of the knowledge that you have, you will have nothing. Aim past them, through them, to where they must go, to where you must go, if you and they are to going to have a life. The students are pages they will write themselves. I teach them to hold the pen, to get the ink flowing. This is all I can really do. It is all I can do for myself! Who will teach us to teach? The work will. The work of learning.

A teacher teaches many classes. In each class, I intend, like Dillard, "several urgent and vivid points," some of which I sacrifice as the class's format hardens (5). The class has a life of its own, and I follow where it leads. Careful plans dissolve and precious points are left behind, unsaid. I linger over them in my notes as the class takes a different turn, goes around a different bend in the road. Maybe next time. The next class, perhaps a new course. Even as I try to create the new, I am recreating the old, the unfinished business, trying to find a way to say it, to do it, to explore these things I feel are so important, so necessary to know. It is what turns teaching into a life. It is how I stay alive.

IN CONCLUSION

The teaching life is the life of the explorer, the creator, constructing the classroom for free exploration. It is about engagement. It takes courage. It is about ruthlessly excising what is flawed, what no longer fits, no matter how difficult it was to achieve. It is about recognizing teaching as a medium that can do some things exquisitely but cannot do everything.

Unlike writing, however, teaching is not a solitary endeavor. Your audience is not imaginary, in your head: It is in your face, every time you walk into a classroom, every time a student crosses the threshold of your office, every time you pass a student you know on the street. You cannot hide behind your book, like J. D. Salinger.

When I am doing it well, I feel energized. I feel free. I want to experiment, to take ideas and actions where they lead me. I feel like I am building my bridge to the moon. But I am often tired because it consumes energy rapaciously. It is an uphill journey; sometimes I fall down. Sometimes students follow me but sometimes they abandon me—they think I am crazy and they take me to the woodshed.

Teaching as a life is a scary thought. I do not win teaching awards; students do not flock to my classes to hang on every word. Oh, I get a small following, now and then, of students who are surprised by how I teach and want another taste. But I am ambivalent about teaching, and no doubt it shows. I would like to be as confident about my teaching as bell hooks (1994), or as able to weave praxis and resistance into critical pedagogy as Mary Boyce (1996), but I am not. Perhaps this is why I am drawn to Annie Dillard's discussion of writing as a life. Dillard is wonderfully direct about the difficulty of such a life, about her flight from the difficulty of writing as well as the relentless and inevitable attraction that pulls her toward it. This is how my teaching life proceeds as well. An ebb and flow, a retreat to recover, sort it out, to renew and ready myself for the next surge forward. This is how teaching creates a life.

The more I think about it, the more I find freedom—academic freedom—to be the crux of the teaching life. Like the writer, the teacher must be free. What hooks (1994) says about the classroom might well be what Dillard would say about the open page:

> The classroom, with all its limitations, remains a location of possibility. In that field of possibility we have the opportunity to labor for freedom, to demand of ourselves and our comrades, an openness of mind and heart that allows us to face reality even as we collectively imagine ways to move beyond the boundaries, to transgress. (207)

19

Too Soon Old, Too Late Smart

GAYLE PEMBERTON

My teeth are still good. My eyes are not. I find myself looking at my students as my father once looked at me: imploringly, routinely befuddled, asking, "Have you seen my reading glasses?" My hearing remains acute, but there is so much that I have heard before—and before and before—that I am aware that my concentration lags. I can hear; I just don't listen sometimes. Occasionally I even find myself opening mail as a student speaks to me from across my desk. I don't recall ever having been that rude in years past. These things happen on days when I wish I were doing anything but teaching. To make matters worse, someone sent me an e-mail this fall that consisted of a long catalog of things that entering students did not know—history, social movements, television, sports, music, and the like from the last fifty years. At first glimpse, it looked like everything. At second, I was reassured; it was only everything that I thought I knew. The problem is an old one and it has to do with history and culture. How do we teach students vital information that we know as we simultaneously learn what they know? The rub comes on bad days, when I have no idea what to do and when they seem so uninterested in my news and I in theirs. Let's call it "Culture Wars 101." There always have been days like that, but I am older now, and I see them from a perspective that I could not have imagined when I first began teaching.

I began teaching American literature twenty-five years ago. In 1973 I was hanging on to the remnants of a 1960s optimism that had ushered me and thousands of black youth like me into predominantly white colleges and universities, mostly for B.A.s and, in time, some Ph.D.s. I had not the heart, head, or stomach for taking my message to the streets, so I opted for the classroom, which, historically at least, has been that terribly contested place—sometimes mountain, sometimes wayside, sometimes pit—of African American hopes and dreams. My activism would come in teaching well, I hoped, all or some of the wonderful writers, white and black, from this side of the Atlantic. (In our highly polarized 1990s fight over curricula, we frequently forget that in some English classes twenty-five years ago even white American authors were rare because American literature was thought of as the weak offspring of Mother England's literary aces.) Looking backward over these years, I am aware of how much has changed in academia and in me.

It is difficult to come up with anything new or fresh to say about aging, about generations, about time. We grow older; we're different from those younger and older than we. And we are the same as all people who have lived. Time passes more quickly than we ever could imagine, our understanding of relativity notwithstanding. We forget a lot. Or better, I've learned that selective memory frequently can be an impulse toward self-protection and healing rather than plain orneriness. I am selective when total recall simply would hurt too much. Watching footage of urban riots from Henry Hampton's *Eyes on the Prize*, I recall telling a colleague how it seemed simultaneously so completely familiar and so utterly foreign. I had lived through those days—been closer to some of the action than my nerves could stand—but how they lived in me was in some sort of translation from the original. I could never lose the knowledge, the feel, or the taste of what had prompted the rioting, but allowing the full measure of my memory to take me back was impossible. Having been witness to urban 1960s rioting is not the equivalent of having been a slave, but my relationship to the past is akin to the act of *rememory* in *Beloved*, where Toni Morrison's former slaves must remember enough of slavery to be freed to forget it. And what I do remember is that I opted for an academic career as an act, both private and public, in answer to the multitudinous questions that the riots raised.

I learned the fields of American and African American literature as "on the job" training, graduate school having done little to prepare me for these ostensibly lesser fields. The great exception was my work with my thesis adviser, Daniel Aaron, who arranged for my first job and showed me, by example, that being an Americanist requires no apologies. For my first two or three years, I stayed ahead of my students—who were only two or three years younger than I—by increments of pages. I wanted them to share my enthusiasm for our national literature, and I wanted them to go beyond mere acknowledgment that an indispensable component of that literature was created by African Americans. It was vital that they see the intricacies of the relationships between white and black as clearly as the white pages of their books require black ink in order to transmit information. I wanted them actually to read *Moby-Dick* and the Puritans, to compare the twentieth-century worlds created by southern white writers like Faulkner, O'Connor, and Welty to those constructed by northerners of a century earlier, Hawthorne, Melville, Dickinson, Emerson. Black writers like Morrison, Wright, Ellison, Hurston, Wideman, and Hughes were of the woof and warp of the great tradition. Twain was in the middle and was the bridge from one century to the next, from white writers to black ones. It was Twain, so much like his own Huck, who risked "going to hell" in telling us that black folk could matter and that the great subject of our country was race. A century later we quibble about the way he went about saying it — in the trademark American fashion of mistaking the image for the thing, which obviates the necessity of thinking.

I wanted them to know that most great writers are very good readers, that black writers from the past and the present have never been anti-intellectual provincials, but voracious students of the classics, the Bible, Shakespeare, the *New York Times,* each other, and all the vaunted European and American white writers they could admire, despise, or merely stomach. They might write of "down home" people, but they themselves were literary sophisticates bent on creating a home in the inhospitable neighborhoods of American belles lettres. I wanted them to know that, try as we all might to make one, there could be no unified field theory of American writing, especially if black writers and the subjects of their novels, stories, poems, plays, and essays were relegated to roles as spectators forced behind the barricades of some premiere called "American literature."

Naturally, most of my students would have none of this. "Reading novels beats reading poetry." That sentiment accounted for a goodly percentage. "Reading novels by black authors is easier than reading novels by whites." I never wanted to discover the percentage who believe that, and I worked hard to disabuse them of the notion. "This course sounds cool." That was code for white students eager to show their liberality in taking a course from a black professor. "I want to relax." That was code for black students who, seeing me at the helm, wanted the opportunity to be something other than anomalous in class. Finally, there was that five percent—a percentage that has remained consistent regardless of the quality of institution, region, gender, class, or racial makeup of my classes—who wanted to go with me on my trip through American writing, who taught me as much as I taught them, and whose names, if no longer faces, are indelibly marked in my memory.

Whatever success we have as teachers is measurable really only by what our students continue to take with them through their lives. And that is something we will never know. Sometimes I was able to teach them how to think and write more clearly. Sometimes it was close reading and listening. Sometimes, and thoroughly beyond my control or intent, it was that a black woman could think fast, speak fluently, be passionate about art from artists of all hues, and have the temerity to judge their work. Responses to me fell along racial, class, and gender lines. In my early years, black women students viewed me with either suspicion or too great a familiarity. Black men avoided my classes completely, and when there, resisted my authority. White women tended to put me on a pedestal. And white men, the most privileged and adept in our society, made sure I was there to answer every question and lend a hand in solving a host of other problems they had. In response, I began to think of myself as "Miss Chips," some black female version of Robert Donat or Peter O'Toole from the movies, desexed, dowdy, reliable, kind. It was a humorously bleak future landscape I drew. I even took up the habit of photographing my first-year student seminars so I might have something to muse upon in my old age.

There is a line from one of those Mr. Chips movies, where the ancient-of-days Chips addresses the school full of young men. He says, "You remain the same age, but I grow older"—something like that. And it was true. The public school English boys who studied with Chips were always the same age, always at the same place developmentally. Apart from having married late only to have his wife, the extraordinary love of his life, get killed, the developmental stages of Mr. Chips are not explored in the movies. After all, movies don't do that sort of thing. But I suspect James Hilton, who wrote the novel, was interested in how Mr. Chips grew. Hilton also wrote *Lost Horizon*, where a planeload of passengers end up in Shangri-La; obviously he was interested in time and space, how and whether we grow and adapt to new things. My mistake in seeing myself as Miss Chips was that I failed to assess the potential of my own developmental changes. Like my young students, I could not imagine myself beyond the person I thought I knew then, and so a faded movie script was my guide. There's something terribly American about that need for a bad script to follow; it must flow from the melodramatic implications of our collective history. Mercifully, for me, if not for my students, I stopped thinking of myself as Miss Chips about midway in this twenty-five-year career. My relationship to my beloved American texts, to my teaching and to my students, began to alter.

Those faces looking back at me in the classroom are of a different generation than my early students. My black female students, in general, are no longer suspicious of me, but rather protective, alternately desperately seeking my approval or wanting to be adopted, nurtured. My black male students, discarding temporarily the misogyny that runs rampant in the culture, see something of their mothers or grandmothers in me; I own a credibility I did not have in the past. My white female students are like their male counterparts: adept at using a privilege they do not admit or sometimes understand as they seek my assistance or challenge my reading of their work. I occasionally get a note from a student attached to a paper, tucked at the end of an exam, or dashed off in an e-mail message, filled with apology for his or her intellectual lethargy. That is new. Course evaluations are more mixed than in the past; those students who resist my message are bolder and sometimes nastier in saying why.

Of course, race matters. Colleges and universities are places where a large majority of white citizens look upon their nonwhite students and colleagues with a mixture of tolerance and racism that mirrors the amount held by the general populace. This means that there is very little progress or commitment to real equity. There is a great amount of duplicity, mendacity, cowardice, meanness, and laziness around issues of race. So much in academic politics is ignominious spectacle that after twenty-five years I am beyond exhaustion in fighting for real fairness. In my mind, the bad guys have won in society and in its educational systems. Since I believe in the quest, if not the grail, I still fight on, but I save my energy for the classroom and my office.

What has been the revelation is my relationship to the material. Literature is more important to me than it ever was. Its message is more urgent. I linger over lines, read them aloud, repeat them, let their beauty or horror run through me from my brain to my toes, around the corners of my present into the interiors of my memory of events in my own life, in those of my relatives, in those of our collective history. My interest in literary theory is in inverse proportion to that of my best students. They want more of it, and I prefer talking about how writing is constructed and what the emotional and psychological weight of the writing means. But my students need to be better close readers regardless of any theory taught. Years ago I so hoped my students would think of literature as a friend to carry through life, whose failures, blunders, triumphs, and laughter help make the arrival of each day portentous of great possibility. That my students still will have nothing of this matters less to me now. At worst or perhaps at best, they will read great literature in my classes, and that is in spite of the fact that fewer and fewer of them find the prospect either enjoyable or even possible.

I keep reminding myself to take the time to learn new technology, to use computers more in my teaching in order to give my students cyber-interaction with chat rooms, graphics, and all sorts of fancy stuff, because it's all the rage and it may excite them further. But I want to try much harder than I ever have to let them know that literature matters, that narrative and storytelling are things we must not lose, that the computer I write this essay on or the elaborate cyber-syllabi of my colleagues are not ends, they are technological means in support of acquiring nontechnological knowledge. My classroom is not a pulpit, but I do want my students to leave my classes with a touch of an old-fashioned humanist education. I am not embarrassed to say that.

I also will repeat, every now and then, my Henry James and Edith Wharton seminar, or my Ralph Ellison course, where I shamelessly encourage my students to find overstuffed chairs in some lost corner of the library and stay there reading, for five hours at a shot. There always will be too many books on the syllabus; I'll always be rushing at the end of the course to make sure we've covered as much as possible. And I will take as they come the next developmental stages in my life, doubtless fumbling for my glasses, sometimes smiling or through gritted teeth, glad for the opportunity to grow, learn, and most importantly, teach—and get paid for it.

20

Ecstasy

Teaching and Learning without Limits

BELL HOOKS

On a gorgeous Maine summer day, I fell down a hill and broke my wrist severely. As I was sitting in the dirt, experiencing the most excruciating pain, more intense than any I had ever felt in my life, an image flashed across the screen of my mind. It was one of me as a young girl falling down another hill. In both cases, my falling was related to challenging myself to move beyond limits. As a child it was the limits of fear. As a grown woman, it was the limits of being tired—what I call "bone weary." I had come to Skowhegan to give a lecture at a summer art program. A number of nonwhite students had shared with me that they rarely have any critique of their work from scholars and artists of color. Even though I felt tired and very sick, I wanted to affirm their work and their needs, so I awakened early in the morning to climb the hill to do studio visits.

Skowhegan was once a working farm. Old barns had been converted into studios. The studio I was leaving, after having had an intense discussion with several young black artists, female and male, led into a cow pasture. Sitting in pain at the bottom of the hill, staring in the face of the black female artist whose studio door I had been trying to reach, I saw such disappointment. When she came to help me, she expressed concern, yet what I heard was another feeling entirely. She really needed to talk about her work with someone she could trust, who would not approach it with racist, sexist, or classist prejudice, someone whose intellect and vision she could respect. That someone did not need to be me. It could have been any teacher. When I think about my life as a student, I can remember vividly the faces, gestures, habits of being of all the individual teachers who nurtured and guided me, who offered me an opportunity to experience joy in learning, who made the classroom a space of critical thinking, who made the exchange of information and ideas a kind of ecstasy.

Recently, I worked on a program at CBS on American feminism. I and other black women present were asked to name what we felt helps enable feminist thinking and feminist movement. I answered that to me "critical thinking" was the primary element allowing the possibility of change. I shared my belief that, no matter what one's class, race, gender, or social standing, without the capacity to think critically about our selves and our lives, none of us would be able to move forward, to change, to grow. In our society, which is so fundamentally anti-intellectual, critical thinking is not encouraged. Engaged pedagogy has been essential to my development as an intellectual, as a teacher/professor because the heart of this approach to learning is critical thinking. Conditions of radical openness exist in any learning situation where students and teachers celebrate their abilities to think critically, to engage in pedagogical praxis.

Profound commitment to engaged pedagogy is taxing to the spirit. After twenty years of teaching, I have begun to need time away from the classroom. Somehow, moving around to teach at different institutions has always prevented me from having that marvelous paid sabbatical that is one of the material rewards of academic life. This factor, coupled with commitment to teaching, has meant that even when I take a job that places me on a part-time schedule, instead of taking time away from teaching, I lecture elsewhere. I do this because I sense such desperate need in students—their fear that no one really cares whether they learn or develop intellectually.

My commitment to engaged pedagogy is an expression of political activism. Given that our educational institutions are so deeply invested in a banking system, teachers are more rewarded when we do not teach against the grain. The choice to work against the grain, to challenge the status quo, often has negative consequences. And that is part of what makes that choice one that is not politically neutral. In colleges and universities, teaching is often the least valued of our many professional tasks. It saddens me that colleagues are often suspicious of teachers whom students long to study with. And there is a tendency to undermine the professorial commitment of engaged pedagogues by suggesting that what we do is not as rigorously academic as it should be. Ideally, education should be a place where the need for diverse teaching methods and styles would be valued, encouraged, seen as essential to learning. Occasionally students feel concerned when a class departs from the banking system. I remind them that they can have a lifetime of classes that reflect conventional norms.

Of course, I hope that more professors will seek to be engaged. Although it is a reward of engaged pedagogy that students seek courses with those of us who have made a wholehearted commitment to education as the practice of freedom, it is also true that we are often overworked, our classes often overcrowded. For years, I envied those professors who taught more conventionally, because they frequently had small classes. Throughout my teaching career my classes have been too large to be as effective as they could be. Over time, I've begun to see that departmental pressure on "popular" professors to accept larger classes was also a way to undermine engaged pedagogy. If classes became so full that it is impossible to know students' names, to spend quality time with each of them, then the effort to build a learning community fails. Throughout my teaching career, I have found it helpful to meet with each student in my classes, if only briefly. Rather than sitting in my office for hours waiting for individual students to choose to meet or for problems to arise, I have preferred to schedule lunches with students. Sometimes, the whole class might bring lunch and have discussion in a space other than our usual classroom. At Oberlin, for instance, we might go as a class to the African Heritage House and have lunch, both to learn about different places on campus and gather in a setting other than our classroom.

Many professors remain unwilling to be involved with any pedagogical practices that emphasize mutual participation between teacher and student because more time and effort are required to do this work. Yet some version of engaged pedagogy is really the only type of teaching that truly generates excitement in the classroom, that enables students and professors to feel the joy of learning.

I was reminded of this during my trip to the emergency room after falling down that hill. I talked so intensely about ideas with the two students who were rushing me to the hospital that I forgot my pain. It is this passion for ideas, for critical thinking and dialogical exchange that I want to celebrate in the classroom, to share with students.

Talking about pedagogy, thinking about it critically, is not the intellectual work that most folks think is hip and cool. Cultural criticism and feminist theory are the areas of my work that are most often deemed interesting by students and colleagues alike. Most of us are not inclined to see discussion of pedagogy as central to our academic work and intellectual growth, or the practice of teaching as work that enhances and enriches scholarship. Yet it has been the mutual interplay of thinking, writing and sharing ideas as an intellectual and teacher that creates whatever insights are in my work.

My devotion to that interplay keeps me teaching in academic settings, despite their difficulties.

When I first read *Strangers in Paradise: Academics from the Working Class* (1984), I was stunned by the intense bitterness expressed in the individual narratives. This bitterness was not unfamiliar to me. I understood what Jane Ellen Wilson meant when she declared, "The whole process of becoming highly educated was for me a process of losing faith." I have felt that bitterness most keenly in relation to academic colleagues. It emerged from my sense that so many of them willingly betrayed the promise of intellectual fellowship and radical openness that I believe is the heart and soul of learning. When I moved beyond those feelings to focus my attention on the classroom, the one place in the academy where I could have the most impact, they became less intense. I became more passionate in my commitment to the art of teaching.

Engaged pedagogy not only compels me to be constantly creative in the classroom, it also sanctions involvement with students beyond that setting. I journey with students as they progress in their lives beyond our classroom experience. In many ways, I continue to teach them, even as they become more capable of teaching me. The important lesson that we learn together, the lesson that allows us to move together within and beyond the classroom, is one of mutual engagement.

I could never say that I have no idea of the way students respond to my pedagogy; they give me constant feedback. When I teach, I encourage them to critique, evaluate, make suggestions and interventions as we go along. Evaluations at the end of a course rarely help us improve the learning experience we share together. When students see themselves as mutually responsible for the development of a learning community, they offer constructive input.

Students do not always enjoy studying with me. Often they find my courses challenge them in ways that are deeply unsettling. This was particularly disturbing to me at the beginning of my teaching career because I wanted to be liked and admired. It took time and experience for me to understand that the rewards of engaged pedagogy might not emerge during a course. Luckily, I have taught many students who take time to reconnect and share the impact of our working together on their lives. Then the work I do as a teacher is affirmed again and again, not only by the accolades extended to me but by the career choices students make, their habits of being. When a student tells me that she struggled with the decision to do corporate law, joined such and such a firm, and then at the last minute began to reconsider whether this was what she felt called to do, sharing that her decision was influenced by the courses she took with me, I am reminded of the power we have as teachers as well as the awesome responsibility. Commitment to engaged pedagogy carries with it the willingness to be responsible, not to pretend that professors do not have the power to change the direction of our students' lives.

I began this collection of essays confessing that I did not want to be a teacher. After twenty years of teaching, I can confess that I am often most joyous in the classroom, brought closer here to the ecstatic than by most of life's experiences. In a recent issue of *Tricycle,* a journal of Buddhist thought, Pema Chodron talks about the ways teachers function as role models, describing those teachers that most touched her spirit:

> My models were the people who stepped outside of the conventional mind and who could actually stop my mind and completely open it up and free it, even for a moment, from a conventional, habitual way of looking at things.... If you are really preparing for groundlessness, preparing for the reality of human existence, you are living on the razor's edge, and you must become used to the fact that things shift and change. Things are not certain and they do not last and you do not know what is going to happen. My teachers have always pushed me over the cliff.

Reading this passage, I felt deep kinship, for I have sought teachers in all areas of my life who would challenge me beyond what I might select for myself, and in and through that challenge allow me a space of radical openness where I am truly free to choose—able to learn and grow without limits.

The academy is not paradise. But learning is a place where paradise can be created. The classroom, with all its limitations, remains a location of possibility. In that field of possibility we have the opportunity to labor for freedom, to demand of ourselves and our comrades an openness of mind and heart that allows us to face reality even as we collectively imagine ways to move beyond boundaries, to transgress. This is education as the practice of freedom.

Re-viewing Our Professional Lives

Talking (and Listening) for a Living

MARGARET MATLIN

The invitation from Phyllis and Jan arrived at an ideal time. I had just completed a chapter on women and aging for my *Psychology of Women* textbook. The next project was to write an invited address for the upcoming convention of the American Psychological Association. This presentation was entitled "Wise and Wonderful or Wrinkled and Wretched? Views of Older Women," and it explored how middle-aged and elderly women are seen by psychologists, the media, and people in general.

However, neither project forced me to explore how I felt about myself and my career as I was growing older. Several recent events had tempted me to glance fleetingly in through the windows at this imposing topic. Two months earlier SUNY had sent an announcement to faculty members who had taught for more than twenty-five years, describing an early retirement option. When should I begin to consider retirement? Several weeks later a letter arrived, asking me to serve on the editorial board of a journal that I admire. A tight schedule of writing textbooks forced me to decline, but I wondered: Could I ever again say "yes" to a new, long-term professional project? More recently, I had walked past a classroom and saw a colleague in her late twenties. She was sitting cross-legged on the table at the front of her classroom, engaging the students in a lively discussion. Would women in their fifties look ludicrous in that informal position?

Phyllis's and Jan's invitation was especially appealing because we humans seem to think especially clearly and comprehensively when we are persuaded to write, rather than speak. We force ourselves to ask questions before we commit our thoughts to paper: "Is this really, honestly how I feel?" "Is this thought about retirement more closely related to reducing my professional commitments or to losing my self-definition as a psychologist?"

Several years ago I had discovered a similar advantage to the written word while exploring some thoughts about teaching. At a superficial level, we professors often contemplate whether a class went well or whether a new teaching technique was effective. However, I had been asked to prepare a talk on my personal views about teaching. The paper I wrote—"Gardeners, Midwives, Bankers...and Barracudas: Metaphors for College Teaching"—forced me to reflect on the most important goals of college teaching. With a clear perspective on these goals during subsequent semesters, I could evaluate whether lectures, discussions, and class activities really met those goals.

The title selected for this current book invites us to look backwards, to try to recall ourselves when we first stood in front of a group of students and began talking for a living. Psychologists who study human development struggle with several dichotomous questions, the nature-nurture debate being the most obvious. To me, however, the more important question is the continuity-change debate. Are we really the same women—now in our fifties—who entered the classroom several decades ago, uncertain where this profession would lead us?

How has my teaching changed over time? When I first started teaching at SUNY Geneseo in 1971, I literally had never taught before. My goal throughout graduate school had been to become a laboratory researcher. Teaching would simply be an acceptable and legal way to find research participants in a college setting.

In the fall of 1971 I was twenty-six years old—not much older than many of my students. My husband, Arnie, had recently accepted a position as the pediatrician in a rural community-run health center in Geneseo, New York, just south of Rochester. We had just celebrated the first birthday of our daughter, Beth. Two years earlier, I had received my Ph.D. from the University of Michigan, and I really hadn't thought through how to combine being a professional and being a mother. However, the SUNY system had a college in Geneseo. Without a real sense of long-term commitment, I decided to apply for a part-time position, teaching two courses each semester. As I discovered a few weeks into the semester, I was pregnant with our second child. Sally was born in May, thoughtfully waiting to initiate labor until three hours after I had graded the spring semester's final exams.

I didn't enjoy teaching at first. In retrospect, the reason is clear. I had adopted the "banker model" of teaching (Brookfield 1990; Freire 1970). The students were merely receptacles—empty vessels into which I must deposit a certain sum of knowledge. With a few exceptions, my undergraduate professors at Stanford had conveyed that same teaching style. I didn't view my students as individuals, partly because as I lectured to them, they looked uniformly bored.

To be honest, I'm not sure how I decided to change both my attitudes toward teaching and my teaching style. Several psychology theorists argue that we humans often make decisions and then later construct post hoc justifications for those decisions. These justifications may not really reflect our actual cognitive processes that were operating at the time we were making the decision. In acknowledging that principle, I'll confess that I can't recall the reasons for changing my teaching style. However, I started to include more real-life examples in my lectures, and classroom discussion began to blossom. I became much more relaxed and friendly, and the students reciprocated by becoming more responsive. In turn, I grew at first to enjoy and then to love college teaching! By then I had become a full-time faculty member at SUNY Geneseo. I was also beginning to formulate my overarching goal as a teacher—to try to make a difference in students' lives.

As I re-view my life as a college teacher, I can see changes in two strands of my teaching. As professors, we have traditionally been taught to emphasize the cognitive components of teaching: What knowledge and skills will our students acquire in our classes? In the first section of this chapter, I will explore the transformation in my goals within the cognitive domain. More recently, however, many of us have begun to appreciate that our teaching can encourage students to develop their attitudes and emotions about critical issues in our courses. This focus will be my second topic. Third, and more briefly, I'll discuss whether students have changed substantially since I first began teaching. Finally, I'll try to explore how I feel about myself as a professional woman growing older.

CHANGES IN MY GOALS ABOUT STUDENTS' COGNITIVE SKILLS

During the late 1970s I began to examine how to improve my students' cognitive involvement with the material in my courses. I was teaching experimental psychology at the time, and I was searching for some way to make the issues of experimental design seem less remote to my students. One especially useful exercise I developed was a course requirement in which students kept journals illustrating how they had applied these design issues to their daily lives.

I really enjoyed reading the students' journals. Some entries were so useful that I asked students if I could quote them in my future classes. One student, who was taking a Shakespeare course at the time, applied the concept of counterbalancing to *Hamlet*. Researchers counterbalance certain variables in order to equate their conditions, so that one condition does not have an advantage over another condition. In *Hamlet*'s second act, my student noted that King Claudius issues a greeting to Hamlet's friends; "Thanks, Rosencrantz and gentle Guildenstern." Queen Gertrude then provides a counterbalanced greeting; "Thanks, Guildenstern and gentle Rosencrantz." Another student applied the methodological concept of confounding variables to her bread-baking project. Another explained how the esoteric concept of signal detection theory could account for a recent observation: He had been so eager to receive a phone call about a potential job that he had set his response criterion very low. In fact, he had even answered the phone when the doorbell had rung.

The responses I received in these journals helped me clarify a major cognitive goal for my courses. Specifically, I want to encourage students to retain knowledge and skills that they can apply in later life, once they have left college. I'm less concerned with their recalling specific details of the psychology research, and more concerned that they be able to think on their own and analyze psychological information appropriately.

In the early 1990s I became convinced of the value of some simple teaching techniques that encourage active learning. The easiest one is the three-minute-paper technique. I ask a thought-provoking question and then instruct my students to write down their responses. Virtually every student adopts a pensive facial expression and begins to write. Then I ask volunteers to answer the question. The pool of respondents is much larger than if I had simply asked the question and acknowledged the first person who elevates a hand. Because students have written down their response, their answers are also more coherent and well-reasoned. If the topic and the time constraints are appropriate, I might also ask them to discuss their answer with someone nearby, prior to sharing their thoughts with the class. When the quieter students see that their discussion partner valued their answer, they seem to feel more comfortable about presenting their answer to the entire class.

About two years ago I was beginning to write the third edition of my introductory psychology textbook. My previous editions had emphasized critical thinking, though I had never formally discussed the critical thinking process. My editor encouraged me to expand my coverage of this topic and also to develop some critical-thinking exercises. In general, these exercises encourage students to decide whether the evidence supports the conclusions. I've subsequently incorporated these exercises into all my classes, often in combination with the three-minute paper. For example, in a recent child development class I proposed a hypothetical study. Suppose some researchers find that the average birthweight is lower for 100 infants born to mothers who had used cocaine than for 100 infants born to mothers who had not used cocaine; why can't we conclude that the cocaine is directly responsible for the difference in weight?

These exercises seem useful because they allow me to shift my role. I'm no longer a banker, whose primary goal is to talk and to worry about whether she can insert two more paragraphs of a lecture into students' minds before the end of class. Instead, I can become more of a midwife, who listens to students' ideas (Belenky, Clinchy, Goldberger, and Tarule 1986). As a midwife, I can encourage them when their ideas are not yet fully formed, and I can respond enthusiastically when they supply innovative answers. My goal is to help students develop the cognitive skills to think on their own. Realistically, very few of these students will use these cognitive skills to analyze a journal article and locate methodological flaws in the research. They are far more likely to be reading *Newsweek* or *USA Today*. I want them to be able to think critically when they read a *Time* magazine article proclaiming that feminism is dead, based on the observation that the lightweight TV heroine Ally McBeal is the new image of feminism. Does the evidence support the conclusions?

CHANGES IN MY GOALS
ABOUT STUDENTS' ATTITUDES

By a series of chance decisions, I am teaching at a liberal arts college with predominantly female students. My students typically do not come from wealthy families. In general they are conscientious and compassionate. Although they are not political activists, they are willing to consider new perspectives on social issues.

I first began teaching in the era of the Vietnam War. My husband and I had formed our political attitudes about national policy in the late 1960s.

During the "doctor draft" of the Vietnam era, the U.S. Army had interrupted Arnie's residency. He had the good fortune to be stationed not in Vietnam but at Fort Hamilton, in his hometown of Brooklyn, as a pediatrician for families in the New York metropolitan area. We attended our first antiwar rally in Washington, D.C., and then helped form a peace group on Staten Island. We were fully aware of the irony of his situation, and the army would occasionally harass us when we participated in antiwar activities near the army base. After moving to upstate New York, we helped form a peace group called Genesee Valley Citizens for Peace. After twenty-seven years, the group's focus has expanded beyond Southeast Asia to include Latin America, more general antimilitary issues, and social justice concerns. Arnie and I—as well as our two daughters—started a Head Start–type program for thirty malnourished preschoolers in rural Nicaragua, and we've now maintained this program for nine years.

In short, international political issues have been an important component of my life outside of the classroom for about thirty years. However, I rarely mentioned these issues inside the classroom during my first decade of teaching. I recall a representative example, though. I had been teaching psychological statistics and wanted some data that would be suitable for illustrating a chi-square analysis. I decided to use data gathered during our army experience: In nearby Fort Wadsworth, one group of soldiers had participated in an antiwar demonstration. The next day most of them received orders to go to Vietnam. In contrast, another group of soldiers had not participated; only a few of them received orders for Vietnam. I asked my statistics students to work out the calculations; yes, there was a statistically significant relationship between protesting and being assigned to Vietnam.

In 1974, with a new full-time teaching position at SUNY Geneseo, I decided to propose a course in the psychology of women. In retrospect, I'm not really clear what motivated this decision. Until then, I hadn't really worried about the fact that only one of my professors at Stanford and Michigan had been a woman. During those early years, we didn't have much research about the psychology of women, and I remember deciding not to discuss issues such as rape or domestic violence because, after all, those problems seemed relatively rare.

My course was also not especially political at first. However, attitudes, emotional issues, and politics inevitably became an integral part of my course. And as the topic of violence against women grew more visible, these issues also became central. I began encouraging students to attend "Take Back the Night" rallies and to write to companies who displayed either appealing or appalling advertisements. My lectures soon included more personal accounts of overt discrimination against women in the workplace, bride-burning in India, and other emotional topics. Class discussions are inevitable in Psychology of Women. The banker model of teaching is not only inconsistent with feminist pedagogy, but it is also—fortunately—nearly impossible to maintain.

Several years later I devised a component for my psychology of women course that encourages my role as a midwife. Specifically, students must design and conduct their own research project. I can encourage them and help them define alternative options in designing their study. However, they must feel the labor pains; I can only be an enthusiastic supporter. This project satisfies some cognitive goals; it encourages them to contemplate research issues as they design their study, identifying potential flaws. Many students report that working on this project forces them to apply the methodological principles they have learned in earlier courses. They also learn that they, as undergraduates, can produce some interesting information about women's lives.

However, an additional benefit for many students is affective or emotional. For example, one student designed a study based on several scenarios of individuals who had been inappropriately aggressive in a social situation (e.g., honking loudly when another driver does not respond promptly to a green light). This student discovered that people judged the individual much more harshly when the scenario described a female named Judy, rather than a male named John. My student was outraged at this inequity, and her emotional reaction was much stronger because she herself had produced this conclusion. Students who merely hear the description of some researcher's study often remain blandly dispassionate about injustice.

Several years ago I attended a meeting in Boston of elementary and high school educators who were interested in social justice issues. One man, a fifth-grade teacher, asked about my profession. When I told him I was a college teacher, he looked dismayed. In fact, he offered the opinion that college students must not be much fun to teach. I disagreed, replying that students in their late teens and twenties are especially rewarding because they have the cognitive ability to think about abstract ideas. They can also care about and become outraged about injustice. And—perhaps most important—they no longer live with their parents.

If I had written this chapter several months ago, I would have said that I had not changed in recent years with respect to my commitment to introducing social justice issues into my courses. However, this semester I am teaching child development, a course I had not taught for about four years. My earlier course had emphasized perceptual and cognitive development.

As I began designing the new course content, it was obvious that I had changed in those four years. In fact, the course now contains more socially relevant coverage. For example, our discussions this semester have emphasized how our health care system does not encourage prenatal examinations for economically poor mothers and how we do not have programs designed to help women with drug problems—women who may well be pregnant. Later in the semester I'll also pay more attention to homeless children, to the demise of the welfare system, and to violence on television and in the community. I'm introducing a new section on ethnicity and racism, and I'll discuss how much our country spends on children in comparison to how much we spend on the military. We'll also examine whether we adults can stand by as passive onlookers while children's lives are in jeopardy.

Interestingly, teaching this course in child development also provided me—quite by accident—with a new pedagogical tool related to attitudinal issues. This particular class of students had been painfully quiet and polite, and they had resisted my efforts to cajole them into conversation. Then I showed a video on babies born to women who had used crack and other drugs. I could sense that the students were being drawn into the problem. Following the video, the discussion began hesitantly. Then one student said she had seen a television program about a project to pay $200 to drug-using women of childbearing age if they would agree to be sterilized. Suddenly the class erupted with passionate questions and statements. Since then, the spirit of this group of students has changed; they are much more willing to ask questions, to engage in discussion, and to voice opinions. I had been teaching for twenty-seven years, yet a college sophomore had taught me that posing a controversial suggestion could transform a classroom.

Have Our Students Changed?

Most of this essay focuses on how I have changed during my years of teaching. A parallel question, which I'll explore only briefly, focuses on how our students may have changed. In particular, have the attitudes of our students shown dramatic alterations? People often claim that students are very different in the late 1990s than, say, twenty-five years ago. Yes, some are lazier, and some seem more shallow. However, the students in my Psychology of Women class really don't appear to have changed. They are still dismayed that little girls receive sexist messages at home and at school. They are still surprised to learn that female college graduates make about the same salary as male high school graduates. They are still outraged at the injustice of rape, incest, sexual harassment, and domestic violence. And my students still show what psychologist Faye Crosby (1984) calls "the denial of personal disadvantage." Although the world may be unfair for most women, each of them believes that she will find a mate who does half of the housework, and she will earn a fair salary in her interesting job, where she is highly valued and respected.

Several weeks ago I was speaking with a good friend, a woman active in the peace movement whose views I value. She suggested that I must find it so discouraging to be teaching college students these days. After all, they must be so cynical growing up in the face of such violence and pessimism. I quickly disagreed. In fact, my students seem to be quite caring and sensitive. Every semester, for example, I ask the students in my introductory psychology course to answer the question "Who am I?" on the back of a large index card. Naturally, the format of this question does not invite confessions of avarice or villainy. Still, I'm always warmed by their answers.

This semester, for example, a great many students describe themselves as studious and hardworking. They say they love to learn or enjoy reading a good book. They often remark that they love and miss their families. Many report that they try to be a good friend or a good listener. Many say they are shy or nervous—many more than the number who say they are friendly or outgoing. Some answer, "I'm in college to discover who I'm supposed to be" or "I'm finding college is a great way to expand my horizons." In short, I still find that students live in the same world that I do—a world that values intellectual achievements, kindness in our interpersonal relationships, and an interest in exploring the individuals we can become.

GROWING OLDER AS A PROFESSIONAL

How do I feel about myself—as a female professor—growing older? Our responses to this question undoubtedly depend on how comfortable we feel with our current situations. In a recent interview, the novelist Anne Tyler noted that she was now in her late fifties, and she still didn't know what she wanted to be when she grew up. How strange . . . a highly talented and successful author, not feeling at home with her occupation?

In contrast, I really do feel "at home" as a professor of psychology. I began my undergraduate experience as a biology major, but my first psychology course quickly lured me away. I passionately enjoy this discipline, with its emphasis on research, its many applications in everyday life, its commentary on social change, and its scope that spans the distance between neurons at the microscopic level and conflict resolution at the international level. Now I feel very comfortable teaching undergraduates, and textbook writing connects me with thousands of professors and students whom I'll never actually meet. A friend recently asked what I would do if somehow I couldn't teach psychology. I had no answer. Psychology teaching is an essential part of my being, and Anne Tyler's dilemma is completely alien to me.

Still, I'm constantly operating under time pressure—certainly an issue for every woman writing a chapter for this book! Until recently I was the solo author of textbooks in introductory psychology, cognitive psychology, and the psychology of women. I also worked together with a coauthor, Hugh Foley, on a fourth textbook in sensation and perception. Each textbook required a new edition every three or four years. Because I teach full time, keeping the four books on schedule had begun to feel overwhelming.

In recent years I had kept adding new responsibilities, engaging in a kind of "magical thinking" that everything could be completed by the appropriate deadline. Did I really want to continue on through my fifties, never feeling "caught up"? I enjoy reading, yet the bookcase holds several yards of unread novels and well-aged *New Yorker* magazines. I feel guilty about taking time to walk in our woods or going to a guest lecture that isn't directly related to my work. As I move through my fifties, time now seems more finite, and living under a constant time pressure has become less appealing.

I'm fortunate to have a husband and two daughters in their twenties who are loving and supportive. All three had begun to express concern, urging me to cut back somewhere. "Letting go" is a difficult and unfamiliar process, but this process is sometimes the only alternative. To decide which project to drop, I thought about my most important goal in teaching—to make a difference in students' lives. The most vulnerable book on this criterion was *Sensation and Perception*. The book had been well received and was now in its fourth edition. However, I didn't believe that many students had altered their lives because of its contents. As it happened, my coauthor Hugh Foley also had been feeling overwhelmed. Together we made the painful decision not to write a fifth edition of the textbook.

Those words "painful decision" glare at me now. What a luxury, when one's most painful decision centers on whether or not to revise a textbook! I shift my mental microscope from my own life to the life of my friend

Nimian, who lives in El Sauce, Nicaragua. Nimian is a few years older than I am, and her husband left many years ago. In 1990 she was devastated when the Sandinistas lost the election. Now she's experiencing heart problems in a country without adequate health care. Nimian must constantly respond to forces beyond her control. She does not have the comfortable option of weighing the benefits and costs of a professional project.

Thinking about women like Nimian certainly helps me regain an appropriate perspective as I continue making choices throughout my professional career. In about ten years, for example, I'll need to make decisions about retirement. In reality, all the options are appealing, assuming that my life circumstances stay the same. I could continue to teach full time, though presumably I would need to learn to let go of some writing projects. I could exit from teaching the same way I entered, by teaching part time. This would seem to be an appealing option because part-time status presumably does not require attending department meetings or other administrative duties. I could write but not teach, an arrangement that is reasonably common for psychology textbook authors. Realistically, though, diminished energy or health problems could limit my options.

Or I could retire, actually retire. The Spanish word for retired is *jubilada,* which captures the sense of jubilation and freedom. I really would enjoy looking up a word in the dictionary and allowing myself the luxury of browsing through the nearby entries. It might be interesting to take an intensive Spanish course, so that my proficiency could rise above the functional level. And we could travel more, even spontaneously, without having to worry about how we would find time to manage the mountains of correspondence that accumulate in our absence. I could even read some of the books that await me on the shelf...

Still, I wonder. What happens to our professional identity when we retire? My father had a career of about fifty years as a distinguished researcher in geology. After the age of sixty-five, he began working part time, and then retired completely. At eighty-one, he still reads *Science* and several geology journals. Do I say he *is* a geologist, or he *was* a geologist? My mother taught fifth grade and seventh grade during the years we three daughters were in high school... and college tuition was daunting. Then she retired, at the age of fifty-five, and she clearly thinks of herself as a former teacher. When I retire, what can I do so that I can still say "I am a psychologist"?

I've just finished glancing through Mary Catherine Bateson's book *Composing a Life.* (And, yes, this is one of many books that I'd like to actually read when I retire.) She concludes this book with a wonderful passage:

Each of us constructs a life that is her own central metaphor for thinking about the world. But of course these lives do not look like parables or allegories. Mostly, they look like ongoing improvisations, quite ordinary sequences of day-to-day events. (241)

As I re-view my professional life after twenty-seven years of teaching, it seems inevitable that I would fall in love with teaching psychology. It seems inevitable that I would enjoy conveying both the cognitive and the affective components of psychology. In retrospect, everything makes sense. I need to remind myself, however, that my career began with an improvisation. I'd like to keep my eyes open and improvise a creative way of remaining a psychologist and yet having the time to walk in the woods, to master the preterit form of Spanish irregular verbs, and to wake up in the morning and decide on a whim that I do not have any pressing obligations for the day.

On Statutes and Dogs, Poems and "Regs," and Life inside the Classroom

JUDY SCALES-TRENT

Is it really possible that this is my fifteenth year teaching law school? I am amazed at the idea. It seems such a short time ago that I moved from the practice of law in Washington, D.C., to a life of writing and teaching in Buffalo. It is almost hard to remember that shaky, unsure woman who arrived at her first class one fall day in 1984. It was a difficult moment of transition in my life. I was not only changing cities and careers, but I also was changing my name from my former married name to one I created for myself. I was putting together the pieces of my life in a new way, and nothing felt solid. I would have to grow into this new name and this new person. At some level, I could hardly believe what I was doing. How could I even think that I was able to teach law school classes? Could I learn all this new substantive material? And even if I managed to learn it, how would I present it to the students? And how would I mask my terror—hide it from my students, from myself? Once installed in the classroom I focused on cases and statutes, agency regulations; I concentrated on control.

But I am a different woman now, and I teach in a different way. I live in a deeper place, a place that is steady, quiet, and rich. I look for the joy in life. I am more kind to myself.

In the past fifteen years I have thought a lot about the different parts of who I am, and about how society wants me to keep those parts separate. In my thinking and writing, I have refused to do this. Instead, I have been working steadily to bring those parts together.

One of the lessons I learned as a young woman was that there were two important, yet conflicting, struggles going on in America—the struggle of *women and* the struggle of *minorities.* Since these two groups were in conflict for resources, I was told, I would have to chose which group I would support...and no self-respecting black person would chose the group "women." But how can this make sense to a person who is both black and a woman? And so I chose them both, together, and at the same time.[1] America says that *white and black* can never be the same? But I am a white black woman, and I say that they can.[2] This country says that the *male and the female* have separate roles, separate spheres, and that "male" and "female" cannot exist in one person? I put together my mother's name (Scales) with my father's (Trent), and insist that America is wrong.[3] *Poets and lawyers* are different kinds of people? How awful life would be if that were true![4] And every time I brought in another fragment of my identity, I became stronger, more centered, clearer about my worth.

And now I bring all this with me into the classroom.

I see fewer lines of demarcation in the world now. *Writing and teaching* are more connected. So when my students talk about their paper deadlines, I discuss my writing problems with them. When we address a legal issue related to something I have studied and written about, I now tell them about my work and distribute copies of the article. The *outside and inside of law school* also merge. The first questions I ask in every class now are "Who has a good joke?" and "Who has some good news"? I tell the students that studying civil rights can—no, should, make them fairly sad: civil rights workers need to find ways to keep their spirits up. And in this way we have not only laughed together, but we also have learned about babies on the way and marriage proposals, new jobs and vacation plans, godparents and skiing. Sometimes students tell of the honor another student has garnered, an honor that student was embarrassed to report. One student brought in a tape of her dog barking because the dog was "good news" to her! And they also learn of my son's graduation from college and my trip to western North Carolina with my sister, to explore Appalachian crafts. In this way we start the class with a smile, and we build community at the same time.

Home and school also converge through food! In my seminars, the student team that prepares questions for the day is also supposed to bring food for the group. My hope is that this will change the law school space into a more relaxed, playful area—the kind of space that is conducive to energy and creativity.[5] Similarly, there is one class party each semester at my home, where it is my turn to prepare the food for them.

In my law school spaces, *poetry and law* are now fused. My office door is a "poetry door": the only thing posted there is a poem, which I change weekly. Seeing the poem as I walk in changes the meaning of my office for me: my spirits lift as I go in. Secretaries, colleagues, students, sometimes stop to read the poem; sometimes someone will tell me whether they like it or not, or ask a question about it. And sometimes they bring me a copy of a poem they love.

There have been many classes where I have supplemented the legal text with poetry, in order to deepen the students' understanding. For example, when I was creating a seminar on the legal and policy issues affecting women of color, I realized that the women who were not African American were strangers to me. So I read their stories and poems in order to understand them more fully, then assigned this literature to the class.[6] Last spring I went a step further. It was April, National Poetry Month, and the director of the American Poetry and Literacy Project (APL) spent that month driving across the country, handing out 100,000 free poetry books at locations as disparate as tollbooths, fast-food restaurants, hospitals, junior high schools, and wineries. He called this journey "The Great APLseed Giveaway." And I tracked his journey every day on the Internet, reading the poems and diary entries about this amazing project.[7] Then one day, it seemed to me that I should be "planting" some "APLseeds" too! So I gathered up all my courage, walked into my class on employment discrimination law, and started the day by reading to the students one of Mary Oliver's poems about spring.

This is what I want in my life every day: hard work and play, poetry, joy, community. And I don't want it to stop for the hours I spend in a classroom. At fifty-eight, I am more and more aware that there is less time now for everything, including happiness. Many years ago I learned something about this from my mother. As we were growing up, she used to make many of our clothes—tailored suits, organza evening gowns, winter coats, she could do it all. And I remember her saying one day, as we were choosing fabric for a dress: "Don't pick that material: if the fabric isn't beautiful, I don't want to work on it." In much the same spirit, I tell my students now that if walking in the classroom doesn't bring me pleasure, I don't want to do it.

Today, fifteen years after coming to this career, I am more aware that the substantive material I present in the classroom is less important than the process. In class, as in life, there is no arrival, only the journey. So I understand better that it doesn't matter how much material I cover during the semester: there is always more to learn. The only important thing to teach, then, is how to think and read and write more carefully: what matters is being rigorous and meticulous about the work. Confuse "and" and "or" in a case you're citing, and your client goes to jail; file the appeal brief one day late, and your client loses her child. The process is crucial.

Since I am clear that the substantive material matters less, I have realized that who I am in the classroom probably matters more. And I am more conscious of what I am trying to present to them personally. Of course, I want them to see careful work, rigorous work, punctuality, organization, responsibility. But they need to see more because I teach very charged subjects about race and ethnicity in a classroom where generally over 95 percent of the students are white. So I also want them to see in me a sense of fairness, an ability to listen to them, to really hear them, even when they voice opinions that are different from mine. I want them to learn that they can do this too. I also want to make the students feel so safe that they can open up their minds to the creative confusion that may bring with it new thoughts about race in America. As I learned once more when I moved to Buffalo and to this new career, changing patterns is hard and frightening, but there is no learning, no growth, without it. Whatever preconceptions about race they bring into the classroom, I want to make change possible. Also, since many of the white students have never had a black professor before, I want them to see me as comfortably in charge, as expecting, and entitled to, their respect. I expect that this may also be very important for the students of color in the class.

Two years ago I started a new grading system in my class on employment discrimination law. Under the old system, the final-exam grade was the semester grade. Under the new one, students who turn in three short essays during the semester earn a five-point grade "boost." I would not grade the essays: my only requirements were that they come in on time and that they be thoughtful. In the first essay I asked them to describe in some detail two examples of employment discrimination they had witnessed. For the second, the students were to discuss two movies they had seen in class. But it is the third essay that is relevant here. This is how I described the assignment:

> I have always wondered if students learn something in this class which
> changes the way they understand employment discrimination, or the law
> in general, or their surroundings, or themselves. Do they learn something
> which changes the way they think about other law courses, or incidents
> that took place a long time ago, or conversations they have had? Much of

what we learn in school stays in our brain until the final exam, and then disappears (... at least, that is my recollection from law school!) In this paper, please describe what you have learned in this class that may stay with you long after the exam is over.

Don't think that you have to describe something personally transformative! You don't. If you learned something important about, for example, the way judges think, or a new way of conceptualizing employment discrimination, that would be fine.

Looking back over their essays, I am surprised once more by what they learned. Several wrote that they finally understood that discrimination took place all the time in this country; a few thought about how they might be complicit in this system, for example, by laughing at racist jokes. One student used the paper as an opportunity to struggle with the concept of affirmative action: as a white man, what might he lose, or gain, by this system? I fully sympathized with the student who wrote that the class had made her think—"maybe too much." A few students were struck by the demeanor of one of our guest speakers, a solo practitioner in Buffalo who specializes in employment discrimination law. They mentioned his integrity, his emphasis on hard work, his self-deprecating manner. One student was so impressed that he decided to try to follow the attorney's career path. Others said that they finally learned how statutes were put together and why it was important to understand legislative history. But the comment that I still can't get over was written by a white student who said she would remember how the students of color raised their hand more frequently in my class than in others, despite the fact that I questioned them in the same rigorous manner that I questioned white students. I hadn't known that the students of color volunteered more in my class, and I wasn't aware that this was one of the lessons I was teaching. But I think it was a lesson about respect, and I'm glad she learned it and told me about it.

During my first year of teaching, I discovered that one of my students had been bringing his dog to class. I was shocked, insulted, enraged. How dare he? The classroom was for serious work about legislation and cases and jurisprudential theories. Certainly his personal obligations or interests should not intrude on our labor. Now, fifteen years later, I wish a student *would* bring a dog to class, and I rejoice when they bring their babies and children. I have been telling my colleagues for a while that I think it should be the dean's responsibility to have a child on each floor of the law school every day, for I have noticed that when we see a child in the law school, we stop and smile a little, as we remember what is truly important in life; as we remember the connections between outside the school and inside, between law and poetry, between love and work; as we remember to make room for the joy.

Exploring Critical Feminist Pedagogy

Revelations and Confessions about Teaching at Midlife

ESTHER NGAN-LING CHOW

This essay offers me an unusual opportunity to reflect on what I have experienced in my intertwined life as a feminist scholar, a professional, an activist, and a teacher in the academy over the past quarter century. Most of my life has represented an interplay between power from within and challenge from without to use that power effectively to survive and to prevail. Peace comes to me when I think that I have stood for social justice and humanity, regardless of the results of my efforts. Some people seek peace in a life that flows along like a quiet stream, spared the ripples of life's vicissitudes. But I welcome the bubbling currents, finding peace when I feel that I stand as sturdy rock in their midst, like the boulders that withstand the onrush of a great waterfall. As with some geologic formations, I think the erosions of time have shorn away some of my rough edges and accentuated what boldness and resilience there is in me. My inner power continues to grow as my life continues to accumulate experiences and to negotiate meanings. Coalescence of the crosscurrents of my private and public lives has very much shaped the meanings and the ways in which I have learned from teaching and have learned to teach.

Midlife signals a rite of passage, a natural process of transition from the life stage of procreation to that of liberation from "anatomy as destiny." I feel elated and exuberant about having made this transition. I find midlife to be a stage of integration, allowing me to blend vision, aspirations, capabilities, knowledge, and experience, which gives me a sense of life fulfillment. It is also a time for reminiscence of the past as I seek understanding of the present and generate hope for the future. Midlife is like a sculpture in progress; its final form is recognizable, but its artist continues to work toward perfecting it. The arts of learning and teaching continue to offer challenges to meet!

In this essay I offer a reflective account of my experience as a social researcher and teacher. I first examine how colonized education and patriarchy shaped the ways that I, as a racialized and gendered subject from the underclass, was taught, and subsequently the ways that I perceive and do teaching. Second, I analyze how my experience of feminist enlightenment and critical pedagogy contests the hegemonic culture, patriarchal rules, and conventional teaching approaches. In search of a critical feminist pedagogy, finally I offer the major results of my experimentation with a dialogic, experiential, and participatory (DEP) approach to teaching students how to research social life.

COLONIAL EDUCATION, PATRIARCHY, AND PERCEPTION OF LEARNING/TEACHING

Growing up as a girl child in the traditional Chinese society of Hong Kong, at first I accepted my very existence as one of being faceless, nameless, voiceless. I became accustomed to invisibility, silence, powerlessness, and devaluation. The credit for my good fortune of receiving any education at all goes to my beloved mother, who herself was deprived of any opportunity for formal education throughout her life. Her misfortune of contributing to the illiteracy statistics in China became a motivating force in her life to contribute differently through me. Thus, in spite of tremendous hardships, she sought opportunities to assure that I would be educated. Her generation paid the awful price for the gain the next ones harvested. My mother, though now deceased, remains my best role model. Although she suffered most of her life, she inspired in me the spirit and strength of feminism, a term that she neither used nor even knew. Our bonding as women and as mother-daughter set the course for our respective life struggles, though we chose quite different paths of resistance to pursue our destinies. My mother planted the seeds for my learning, teaching, and researching of life and later helped me to transplant them to the North American soil in which they could thrive.

My educational experiences from early childhood through adolescence were highly regimented and disciplined. They fit the "domesticating" rather than the "liberating" mode of learning and teaching insightfully distinguished by Paulo Freire (1970, 1985). Literacy was taught for the sake of knowledge that focused primarily on a prescribed abstract understanding of the world that did not always accord with reality. My experience in marketplace and factory work while I was attending school offered me ample opportunities to observe this disjuncture. Education was an act of transferring textbook knowledge, a blend of traditional and modern ideas, from teachers, who commanded absolute authority, to students, whose minds were regarded as empty vessels to be filled. Learners were expected to be passively compliant, denied or restricted in self-expression, voice, and creativity. Schools provided formal, rigid classroom settings that seemed to me to imprison students' young minds.

The domesticating mode of teaching often produces a "culture of silence" among the dispossessed and mass ignorance as direct products of situations of economic, social, and political domination and paternalism. The would-be learners are the victims. Instead of encouraging students or the masses to know and respond to the concrete realities of their world, the domesticating mode imparts a false consciousness to learners, a distorted view of reality, enabling the British in Hong Kong, for example, to maintain their racial superiority and exert their political and economic domination over the Chinese there. The colonized education system conspired to place a higher premium on the English language and instruction in it; in fact, English was the only officially recognized language until the early 1970s. This policy privileged not only the British governance, but also the urban Chinese elites (mainly upper-class males) and their offspring, who possessed the highest English-language proficiency, enabling them to serve as middlepersons (or middlemen) to advance the colonizer's interests in capitalist expansion in East Asia. The majority Chinese, who comprised slightly more than 98 percent of the population of Hong Kong, were largely marginalized, their indigenous culture devaluated, and their voice subverted.

Throughout my schooling, there was no free compulsory education at any grade level (although that did change later). Schools emphasizing English instruction were more expensive and thus less affordable than those offering primarily Chinese instruction. Under British rule, Chinese parents had to work diligently for family survival, earning wages out of which they had to squeeze the resources somehow to pay for their children's schooling. Since Chinese culture placed high importance on both education and achievement, parents willingly sacrificed toward these ends. The costly education imposed by a racist and class-biased educational policy was compounded by a patriarchal ideology that prompted parents to give sons a higher priority than girls for schooling. Uniform examinations given at different grade levels from primary school to college were used as mechanisms of control to weed out seemingly incompetent students at the onset of the educational process, thus depriving millions of students of opportunities to grow intellectually and mature academically at their own pace and on their own terms.

Acting "in loco parentis," teachers had omnipotent power to exercise mind control through persuasion, coercion, and even physical punishment, using a top-down approach to instill values, to pass on knowledge, and to train in basic skills. Defiance of authority was a sinful act that very few dared to try; critically questioning what was taught was unthinkable. Passive learning was further reinforced by requiring memorization to lay a basic educational foundation. However, what had to be memorized was mostly devoid of meaning for students; it did not correspond with the social reality they knew outside the classroom.[1] The teaching and learning methods functioned well only to enable diligent students to survive the school system and consequently to pass the uniform examinations imposed by the British in order to get the credentials to increase their life chances in the labor market.

Did this education system nevertheless liberate young women like me in Hong Kong? My answer is that it was a mixed blessing in this regard. There is no doubt in my mind that my schooling served as a vehicle of social mobility to get me out of poverty, but only in a very limited way did it empower me and liberate me from my state of invisibility, powerlessness, and subjugation. My state of being was epitomized for me when the college dean told me bluntly upon graduation, "Everything being equal, men are more qualified than women and deserve employers' job preference because they will be the breadwinners of their families." Educated college women thus remained devalued, silenced, and powerless, with only limited opportunities and options to improve their lots. For these reasons, I made a transoceanic flight from the repressive circumstances I found so denigrating, hoping to find a better life in the United States.

AMERICAN EDUCATION, FEMINIST ENLIGHTENMENT, AND CRITICAL PEDAGOGY

In the mid-1960s my graduate school in the United States offered a modified version of the domesticating mode of learning and teaching, although with greater freedom than I had had before to question and to explore subject-matter areas in sociology and across disciplines. The emphases remained on abstract knowledge, objective truth, and the positivist approach to empirical research. The curriculum valued "pure" over "applied" science, theory over method, content over process of knowing, and credentialism over lived experience. The dual roles of students as passive learners and teachers as omniscient purveyors of knowledge formed the implicit ruling relationships in the intellectual process. Students were still treated as empty vessels to be filled to the brim rather than as buds with their own potentials that needed nurturing to unfold and develop. I was well trained primarily in quantitative methodology following the natural science model of positivist thinking and empiricism, which treated women or gender as one variable in statistical analysis. This modified domesticating mode shaped my process of acquiring knowledge credentials, a professionally certified identity, and an unreflexive subjectivity. I must confess that this mode also indoctrinated my ways in turn of teaching and research for nearly a decade. I had difficulty letting go of my heavy teaching and cultural baggage. This not only weighed me down to some extent, but also overpowered the students whom I tried so hard to connect with and teach. All involved, teachers and learners, researchers and researched, were entrapped in a culture of one-way communication and top-down power, longing for emancipatory possibilities.

Two major liberating forces, feminist scholarship and critical pedagogy, stemmed from contesting this institutional discourse and have illuminated my lifelong process of learning/teaching. The second-wave feminist movement that swept academic campuses like a tidal surge in the mid-1960s began to challenge conventional knowledge about women, culture, and social institutions and to protest that knowledge was distorted by the exclusion of women from theory, research, and praxis. Historically, Luke and Gore (1992) think that critical pedagogy in the 1980s could be seen to constitute a "third-wave" new education emphasizing liberation, raised consciousness, agency, and equality. Fundamental to feminist epistemology is that knowledge is socially constructed and must be analyzed in the context of the social relations in which it is produced. The advocacy of standpoint theories and situated knowledge became central in feminist pedagogic discourses (Haraway 1988; Hartsock 1987; Smith 1987). Using standpoint theory, Dorothy Smith (1987) argued that sociological research and theory must situate women as social actors within their everyday world as problematic and place their standpoint as the central focus of theoretical analysis, for women are knowers from whom researchers derive knowledge. Sociological analysis must begin with the everyday life experience of social actors as situated in particular social relationships between the researcher and the researched or between the learner and the teacher and must proceed to discover the social and institutional contexts of their respective lived experiences.

In teaching women/gender-related and research methods courses, I began to incorporate women's perspectives and the experiential approach in designing syllabi, in developing curricula, and in exploring with methods of active learning inside and outside of the classroom. To study different forms of social inequality, for example, I first assigned students to volunteer at least one-half to one full day at community service agencies such as soup kitchens, homeless or women's shelters, and rape crisis centers, where they were to do field observation. In a written assignment, they were then asked to analyze their field observations and experiences and to compare these with what they had learned about theories, concepts, and analyses of social inequality in assigned readings, lectures, and class discussion. Through such efforts at curriculum transformation, I questioned the objectivity of research, explored alternative ways of teaching and learning, and made knowledge acquisition more relevant and meaningful, illuminating students' experience of the social reality of which they had been a part.

By the late 1970s I had become critical of the omission of the perspective of women of color from Western-, white-, middle-class-dominated feminist scholarship and pedagogy. I had begun to emphasize the importance of and the ways in which the perspective of women of color could be incorporated into the study and teaching of women/gender-related courses in sociology and to examine systematically and substantively how various dimensions of gender are compounded by the intersectionality of race, ethnicity, class, and culture (Chow 1985). Social diversity and multiculturalism emerged as critical issues when the needs and interests of learners and teachers of diverse backgrounds were taken into consideration in the educational process. Promotion of inclusive knowledge and curriculum transformation has deepened my understanding of the complexity of these issues, which reach beyond national and sociocultural boundaries to include also the lives of women and others worldwide regardless of nationality, age, sexual orientation, or physical ability.

The second major force that has offered me liberating revelations is critical pedagogy, which is founded on critical theories of the first generation of the Frankfurt School, on Gramsci's (1971) concepts of hegemony and hegemonic subjects and practices, on Paulo Freire's inspirational work *The Pedagogy of the Oppressed* (1970) regarding critical theories and practices in education, and on Giroux's (1983) emancipatory rationality and citizenship education. Reading Freire on the critical pedagogy of conscientization, in particular, has steered me to appreciate the meaningfulness of teaching critical literacy as a prerequisite for critical consciousness and to explore the liberating mode of teaching. As profoundly influential as these male authors of critical theories in education have been, however, they fail to emphasize women learners' interests or women's critiques and actions in public and private life (Luke 1992). These weaknesses create an opportunity, however, to rethink critical feminist pedagogy.

THE DIALOGIC, EXPERIENTIAL, AND PARTICIPATORY APPROACH TO TEACHING

Central to the integration of feminist thinking and critical pedagogy in my teaching of sociology are three major concerns relating to knowledge production, curriculum transformation, and the learning and teaching process. The first concern is for the relevance and meaning of sociology and the ways in which sociological knowledge is produced and transmitted. How do we consider the gaps as well as the linkages between the subject matters that we research and teach on the one hand, and the life experiences of those from whom we derive our knowledge and understanding on the other (whether they are research subjects or students as learners)? How do we make connections between abstract theory and research technicality and between knowledge and life experience?

The second concern is to understand social diversity in ways that reflect how social actors' locations, consciousness, and sources of knowledge shape their thinking, subjectivity, meanings they derive, and their relationships in the process of learning and teaching. Critical perspective directs our attention to scholarship on the social construction of differences, domination, and meaning that is based on race, ethnicity, class, gender, age, sexuality, nationality, culture, and physical characteristics. Thus, transforming curriculum for inclusive situated knowledge necessitates incorporating social actors of diverse social backgrounds and their multiple voices. How do we utilize a course as a pool of human resources among whom some have traditionally been excluded, marginalized, or characterized as "other" because of their diverse backgrounds? More specifically, how do we incorporate multiple voices into the goals and objectives of the course and into course assignments and projects?

The third concern is with the empowerment potential of learning and teaching for theory, research, and praxis. How do we design curricula that invite participation by learners? Can we sociologists empower those we teach and research? These three key concerns emphasize making connections, diversity, interaction, lived experience, and agency as constitutive elements in the production of knowledge, skills, and meaning to achieve critical consciousness and empowerment.

A central question here is, how do I as teacher (and learner as well) incorporate these constitutive, potentially liberating elements into teaching and learning? A teaching method I am devising that I call the dialogic, experiential, and participatory (DEP) approach is the direct outcome of my pedagogic exploration and experimentation in teaching about life in several courses that I have taught during the past three years. The educational character of each of these three dimensions is unique, yet they are intricately related to each other and in some cases overlap. My application of this approach received mixed results. It was more successful in a focus group training module and a research methods course, from which I draw many examples in the following discussion. Since the positive learning/teaching outcomes and experiences were based on the collaborative efforts of students as well as myself, I illustrate the following discussion of the DEP approach by including their own voices (i.e., those of Chad, Deanna, Fan, Jamie, and Kay).[2]

The Dialogic Dimension

Rooted in the philosophical traditions of the West, the East, and the Global South, the dialogic approach to education uses group discussion as a means of exploring how teacher and learner communicate the sources, the content, and the meaning of their knowing and experience as well as act on the problematic nature of everyday life.[3] In contrast to the domesticating mode of teaching, the dialogic approach, based on the popularized work of Freire (1985), is a liberating mode seeking a critical consciousness that redefines the purposes, the process, and the outcomes of teaching and learning and thus alters the roles of teacher and student. Education is regarded as the knowledge to liberate both teacher and learner by providing them with the freedom to observe social phenomena critically and to engage in the process of transforming action. Education's aim is to develop knowledge, concepts, and discourse to understand the sources of oppression and disempowerment and to develop an agenda for critical agency granting power to speak, to critique, and to act for emancipatory interests. Language is an effective means not only for basic communication, but also to examine critically the reality, hidden or overt, of the learners' social locations and the structure of their social world. Thus situated knowledge is created, experienced, and acted on to articulate individuals' understanding and to derive shared meaning as to the things, events, and phenomena surrounding them. The role of teacher becomes that of a facilitator of group discussion who uses the power of dialogue to aid group members in giving voice, sharing viewpoints, and making connections between individual and structural conditions. In this way, the dichotomous roles of teacher and learner become blurred or are even deconstructed and redefined.

Teaching a focus group research training module and a research methods course has offered me ample, valuable opportunities to translate these pedagogic ideas into action. The focus group represents a valuable qualitative approach to collecting data through spontaneous discussion and social interaction on a defined topic area with the goal of describing and explaining how people regard their perceptions, ideas, attitudes, feelings, and events (Krueger 1994). Knowledge generates power by constituting people as subjects or participants (Foucault 1980) through language and simultaneous interaction in a group setting. All fourteen graduate students in the focus group training module strongly agreed that the class atmosphere gave them a forum in which to express opinions and led them to experience empowerment in the learning process.

The dialogic approach to research also recasts the role of the researcher as a facilitator or a moderator and situates learners or research subjects as active participants in ways that lead to empowerment of all parties involved. Language matters! Social interaction enhances understanding by aiding learners or participants to negotiate reality and share meanings. Knowledge is neither possessed nor controlled by the teacher, but comes from the liberating, dialogical speaking of words conveying learners' voices and views. As graduate student Deanna remarked, "During... discussion of what it means to conduct a focus group, I was excited to hear the stress placed on the need to tap the participants' knowledge. The participants, themselves, are the experts. The researcher relinquishes her power and realizes the power in the experience of the individual at hand." Instead of feeling that power had been taken away from me as a teacher, I myself became a learner, taught and empowered by what the learners brought to the discourse. Treating teachers and learners as knowers in a less hierarchical way, we sought to develop more collegial, collaborative, and reciprocal relationships. By suggesting that the class conduct real focus group sessions involving research subjects recruited in the field rather than mock focus group sessions among the students themselves, I learned valuable lessons about the utilities of this research method and the emancipating potential of teaching. In this way, teaching becomes learning and learning becomes teaching—the two processes converging and illuminating each other.

The Experiential Dimension

In conjunction with the dialogic approach, an invitation to learn brings increased sensitivity and flexibility to the lived experience of group members, especially the disempowered of diverse backgrounds, as they articulate their multiple voices. Using feminist standpoint theories, the experiential dimension stresses the problematization of everyday experience as the focal point in dialogue and as the research question for social inquiry. It is also important to understand that to be human is to be interpretive. This dimension, searching meanings from inside out, captures the hermeneutic or interpretive understanding of people's life experiences, viewing reality through the lens of the learners or research participants and generating ideas and information through their own voices. Then the linkages of objectivity and lived experience, intersubjective construction of meaning, and identity formation are authenticated and illuminated.

Whose voice? The experiential dimension offers the content and the form of substantive knowledge informed by multiple voices articulated by participants from diverse backgrounds based on race, ethnicity, class, gender, age, nationality, sexual orientation, and physical capability. Discussion in teacher education has paid more attention to the diversity of students than to that of teachers. The general assumption is that the teacher has more formal authority than the students; that oppressive conditions may also denigrate the teacher is seldom considered. If s/he is of minority background and interacting with students from dominant groups, this may to some extent undermine (or even challenge) her or his authority, affect her or his teaching effectiveness, and alter classroom dynamics.[4]

Social diversity and cultural pluralism imply that knowledge is provisional, relative, and open-ended and that there is no finite and unitary truth. Learning is also derived from multiple sites of pedagogic practice, be they inside or outside of the classroom. I use various strategies emphasizing field observation (e.g., of battered women, and ride-on experience in a police patrol car) as well as written assignments designed to acquire hands-on experience in practicing social research, to create an active environment for self-exploration and mutual aid among learners in social research method courses. Many of the assignments encourage or require students to employ a comparative approach to understanding the complexity and intersectionality of diversity (e.g., compare a selected gender phenomenon cross-culturally or across race or class boundaries). I sometimes weigh students' ability to complete a research project heavily over or even as replacement for in-class examination.

The focus group offers the versatility of a setting in which social diversity can be explored and cultural similarities and differences assessed while simultaneously advancing theory and research. My course entitled "Focus Group in Cross-Cultural Research" attracted a group of international students and others with rather mixed backgrounds to share a variety of ideas, opinions, information, and experiences through multiple lenses. Special attention was paid to the practice of feminist caring and sharing among the participants and to the use of a feminist ethic in selecting and protecting the human subjects of focus group research. An icebreaker exercise and its attendant introduction of students to each other turned out to be a useful classroom technique for building rapport among learners at the outset of the course. Graduate student Kay commented on this technique, "I firmly believe that this an effective way to give voice to every student. It affords us all an opportunity to share our respective academic interests, as well as learning about each other's ethnic and cultural backgrounds." Students were asked to write weekly journals reporting their reflexive thinking regarding how they reacted to lectures, what they read and discussed inside and outside of the classroom, and how they acquired personally evolving experience through learning, dialoging, and interacting. After each focus group session afforded students opportunities to study gender and cross-cultural differences in media impact on society, a debriefing technique was used to allow everyone to take a turn at discussing the results of their observation and contrasting their research experiences.

The Participatory Action Dimension

Participatory action is an invitation to learn by reflexive teaching to promote emancipatory and active learning in democratic settings, whether they be inside or outside of the classroom. An important goal here is to relate theory, research, and praxis to ensure a unity among reason, reflection, and action. The means to achieve this goal is to employ the bottom-up approach to ground learning experience from all the people involved as they take charge of the learning process. In the syllabi of all my research courses, I state that "the course is aimed not only at introducing students to knowledge and methodological know-how for doing social research, but also at helping them develop conceptual, analytical, critical, and creative abilities as they conduct their rudimentary sociological inquiry. The ultimate goal is to train students of sociology to be working sociologists." I have increasingly employed the pedagogic practice of giving only the first half of the syllabus to students on the first day of class, then in the second class providing them a final syllabus that incorporates students' ideas, interests, and input into the design and development of the course.

My focus group training module epitomized application of the participatory component in the active process of creative learning and teaching. Students were mobilized to engage in and take charge of every stage of the focus group project, from conceptualization to implementation and final report writing. They functioned like nuts and bolts. Without each one's effort to complete her or his own tasks, the whole scheme of things would have fallen apart. Graduate student Jamie appreciated the praxis aspect, commenting, "I think I learn something better if I am able to actually practice the new skill . . . but the best learning comes from taking that new skill and teaching someone else. . . . This [DEP] approach does seem to work very well with this type of hands-on class where we need to come away from the course with the skills to actually conduct focus groups." Fan, a graduate student from Taiwan, agreed: "I believe learning from doing is always a good way of learning . . . this is the biggest advantage of this class."

I exerted concerted effort, though still more would be desirable, into putting the feminist principles of caring, fairness, and equity into practice to ensure gender balance among students with regard to interests, resource allocations, task assignments, rewards, and accomplishments. Aware of women's marginal position in society and the subjugation of their voices in the public sphere, students considered the disadvantage of a mixed-gender group that would have the potential of silencing women participants in group discussion. An important decision was made to have one all-women and one all-men group for equal representation in the focus group sessions. Within each group, we also took race, ethnicity, nationality, and cultural background into account to make another decision concerning whether to recruit a more or less equal number of American and international research participants to study cross-cultural communication. Each group was co-moderated by two students who matched the gender and international backgrounds of its participants.

Striving for a democratic process in which learners played a main part, we emphasized teamwork, a spirit of cooperation, and community building in the classroom. To achieve this, some basic principles of group dynamics were carefully considered and efficiently carried out. To build group cohesion and solidarity, I also developed a slogan, "TRUE PALS," an acronym for Teamwork, Respect, Understanding, Equity, Politeness/Courtesy, Awareness/Sensitivity, Leadership, and Sharing. Although the time, energy, and effort invested in participatory mobilization, task coordination, and team building were considerable for both myself and other learners throughout the course, we all reaped the benefits of active learning, collaborative research, and collective action. Graduate student Kay commented, "The introduction of this [TRUE PALS] to the class I believe was an ice breaker.... Everyone should be given the opportunity to voice their opinions."

CONCLUSION

Midlife signifies the coming of an age in which to reflect on and explore the self and teachings about life. The Chinese word for "crisis" consists of two main components, meaning "danger" and "opportunity." Midlife, to me, symbolizes more the "opportunity" than the "danger" of engaging in a natural process of maturity, integration, and empowerment to face the changes and transformations awaiting me. At midlife, I have come to realize that I have been imprisoned by the domesticating mode of teaching and engulfed by a sea of silence for most of my life. My teaching struggle now is a tug-of-war between the domesticating and liberating modes of teaching and learning; and I draw power from within myself, and, along with my students, face the challenge in search of a better pedagogy.[5]

As my graduate student Chad observes so clearly in his journal,

> Often on campuses or in journals critics will claim that education in America, and life here in general, has become too fragmented. I see some truth to this claim. However, I think that these critics underestimate the student's role in synthesizing all that s/he learns from many, many fields s/he is exposed to. As Paulo Freire would say, education is not something put into students like money into a bank. I, the learner, play the greatest

ESTHER NGAN-LING CHOW

role in my own education. I have the power to synthesize all the greatest concepts and dreams from the greatest thinkers of all time. A book cannot do this, a computer cannot do this, and a professor cannot do this for me. I will carve my education into the marble mind of myself!

To the extent that students and teachers succeed in this mutual exploration, not only students but also teachers as well will find themselves transformed and truly empowered.

Community ❧ Generativity

... Your mother ... would braid your hair while you sat between her legs, scrubbing the kitchen pots ...

When she was done she would ask you to name each braid after those nine hundred and ninety-nine women who were boiling in your blood, and since you had written them down and memorized them, the names would come rolling off your tongue. And this was your testament to the way that these women lived and died and lived again.

Edwidge Danticat

What are our preoccupations as women?

Perhaps here: It would begin with each woman carrying a deck of cards—wild cards—cards that could not only portend the future but create it. If a woman saw an act that violated the health and integrity of her community, she would leave a card onsite.

Terry Tempest Williams

The sea rises, the light fails, lovers cling to each other, and children cling to us. The moment we cease to hold each other, the moment we break faith with one another, the sea engulfs us and the light goes out.

James Baldwin

24

Themes That Link
through Time

S U E   V .   R O S S E R

As I reflect upon my teaching to begin to write this essay, I realize that I received my Ph.D. in zoology exactly twenty-five years ago. At age fifty-one, it shocks me somewhat to recognize that I have been teaching for a quarter of a century. In the mid-1970s, while I was still a postdoctoral researcher, teaching in women's studies provided the venue for me to begin to integrate what had previously stood as separate personal and professional pursuits in feminism, the science of biology, and women's studies.

After two years of learning a new area of biology, my postdoctoral research finally appeared to be on track. When I became pregnant with my second child, the professor supervising my research suggested that I get an abortion, since it was "the wrong time in the research and we needed to obtain more data now to have the grant renewed." I did not have the abortion; I rationalized that taking minimal time off for childbirth meant that everything would be fine in the lab and with my scientific career. One day when I was out at noon to breast-feed the baby, a call came that focused on my area of research. Although many of the other postdocs and graduate students (all males) used their lunch hour to play squash, I later learned that the professor had made comments to others in the lab about my being off nursing again. Those comments coupled with related incidents made me decide to accept the offer of the new women's studies program to teach a course on the biology of women.

Women's studies gave me new space, perception, knowledge, and connections to understand my bodily identity and the reactions it invoked. In the mid-1970s, only women were involved in this first year of the program; they welcomed me because I was a woman and even encouraged me to bring the baby to some meetings. From the stories of the more senior women in the academy, I learned that much of the discrimination I had experienced was not unique, but resulted from being a woman in a patriarchal university that only the previous year, under court order, had dropped its official quotas on women medical students and nepotism rules against women faculty. From teaching biology of women, I began to read the evolving critiques revealing bias in research developed by men, using only males as subjects, and with theories and conclusions extrapolated inappropriately to the entire population of both men and women. While developing a new course in women's health, I recognized that despite having received my Ph.D. in zoology and having given birth to two children, I knew almost nothing about my own body and its functioning. When I sought materials to fill this knowledge gap, I learned that very little research had focused on women and their bodies in health and disease. Recognizing this dearth and that any research that existed had been undertaken by men from their perspective, I began to work to create materials that reflected women's experience of their biology and bodily identity. Suddenly I felt a connection with teaching this research and with my search for materials from medical textbooks through scientific journals to fiction to convey the information to students. Trained in the humanities, social sciences, and fine arts, my colleagues in women's studies helped me to uncover the interdisciplinary resources needed to understand the components of women's health.

In retrospect I realize that common themes unite both the aims and curricular content that I have taught during these two and one-half decades. These themes include the attempt to bridge women's studies and science by using feminist perspectives to analyze and to teach science courses and by integrating science into the women's studies curriculum; the evolution of innovative techniques by applying feminist pedagogy to the teaching of science and using methods traditional for teaching science in the women's studies classroom; and a focus on interdisciplinarity coupled with a commitment to team-teaching.

While these themes have remained constant, what has changed very much over the years is the actual curricular content, the particular pedagogies, and the insights and perspectives from different interdisciplinary and team combinations. The rapid evolution and increasing complexity of both feminist theory and innovations in science and technology have changed the curricular content quite dramatically and have suggested productive interdisciplinary combinations. My own maturation as a scholar and teacher, influenced by research on authority in the classroom, feminist pedagogy, and student learning, has led me to lecture less, to give fewer exams, and not to attempt to cover the entire breadth of a topic. In contrast, the students in my classes now engage in more group work and projects, deliver more oral presentations based upon papers they write, and explore subjects in greater depth.

Integration of Feminism into Science and Science into Women's Studies

A glimpse of some of my earlier published writing about teaching compared to what I now write about a similar subject may provide the best revelation of the evolution of my teaching. In 1986 I wrote the following passage, which reflected my attempts to integrate women's studies into biology:

> Teaching science from a feminist perspective should make young women realize that science is open to them. . . . The question for the introductory biology teacher then becomes how—at the present time—does one incorporate the nascent scholarship on women and science into the biology curriculum in a manner that will inspire further critiques and theoretical changes? How can one integrate into the standard biology curriculum the considerable, but diffuse information constituting the contemporary feminist perspective: the critique of biological determinism and androcentric "objectivity," the substantial information about famous and lesser-known women scientists and their discoveries, some remarks about the obvious influence of masculine thinking on the descriptive language of biology, the feminist theoretical changes that have already taken place, and those areas where the theoretical changes are still needed? (Rosser 1986, 24–25)

I saw the inclusion of material about women in science courses as a way to attract women to the sciences; introductory biology stood as an important opportunity because it often serves as the gateway to other science courses that determine a student's decision to pursue work in science or abandon it.

Simultaneously I was equally committed to developing science and health courses to fill the void in the women's studies curriculum. In the same 1986 volume I described my reasons for teaching such courses: "The goal of Women and Their Bodies in Health and Disease is to help women regain control over their bodies through learning the language and understanding the theories of science and health. . . . Women and Their Bodies in Health and Disease is an introductory course without any prerequisites. . . . In brief, this course is likely to attract a group of students who feel very unsure about their science ability, very unwilling to question authority, and rather fearful of talking about these issues" (84). Empowering women through providing them with scientific vocabulary and some knowledge of their bodies stood out as a strong motivation for my offering this course.

My desire to bring women's studies to science and science to women's studies because of the potential to empower women and reveal new perspectives in each field becomes clear in these 1986 writings. They also suggest my struggle to bring these disparate aspects of my own intellectual interests, background, and personal experiences together in my teaching and research.

Integrating biology and women's studies into my teaching using interdisciplinary methods and materials seemed exciting and natural to me. This evolution of new curricular content and new teaching methods interwove the threads from my undergraduate humanities background with my years of training in the sciences. For example, I asked students to keep a body journal in biology of women courses that I taught. They wrote about the psychological, social, and physical interactions that they noted in their bodies. In addition to reinforcing the interdisciplinary nature of health, the journals exemplified the use of a pedagogical technique more commonly used in the humanities than in a science class. Similarly, such approaches as cooperative learning, placing science in its social context, and including the history and philosophy of science that I advocated in *Female Friendly Science* (1990) were perceived as pioneering and groundbreaking by the scientific community. I adapted feminist curricular and pedagogical initiatives, borrowed from women's studies, to the teaching of science.

This theme of bringing science and women's studies together continues to characterize my work. In the introduction to my forthcoming book, I write the following:

> A few scholars within women's studies have developed feminist critiques of science, but until recently the humanities and social sciences served as sources for most of the scholars and research in women's studies. Science has remained on the margins of women's studies. Women now receive almost half of the undergraduate and 45 percent of the graduate degrees in the life sciences and constitute 41 percent of medical student enrollments. Although women scientists may recognize on some level that the women's movement may have generally contributed to removal of quotas and encouragement for women to enter science, many remain unaware or

uninterested in women's studies and feminist critiques of science. In short, both women scientists and women's studies scholars have developed along parallel paths, with little crossover between them. Although the life sciences and women's studies have contributed the most exciting research of the late 1990s, scholars in each field have not crossed the threshold to learn how work in the other can enhance and bring their own work to fruition....

The confluence of these three factors—critical mass of women in biology and medicine, the life sciences as the frontier for research in the next millennium, and the readiness of women's studies to place gender and science in central focus—provides a unique opportunity. Working together, scholars in women's studies, scientists, and physicians can use feminism to examine the frontiers of biotechnology and reproductive technologies. Without feminist lenses, women, society, and science may all suffer as the development and application of these technologies proceed and expand. (Rosser forthcoming)

Different feminist theories provide lenses that reveal different facets of who experiences beneficial and harmful impacts of biotechnologies and their applications. For example, socialist feminist critiques expose how the decisions regarding which products are developed from the numerous patented genes isolated and sequenced by the biotechnology industries fall as much under the influence of capitalist interest in profit margins as they do needs of people in developing countries for nutritious foods. Reproductive technologies have different impact upon people of different classes and in different countries. The capabilities opened by in vitro fertilization have led to an industry in which poor women are paid to gestate the developing fetus, who may represent the genetic offspring of a rich man and a woman who does not wish to and/or can't carry a pregnancy to term—the so-called Baby M phenomenon. On a worldwide scale, particularly in India and China, amniocentesis is used for sex selection to abort more female than male children because traditionally in those cultures, sons are valued more, partially because of their economic contributions to the family income and to the care of their elderly parents. A person born in an overdeveloped country consumes about thirty times as much as a person in an underdeveloped country. Despite the fact that children born in industrialized, first-world countries, especially middle-class ones, are encouraged to have children, women in developing countries may be sterilized against their will. Infertility becomes the issue in first-world countries, while fertility signals the problem in developing countries.

In contrast, the lens of postmodern feminist theory reveals that no universal research agenda or application of bio- or reproductive technologies will be appropriate and that various women will have different reactions to the technologies depending upon their own class, race, sexual orientation, country, and other factors. Because postmodernism recognizes different, yet valid, standpoints from which various individuals view the same activities, the theory is often criticized for leading to political inactivity. Postmodern feminists would be unlikely to have a unified position on a biological research agenda, applications of various reproductive technologies, or whether bio- or reproductive technologies should be pursued at all. Postmodern feminism may explain why many feminists oppose in vitro fertilization and other reproductive technologies while many women eagerly seek them out in their desire to overcome infertility and produce "perfect" children.

THE INFLUENCE OF INTERDISCIPLINARITY ON THE PRESENTATION OF TOPICS IN THE CLASSROOM

During the 1980s I became keenly aware, primarily from my colleagues in the humanities and social sciences, of the debates erupting over diversities among women. Critiques by women of color, working-class women, and lesbians made me explore ways to incorporate into curricular content and teaching approaches the recognition that gender does not represent a homogeneous category of analysis and that it must be studied in relationship to other oppressions of race, class, nationalism, and sexual orientation. In describing courses I had taught in the biology of women during the previous nine years, I wrote the following in 1986:

> Unfortunately, some women's studies classes tend to present sexuality and reproduction only from the perspective of white, middle-class heterosexual women. Many of the facts were gathered from this group, and most of the research is based on them. Quite frequently, given the structure of academia, the instructor is also from the group. As a result, the experiences of only one group of women are held up as the "fact" and models for sexuality. At best, this leaves nonwhite women, lesbians, women of other socioeconomic classes or religions, and physically challenged women feeling that the model does not describe their experiences. They may discount the course as taught from an oppressive, normative viewpoint (Dill 1983). At worst, women who are not white, middle-class, and heterosexual may instead discount their own experiences. They again realize that they deviate from the standards and wonder why they fail to conform in this area, too. (52)

Later in that same chapter I specified, using a particular example, how I had redesigned the course. While attempting to "decenter" the white, middle-class, heterosexual perspective, I still used the lecture, preferably delivered by a professional woman from one of the previously marginalized groups, to express her own "voice" and move her experience into central focus.

More recently, I attempt to organize a more student-centered classroom. While I have personally advocated an emphasis upon group work, collaborative learning, and hands-on experiences in science classes as better for women (Rosser 1990), I now worry about the impact of the group dynamics on men of color and women. Too many faculty from the sciences remain unaware of the research from women's and ethnic studies demonstrating how racism and sexism from the broader culture become replicated in classroom and group dynamics. In 1998 I expressed my anxieties in "Group Work: The Consequences of Ignoring Race and Gender":

> Four females and sixteen males would not be an uncommon gender distribution in an introductory calculus-based college physics class. Four groups of five individuals each, with one female in each group, appears to represent an equitable (or at least representative) division along gender lines. From the research on study groups at Harvard (Light 1990) and other work, evidence suggests that women are more likely to drop out of the group if they are the only female, particularly if the subject is a nontraditional one for women, such as science, engineering, or mathematics....
>
> The intersection of race and gender further complicates group selection. While assigning an African American woman to a group whose other members consist only of white men clearly constitutes isolation, questions arise about whether the African American woman is still isolated when another woman (not African American) or an African American male is assigned to the group along with the white males. (Rosser 1998, 84)

INTERDISCIPLINARY TEAM-TEACHING

Team-teaching with colleagues from other disciplines has provided students with very different perspectives on complex issues in women's studies and science while simultaneously giving me valuable insights for my own scholarly work. During the last twenty-five years, I have team-taught with colleagues from French, English, sociology, art, music, anthropology, psychology, history, philosophy, religion, ethnic studies, as well as the natural, physical, and health sciences. Although sometimes the struggle for common vocabularies and understanding of approaches becomes difficult, especially when I team-teach with someone from the humanities or fine arts, the discussion and its rewards, especially for the students, justify the difficulties.

In 1986 I wrote the following about team-teaching:

> Although coteaching may take more time than teaching alone, it is definitely more rewarding for both students and faculty, since issues can be explored in greater depth and complexity and from more perspectives. (113)

In 1998, looking back upon twenty-five years of team-teaching, I assessed some of its rewards:

> Different colleagues relate to one or more parts of my identity which they share; often because they share some parts of my identity, they willingly attempt to understand parts with which they do not identify. Since other women scientists understand the discrimination I have experienced because of being a woman in a male-dominated field, they listen to my critiques of gender bias in science. Heterosexual women and mothers, who appreciate my revealing the exclusion of women from clinical trials of drugs and the lack of attention to women's diseases, attempt to understand my critiques of lesbophobia within medicine. Trusting my training as a scientist and my rank as a female who has achieved some professional status, male science faculty and administrators give some credence to what I say about women's studies and interdisciplinary work. Because of my French degree and feminist credentials, some women faculty in the humanities heed my plea that they read and understand some science. (King, forthcoming)

CONCLUSION

Coalitions between women scientists, physicians, and women's studies scholars in the humanities and social sciences provide the lifeline that each group needs for its own professional and personal survival. Without coalitions and interdisciplinary interactions with other women colleagues, even dedicated scientists who are knowledgeable feminists may experience an isolation that may lead to alienation and self-destruction. As a woman, a feminist, and a scientist, I have found that my interdisciplinary coalitions among colleagues in women's studies, the humanities, social science, science, and health have been critical for my twenty-five years of teaching and to my professional and personal survival.

25

Naming, Sharing, Speaking

Teaching in Midlife

JEAN F. O'BARR

At fifty, I entered menopause. My cycle stopped suddenly. Anticipation rewarded: one less thing to clutter a full life. I felt a surge of energy and rushed into what I believed to be the next phase of my life. I cheerfully helped my younger daughter off to college. I insisted we finally renovate the kitchen after twenty years in the same house. I began a serious rehabilitation program for lifelong leg injuries. Challenging cultural prescriptions always has energized me, and I was ready for the ones on aging!

And in the process, I went to a new OB/GYN, my first female doctor, for a checkup. I had learned through talking to her at a party that she liked seeing older women. I was tired of the kindly male who had guided me for twenty-five years through two children. His waiting room bulged with stretching bellies. I no longer felt comfortable there, and he seemed completely uninterested in the emergent me. The new doctor listened patiently to my medical history, examined me, and then looked me straight in the eye. "Jean," she said, "medically, you appear in good shape. I think all of your symptoms are stress-related. Are you getting any help with that side of your life?" "STRESS!" I practically yelled, "I'm not under stress—everything's great."

Out in the car, my mind raced over all of the personal and professional episodes of the last few years. I remembered visiting doctors and being told they did not see anything to treat—"Let's just wait and see." Nothing ever developed. But headaches, stomachaches, chest pains, sleeping problems, continued. Did this new doc see something I had not? Acknowledging to myself that I "believed" in stress as a physical illness, I decided to seek help from a psychiatrist friend.

We met for lunch. I reported on my trip to the new doctor and her recommendation. My friend looked at me in wonder, in much the same way the doctor had, but she put it more gently. "Jean," she said, "given your hectic personal and professional life and its demands, are you telling me that you have never sought psychological support of any kind? How have you managed? I can tell you that almost everyone we both know sees someone, at least occasionally." Click!

I went to the psychotherapist she recommended. We began talking, using language in new ways. As a scholar, I was accustomed to using language for scholarly analysis. It was new to me to use language to express experiences and emotions. Speaking those experiences and emotions contributed directly to physical changes. My aches and pains lessened, then vanished. Within the year, my menstrual cycle returned after a two-year absence and began its slow meandering to an end.

The reversal of the physical signs of menopause was a wake-up call for me. I had thought midlife came through a simple physical act. I now know that life transitions are a much more elaborate set of processes with physical, mental, emotional, and spiritual dimensions all taking place at the same time. Midlife is as much a developmental process as any other life stage, albeit neglected in cultural myths, academic study, and much popular discourse. Getting to know myself, fostering many relationships, recognizing the fusion of mind, body, and spirit in all that I undertake, were the rewards of exploring this transition time. My body became more than a convenient place to carry my head. And most importantly, I came to understand that what I do in one sphere of my life has profound influences on what I do in others.

For this essay, I want to describe and reflect on what this journey has meant for me as a teacher, in the classroom, with individual students, and on the myriad of committees universities create to do business. Without the naming process that identified stress for me, the tools that I acquired to deal with the situations I encountered, and the understandings about myself in relation to others that were released by those tools, I would have missed midlife and its riches. I would have missed the opportunity to use life experiences in exhilarating ways in my teaching. With them, I have released energy and ability that have me bounding around classroom, office, home, and community.

A brief bio is in order here. When I graduated from college in 1964, higher education was looking for new talent. I received a Woodrow Wilson

Fellowship to graduate school. Not knowing what I wanted to do, and without the ideas the modern women's movement would offer in several years, I accepted their description of me: college teacher in the making. I know now that I made it through graduate school because I married at the end of the first year. I always recognized the personal support that came from a life partner. What I could not have understood then but now grasp is that with the move to "wife," I was able to be "female" and "scholar" simultaneously in a culture that then refused to allow the two to inhabit the same persona. As we completed our dissertations, my husband sought a university position, and I had a baby. Then, suddenly, this same university needed an instructor. One month into motherhood and moving, I was in the classroom. I have been here ever since.

But I have been here in a particular way. Because I was first hired as a fill-in and then later retained as an administrator, I was never on a tenure track. First, I developed a continuing education program that flourishes today. Then, under the mentorship of the first female dean I ever had, I was asked to found a women's studies program. Throughout I taught and wrote, but never with the security of tenure. Feminist scholarship enabled me to see the connections among my unusual status, my academic abilities, my political passions, and my rich personal life. It gave me the space to explore them theoretically as well as practically. It is in midlife that I could look back on a career path that was "not normal" (according to conventional wisdom based on male standards, of course!) and see it as perfectly normal (according to feminist knowledge that assumed diversity). Feminism and experience in midlife interconnect in such a way that I have enough hindsight to see where I have been and enough perspective to know where I might be heading. All of these interconnections have infused my teaching.

The first connection revolves around the insights I obtained from a number of therapists. The second comes from a rich circle of women surrounding me. The third rests deep within me—an intuitive sense of how to use my gray-haired power. I want to explore each in turn as it has manifested itself in teaching.

Naming

Over the years I have utilized the talents of an individual psychotherapist, a marriage counselor, and a consultant on group process, as well as physical therapists, massage therapists, and body workers. I have worked with these women as an individual, as a member of a family, and as the head of a staff. Although they do not know one another, there has been a strong convergence in their observations. Those observations have helped me express and resolve both personal and professional issues. But what strikes me so dramatically about the tools I have gained from these insightful therapists is how the very same strategies they are urging for self, family, and staff transfer to teaching. Given that I have now been teaching for some thirty years, I often wonder if I could have acquired these insights earlier. Certainly, some could have been grafted on sooner. But by and large I have come to believe that only in midlife was I rich enough in experience and secure enough in status to listen and to utilize. What did I hear?

I heard about the power of naming. I heard each of these professionals name a feeling, a belief, an interaction, a practice, and give it a context. I heard them take my experiences, put names on them, and offer me a reality check. Reality check in hand, I engaged in naming in return. *Yes, I was upset* when that happened. *No, I did not believe* that the person holding an official position necessarily had the authoritative answer. *Maybe I could reach my goals* more readily when I enabled others to buy into the agenda. *What if I tried another approach* rather than the one I had always followed? Pretty simple stuff when spelled out in these straightforward sentences. But very complicated stuff when buried under frameworks that evolved and that proved adaptive, unexplored, and unaltered.

This process of naming had immediate applications to teaching in every kind of setting. In one sense the examples might seem trivial to some. "You seem to me uncomfortable talking in class. What's going on?" Said privately and carefully outside class, naming a behavior I have seen repeatedly almost always opens up a conversation and results in changed classroom behavior. What's going on for any given student is not the issue. Naming how she is affecting the classroom as well as herself is the issue. Once named, a student usually takes the responsibility to change the classroom dynamic.

Before I understood and used naming as I do now, I tried many other strategies. I might look expectantly and frequently at her, giving her every opportunity to volunteer. I might comment on a contribution she had made in writing and ask her to share the thought in class. I might simply call on her. And many of these things might work. But I have learned that for me nothing works for me as effectively as active listening, naming, and then suggesting some of the strategies that she might employ to move to a different place. I now see it as my responsibility to give her some tools to make that move. "You can always ask me to elaborate," I say. "You can usually ask how what we are doing today links back to what we did last week." "You can often observe that John said this and Tom said that and you wonder what they think of each other's position." "By simply asking questions you use your voice. And once you use your voice, you create a space, a space with your name on it. And once created, thoughts as well as questions usually flow." I have applied the skills that I have gained in therapies about mind, body, and soul, the skills that I cluster under the rubric of naming, to the classroom. Without these skills learned through midlife development, I would be a less effective teacher.

Sharing

For many years I had few friends. As a young mother and busy professional, I knew many people, and we cooperated on the tasks at hand. We got our kids to school and to events. We figured out how to organize programs, projects, conferences to foster our careers. We chatted as neighbors. I stayed in touch with family and a few old friends. But for the most part, my list of roles did not include that of friend. I had no one with whom I shared my more intimate thoughts, no one that I felt I could ask for advice, no one who gave me honest feedback as I went about in my worlds.

In midlife, with fewer responsibilities for offspring and a career more or less in hand, I began to feel the absence of friends. And I realized I was surrounded by the most wonderful women, most of them friends in the making. That is, if I made the time for these relationships, they could blossom. I found new friends among university colleagues, the women I knew nationally from professional associations, the graduates of the university who had come together over the years in support of women's studies as well as the dozens of women and men I knew who had been students and were now pursuing their own lives.

I made a point of making time for them—of sitting down to talk when we were together, of meeting them when they were in my town or I in theirs. And I wrote letters, thousands of them, to exchange feelings, experiences, reactions. My outreach to friends, mostly women, was quickly encouraged as I learned to support and be supported. I realized I was abandoning two models that had been implanted early in my twenties—the monastic model of the solitary scholar huddled in the library who occasionally emerges to speak the truth unchallenged and the supermom model of the world of popular culture who smiles while doing everything splendidly without anxiety or assistance.

As I worked more and more in the scholarship on women, I wanted to behave as well as think as a feminist. I wanted to have strong beliefs and work them out in a community of people dedicated to those beliefs and to the social change that was necessary for those beliefs to make a difference. Above all, I learned from these women how to put balance into my life. How to work and to play. How to do one thing, then another, rather than drive myself crazy. How to dive in and how to pull out. How to figure out what I wanted and go for it, leaving other things aside. How to look at a situation from many angles and enjoy it, challenge it, ignore it, according to needs, both individual and collective.

All of these friendships reformulated my teaching. No, I did not make students my best friends. But being more actively engaged with friends helped me to see how to interact with students. Yes, I still gave lectures, wrote syllabi, graded written work. But I watched myself move from the hub of the wheel to being a prominent piece in the kaleidoscope. I saw this most in my individual interactions with students when they came to my office or when we encountered one another on campus. When they sought advice about courses, study-abroad plans, postgraduation decisions, expressed their curiosity about life as an adult in general, I found myself telling stories. The stories came from this vast array of people I knew and their journeys through similar times. I no longer gave answers, I gave possibilities in the form of stories and suggestions for who to contact for further help. And it seemed to work.

One of my most successful stories revolved around graduation, a time of stress for every student who has not yet decided what to do and does not have the job or professional school placement that is supposed to be the outcome of an elite education. The students and I joke. There are really only two questions in college. The first week everyone asks everyone else where they are from. And the spring semester of your senior year revolves around the question: what are you going to do now? For those who don't know, this question looms particularly large over graduation weekend. My suggestion to them for several years now is to turn the query around. "I'm exploring lots of options. Tell me what you did when you graduated from college." I am told again and again that this simple reversal makes all the difference in the world. The student is no longer on the spot for being unable to utilize this expensive education. Rather, he or she is now an active learner, getting advice—and getting off the hot seat.

My friends and their strategies for living taught me how to do this. Use experiences, tell stories, draw observations, locate resources, suggest approaches, point out mistakes, map out possibilities. In the process, pathways open up, often moving each one of us from the place where we are currently stuck. The richness of my friends' lives in some ways channels through me to younger women and men who are facing similar questions, albeit in varying contexts. I have come to see that the connections I have made with friends are valuable resources for students as well as for me, and I am enriched when I connect the two through stories.

I understand this process of sharing stories to be based on the new position of authority I inhabit in midlife. I have not surrendered authority in teacher-student relationships, in or out of the classroom. Rather, I have tried to reposition authority within a larger framework of listening, asking questions, relating one person's query to another person's responses in a similar situation—all mediated through my own life but not structured exclusively by it. I think a lot about the whole student now that, in midlife, I see myself more frequently as a whole person (not just the head on the body without a spirit! or the mom/wife who leaves what she knows in her briefcase! or the activist who does not consider bringing "real" life into "academic" analysis!). I see the questions asked in the office as just as important and valid as the questions asked in class. Seeing learning as a continuous rather than a fragmented process comes, I believe, from seeing myself at midlife and my friends at all life stages as part of larger stories that must be shared.

SPEAKING

Feminists use two phrases frequently. One comes from the early days of the women's movement when most women were outside the places of power. The statement *the personal is political* explained a fundamental premise—that the condition of individual women as well as culturally employed categories of women was the result of sociopolitical systems and that those systems had to be confronted. With the conservative backlash of the 1980s, feminists reversed the statement and pointed out that *the political is personal*. That is, the changes in the American national political agenda (restrictions on abortion and the emphasis on family values being the two that resonated most loudly to the undergraduates I knew) had profound influences on the opportunities women had to shape their lives.

In class, I often tried to go a step further in the late 1990s and explain that *both the personal and the political are conceptual.* What we knew about events, how we thought about issues, and what we did about them mattered. Words, ideas, approaches to what we do and do not learn, how we interpret that knowledge or lack thereof, what we pass on to one another and to the next cohort, all affect us as individuals and as a community.

The second phrase that feminists have in their backpacks and briefcases is simultaneously both older and heard more in the later stages of this phase of the women's movement. It has proved most useful once women were inside institutions and able to speak from those positions. *The necessity to speak truth to power.* Feminists often feel they have experienced truths and that those in positions to make decisions, usually male, are unaware of those truths.

In class, I explain this concept by talking about how letting women into social institutions is not the same thing as enabling those women to assume decision-making positions and changing enough of the policies so that more women can enter the same institutions with fewer restrictions. I emphasize that "trickle-up" has a spotty history and that social change is not just about who got what but also about who got to say who got what as well as when they got it.

In short, in class and with individual students, I talk about speaking up. Over time, I have done so within the feminist community. It has proved harder to do so outside that community. The conditioning to female silence of my undergraduate days coupled with the absence of a feminist voice in graduate school were overlaid with a precarious professional position. I valued feminist scholarship when the institution did not. I occupied positions deemed without authority in the eyes of the institution. It took years to connect and use what I knew to the places where I found myself on campus. In the classroom and in my office, students agreed that I had knowledge important to impart. And that agreement rendered me authority. On the campus, feminist knowledge was questionable at best. On campus, my status was equally so. Over time, acceptance of feminist knowledge spread through the academy. Simultaneously, I gained authority through acquiring power on campus. The programs created through women's studies drew good students, popular support, national recognition, and insights that came to be sought by other academic enclaves. I had had the autonomy and power to make this happen. Over time the institution legitimized the power by granting it authority.

With authority outside the classroom, I found myself speaking truth to power. Institutional power makes for a stronger voice on my part. At midlife, with this power, I am able not only to use it but also to have a perspective on it. That perspective involves using it responsibly, but frequently, in how I teach in all the settings where I find myself.

I find myself on committees, advising colleagues, heading an effort and drawing on the resources that I had been accumulating for a long time. Comparative experiences from visiting other campuses as lecturer and consultant. Observations of students, practices, cultures, over almost three decades. Insights gleaned from conversations with other people pursuing similar agendas. Confirmations and revelations from reading. Connections from one situation to another. All combined to help me use my knowledge while I was still acquiring knowledge. It is that sense of process, of being in a particular place, using that place, and knowing that there are still other places to go that empowers me. I talk more now in public places, enabled by the talk of the classroom and of my friends. And I think I talk more now that I am in midlife, connecting what I have gathered to what I see around me as well as what I look forward to figuring out.

I began with a personal story and I will end with one. Three years ago last summer, I was giving serious thought to the accomplishments of women's studies at Duke after a decade and contemplating what the next decade would bring. My ruminations led me to the conclusion that those who knew women's studies well valued it—and those who were unfamiliar with the contributions of feminist thought to institutional culture ignored if not dismissed women's studies. I decided that the program needed to partner with another university unit, completely removed from ours, so that we might learn the various ways in which feminist insights could be applied elsewhere.

The opportunity came in the form of a new program for affiliating faculty with residential units called the Faculty Associates Program. The details of FAP are not important to the story. What is important is the fact that as the director of women's studies, I agreed to codirect this program with a faculty colleague for its initial two years. I did so very deliberately, thinking that by working with the upper administration, student affairs, and over one hundred faculty members from other university schools and colleges that I did not know well, I would be able to insert information about women, gender, and feminism into campus discourse and simultaneously would be able to alter some institutional patterns that were in place that made the climate chilly for women. With every chance I had—workshops, newsletters, small group meetings, large gatherings, administrative sessions—I used what I knew from women's studies and named it as such. Working toward equity: how many of the student representatives selected by the dormitory to work with the faculty are women? Including new perspectives: if we have a program on the religious life of students for the faculty, we need to address gender questions in faith communities. Challenging paradigms: recognizing that all students on campus do not have the same experiences, one of the panels ought to be made up of women, including women of color, talking about what it is like to live as female undergraduates here. Changing practices: before the lecture, let's have all the members of the group introduce themselves and name a question that is on their minds about first-year students so that we can be certain to address the concerns they bring to the session. Reflecting on our own practices: in writing this job description for our staff member, we need to be certain that we recognize her contributions as a member of the team and resist the way wage and salary have defined her roles and responsibilities.

In midlife, with feminist frameworks, using experiences, I have found not only a voice, but also many kinds of voices and ways of speaking. The skill and power of naming, the reinforcement of friends' stories, the authority that comes from having abilities legitimized with institutional power, have come together. They complicate what it means to hear and be heard, making listening and being listened to all the richer. The physical signs of menopause need mental, emotional, and spiritual nuances to be an authentic marker of midlife. Naming, sharing, speaking, are the processes of midlife that for me have made teaching classes, students, and colleagues fuller and, I think, more meaningful—for them as well as for me.

My appreciation goes to former student and now colleague Mary Armstrong for her thoughtful reading of the first draft and the ways in which she suggested putting many thoughts more directly. And, as always, none of these insights would have been possible without the superb assistance of the Women's Studies staff: Stephanie Sieburth, Nancy Rosebaugh, Juliana Smith, Cynthia Bunn, and former staffer Vivian Robinson.

26

"Thinking Back through [My] Mother"

Reclaiming Anger, Advocacy, and Pleasure in Teaching

JUDITH A. DORNEY

INTRODUCTION

Toward the end of her text *Bitter Milk,* in which she explores profound connections between gender and teaching, Madeline Grumet poses a most provocative question. "What would thinking back through our mothers mean to us, we the women who educate?" (1988, 191). At this point in my life I find that this is precisely what I must do in order to understand something about how my development as woman and as teacher have informed each other. I believe, however, that this is not an exclusively personal journey. For I learn, in thinking back through my mother, something about what has been lost in teaching and something about what might be done to restore it.

IMAGES IN MEMORY

I was eleven. It was evening, around dinnertime. My mother, Betty, a teacher at St. Eugene's elementary school, was explaining to my father an incident that occurred in school that day. It was an exchange between my mother and the school principal, Sr. Jean. Apparently my mother and Sr. Jean were arguing in the hall outside my mother's third-grade classroom. Class was in session, and my mother stepped outside to speak with Sr. Jean. She and Sr. Jean disagreed about something and in describing the exchange my mother backed herself up against the kitchen wall, put her arm up to her head, and let out a sound that I had never heard before. The sound startled me. It did not seem like a human sound. It was more like an animal sound, a kind of roar. It was not the sound of a woman, certainly not the sound of my mother—a woman whose family had drilled into its female members that the first sign of a lady is a well-modulated voice. The sound was dark red, like drying blood, and deep. It seemed to come from her intestines. It was uneven, shocked. It was anger. That was Friday night.

The next afternoon my mother was talking on the phone to her friend Rosemary Callaghan. I heard another loud noise—this one a thump—from the room where she was. A short time later my father found her on the floor. She complained of a terrible headache. She was taken to the hospital in an ambulance. She had suffered a cerebral hemorrhage. That was Saturday. Sunday afternoon my mother was dead. She was fifty-two.

I am now fifty years old, two years from the age at which my mother died. I have wondered how much of my mother's death was precipitated by her anger and how much of her anger was related to her work as a teacher. Anger was not all I saw in my mother, the teacher. I saw compassion, patience, and generosity toward her students, but it is the anger that has stayed with me and challenged me.

While I was not aware of it at the time, what merged in my psyche were images of anger, women, teaching, and death. On some very real level school must have seemed a dangerous place to me. Certainly anger was a very costly emotion. While on one level I have been able to consciously disentangle these messages and defuse their psychic power, on another level I see certain wisdom in recognizing that expressions of anger can be and have been dangerous for women—not necessarily because the expression itself is problematic but because of the social sanctions against such expression. On the other hand, the repression and loss of knowledge resulting from such sanctions are perhaps more costly to individual women and to the culture at large.

IMAGES IN PHOTOGRAPHS

The week before my father died I gathered and looked through the photographs that he had collected and stored during his seventy-eight years. Scores were of my mother and her family of origin, which was large and handsome. She had five siblings, three brothers, and two sisters. By the time my mother was forty, when I was born, only one remained alive.

Among this collection was a picture I now have framed in my living room. It is a photograph of my parents, probably before they were married. They are with another couple I do not recognize. It is clear that these people are friends and that they are enjoying each other. My mother and her female friend are sitting on a stone wall. My mother holds her friend's hand on her lap. They are both smiling broadly. The two men are on either side of the women. My father, a pipe in his hand, leans in toward my mother. His pleasure, too, appears bountiful. My mother's hand rests high on his shoulder, near his neck. There are hills in the background and perhaps a lake. Although it is a black-and-white photo, I can see it is a sunny day.

This may be my favorite picture of my mother. It is the one image I have of her where she appears to be experiencing genuine pleasure. She radiates warmth as she physically connects to both her friend and my father. My brother, Paul, once said of our mother that she "had a great capacity for joy." It is the realization of joy that I see here.

That same day I also found what may have been one of the last pictures taken of my mother. The setting here was my brother's college graduation. This snapshot, printed in color, reveals another sunny day. The sun and the presence of my mother offer the only links to the previous image. I am not a parent, yet I imagine this must be a powerfully proud day for parents—the graduation of a child from college. My brother had done very well academically at the University of Notre Dame, which was, at the time, a popular college among Catholic working- and middle-class people. He had also succeeded socially, establishing relationships there that have lasted to this day. In order to support his way through school, Paul had joined ROTC. It was 1959. Our involvement in Vietnam had not yet complicated our pride in his military connection. For graduation he wore his navy blue uniform. My father, wishing to capture his son and his wife, caught, with his camera, a strange-looking pair. Paul is very handsome. He stands, almost grinning, with his arms behind his back. He appears proud and happy. Wearing a wide-brimmed black hat, flowered cotton dress, and sunglasses that literally shield her from exposure, my mother stands next to him. Her position and facial expression strike me and make me sad. Her body is rigid; her arms folded across her chest as if to protect her heart. Her lips are tight. There is more of a scowl than a smile on her face. I see such unhappiness there. She does not touch her son. They stand side by side, but there is no evidence of a relationship. This picture has confused me for a long time, as it does not appear to me to be a picture of what it is, a mother and son at his college graduation.

As I reflect on these two images, I wonder what has happened to this woman. I know her life was difficult and perhaps not what she had hoped it would be. As a girl she had wanted to be an actress. Her mother wouldn't allow it. She was madly in love with my father, but her life with him was fraught with money worries. When she was thirty-four, she gave birth to triplet boys; they all died within two days. But, it seems, there was more to this profound shift than a very difficult life. I think my mother lost the capacity for pleasure. But I do not think this loss is solely due to the tragedies and disappointments of her life. I believe she lost the possibilities for pleasure because she was encouraged by church and culture to deny her anger. When she finally did tap into the anger, in her exchange with Sr. Jean, it may have been literally too much for her body to bear.

But how do I come to this? There is scant evidence here to support such a conclusion; it appears that I offer only a few photographs and a memory. However, I also bring to this interpretation an almost twelve-year relationship with Betty and the knowledge and understanding of the world embodied in my fifty years of life. Embedded in these shards of image and memory are my witnessing of my mother's life as her daughter and her student, and my experience as a female who also learned through church and culture that goodness and self-sacrifice were traits to be cultivated. Certainly the expression of anger and the pursuit of pleasure would interfere with such standards. The only times I saw my mother angry were in situations where she was mad at me and in her reenacted exchange with Sr. Jean. I never saw her capacity for joy. I have come to see the relative absence of these two feelings as inextricably linked in her life and in my own. I believe, as well, that they are elementary dimensions of teaching because they are central to the identity of the teacher. Many might argue that anger is an emotion to be avoided in teaching. My point is not that anger should or should not be present. It simply is present in our lives. To ignore this reality and to suggest that there is no place for this reality in teaching is, I believe, to lose a portion of the power and the possibility of the work itself and the relationships inherent in the work. In making this case I find it appropriate and helpful to call upon the voices of other women who have also considered the meaning and significance of anger.

Anger is essentially a relational emotion. When anger flares, something is going on. The anger is a signal or clue to this occurrence. The feeling contains information. But, like a detective, one has to attend to the clue in order to discern the message. It is not always readily apparent why one feels angry or to what it is a response. For the most part, I believe, anger signals some kind of violation, mistreatment, wounding, or injustice. Underneath the anger there is often hurt, sadness, or loss. Once it is decoded, a person can act to heal the wound, restore what has been violated, or create justice where it is undermined. However, without acknowledging the feeling that reports this to us, the problem cannot be known, nor the advocacy undertaken to restore harmony. The theologian Beverly Harrison was the first person I found to give anger a positive value. She describes anger as a powerful ingredient in the work of love precisely because it informs us where work needs to be done. Without attention to anger, relationships don't grow (1985) and individual self-knowledge is stifled.

Psychologist Carol Gilligan identifies anger as the "political emotion par excellence" (1991), providing the fuel for activism or advocacy. Thus it is a catalyst for change—it is energy. Anita Barrows blends the concerns highlighted by Harrison and Gilligan in addressing the distinction between rage and outrage.

> With outrage anger takes a leap into the arena of injustice.... Outrage leads to resistance...we have learned that the oppressor may be undermined by resistance; not by superior force, but by fortitude, faith, conviction, defiance of authority. Outrage is the *coniunctio* of rage and eros, where what informs rage is love and the absolute determination that what we love shall be preserved...its aim would be not to continue the cycle of suffering, but rather to interrupt it and establish something new in its stead. (1996, 56)

Acknowledging the transformative potential of anger, Barrows asks, "Can we allow our anger not to dissolve, not to lose itself, until we have found what it is asking of us?" (56). In joining anger and the work of love, these women evoke the insights of Audre Lorde, a writer whose work has been most meaningful to my consideration of teaching. While Lorde does not focus on anger in her essay "Uses of the Erotic" (1984), she does identify the centrality of feeling at the heart of passionate living and working. In fact she characterizes the erotic as, in part, a process of naming our feelings and scrutinizing them for the insight and knowledge they contain. Because I believe feelings are inextricably linked to all activities of body, mind, and spirit, they will be a significant part of our teaching practice and relationships. Along with those feelings, like love, which we are likely to view in a more positive light, fear and anger are very present in teaching, and while we may think the anger is likely to be evoked by students, I suggest that much of teachers' anger is roused by administrative policies that limit their capacities to do their most imaginative and passionate work. Teachers who burn out are not, for the most part, angry at students but at structures that don't honor and support their efforts to teach. This is not to say that there are not times when teachers are angry with students. But I do not believe that is the largest source of teacher anger. And if we accept that anger is a sign of a problem in a relationship no matter who or what stirs the anger, it needs attention. Ignoring the natural anger that comes from relationships both personal and institutional means that nothing will change externally and the individual who has the anger is likely to become bitter and cynical, or at the very least simply worn out. The possibilities for advocacy and pleasure are lost. Arguing that relationship is the medium from which knowledge is born, Madeline Grumet extends my own concern about such effects: "Because knowledge encodes the human relations that are its source and ground, it is pointless to design a tolerant curriculum without examining the relations that create and sustain it" (1988, 162–63). To think of curriculum without thinking of relationship is, as she says, "pointless"; and to think of relationship without acknowledging and honoring a complexity of feelings is counterproductive and possibly destructive. Thus the loss of the wisdom embedded in anger and the absence of pleasure and advocacy in pursuing, engaging, and constructing knowledge have grave consequences for the educational domain and the world at large.

Part of the rub here is that, for reasons I have already cited, anger is a particularly challenging emotion for women; indeed, Alison Jagger refers to it as an "outlaw emotion" (1989, 160). If we are not socialized to lose the voice of anger within ourselves, as indeed some women are not, women may simply be punished or ignored for expressing anger. This can isolate us further and result in a loss of our ability to express and learn from it. Based on my three decades as a teacher and my work designed to reclaim lost knowledge and voice with teachers across the country, I have come to believe that perhaps the most effective and safe way to reclaim anger is with the support of small teaching communities, "outlaw" communities of sorts, where teachers can have feelings valorized, work together to scrutinize their insights, and strategize for change.

CLAIMING ANGER THROUGH CONNECTION

As a doctoral student I was a member of the Harvard Project on Women's Psychology and Girls' Development. My research on this project involved me in extensive interviewing of girls at a private girls' school and at an urban high school. The project at the Laurel School for Girls is detailed by Lyn Mikel Brown and Carol Gilligan in *Meeting at the Crossroads* (1992). While the project focused on girls' development, we found that this phenomenon was inextricably linked to the development of the adult women in their lives, their mothers and teachers. It was, in fact, some of the teachers who brought this to our attention when they acknowledged that they could not help the girls hold on to the feistiness and confidence they exhibited in their younger years because a number of the female teachers felt that in the process of their development they had lost these things as well. Several of the teachers requested a retreat with the researchers to discuss this dilemma. Drawing heavily on the work of Maria Harris (1988), and with the assistance of upper school dean Pat Hall, I designed two retreat weekends in which we identified and explored the silences embedded in our socialization and how those silences informed our knowledge and our relationships as teachers (Dorney 1991, 1995, 1997). Central to this process was an examination of the place of anger in our lives as women and as teachers. One woman admitted that she had learned to be "the good little girl," which translated into "really hav[ing] a hard time being angry" (1991, 74). Another said that her anger often had been "a source of energy" for her but found that there was no place to be angry at the school. The result was a disconnection between what she felt and what she said and did. A third woman recounted a time when she disagreed with the head of school at a meeting and was publicly silenced by her. Feeling humiliated and alone, she decided not to speak her mind again.

In light of these comments, Anita Barrows raises a pertinent question; "Is our longing to be 'good' greater than our longing to be whole?"(1996, 55). Her words challenge me to consider how opting for goodness and conformity in teaching has constrained women's relational development with students, colleagues, and curricula. However, I also am aware that choosing wholeness purely on an individual level can be a lonely and consequently less desirable alternative for many women. This realization vividly was borne out in our third and final retreat meeting, where we spent a good portion of our time problem-solving around a recent decision made by the head of the school. About six weeks after this last retreat, there was to be a national conference to report the results of this study to a wider audience. The conference was being held on a day when school would be in session, which meant that none of the teachers, who had generously worked with us, and whose students had been involved in the study, would be present. The teacher-researchers on the retreat felt this was highly problematic and dismissive in a general way of their role as faculty, and in particular because of the work they had done as teacher-researchers on the project. They were angry. Through much group discussion, they agreed that all faculty and staff should be able to attend the conference. They devised a plan proposing to switch an upcoming professional day to the day of the conference so that all the teachers would be free. One representative consulted with the hotel to ensure that it could accommodate another seventy-five people for sessions. Rather than choosing one member to meet with the head of school, they decided they would all arrive early to school one day to present their case together. Each woman spoke, giving her reasons for why she felt this change was important. They also agreed that if the head of school refused to go along with their position, each one of them would take a personal day to attend the conference. The meeting was successful. The head of school thought it was a wonderful idea: on the day of the conference all faculty members were in attendance, and the women retreat participants were discussion group leaders for the workshops on the retreats.

What moved these women initially was a sense of injustice, to some extent outrage, that faculty would be overlooked. Because they had been able to form a kind of "outlaw" community where they could identify anger and face the fear that would prohibit them from speaking and acting, they became advocates for themselves, their colleagues, and for the many who attended their workshops. Their work that day was infused with passion and deep pleasure in their accomplishments. I do not know how or if they have managed to hold on to that work, but I know I certainly have. That experience of community has been a significant part of the foundation for almost all my later work and insights about teaching.

CONCLUSION

Thinking back through my mother helps me to know what I have learned from her. It helps me to understand how I teach and why I teach teachers. Although I did not begin my teaching career with this awareness, I have come to see teaching as an activity dedicated to development. Aside from a depth of subject-matter knowledge, teaching requires imaginative capacity, collaborative effort to construct meanings and knowledge, and the abilities to nurture the psyches of students and generally to contribute to the cultivation of a member of society who is just, active, creative, and responsive. Pleasure and advocacy are at the heart of teaching.

However, we do not get to the heart alone, especially within institutions of schooling that are often toxic for the heart. I do not know if a community of outlaw teachers could have saved my mother. But I do know such communities have saved me. With their help I have found that the pleasure and passion in teaching are often dependent upon attention to anger. I teach with this knowledge that has taken my lifetime and my mother's lifetime to learn.

27

Charis = Light = Grace

PHYLLIS R. FREEMAN

MUTUAL RECIPROCAL PLEASURE...AN ENCOUNTER WITH
BEAUTY...A BELOVED...A RADIANT VICTOR...A POET'S WORDS
OF PRAISE... ALL ARE EXPERIENCED AS *CHARIS*. ALL CONFER PLEA-
SURE AND THIS PLEASURE PRODUCES A RESPONSE LIKE THE UNSET-
TLING PLEASURE PRODUCED BY A GIFT OR A FAVOR.

Adapted from Bonnie MacLachlan, The Age of Grace *(1993, 10)*

I first saw the Three Graces and Venus portrayed in Sandro Botticelli's *La Primavera* (1477–78) in January 1977 in the Uffizi, where it hangs across from his Birth of Venus. Although the painting had not yet been cleaned, it was an unforgettable, visceral viewing, and I remember much preferring it to its companion piece, the Birth painting. At fifty the Three Sisters and Venus return to my life, memories sparked by their image on a recent card from a long-lost friend. Through the prism of my midlife, I again am drawn almost chemically to the image of the Graces: their luminous faces, their beautiful uncovered flowing blond hair, their pearls, their fleshy bodies, their garments, their intricate hand gestures, and their barefooted leg placements. I am moved most particularly by the one Grace (on the right) who seems a bit older (although still very young) and whose slightly haughty demeanor is different from the aspects of the other two. Of the remaining Graces, the middle one appears very young and the last one (on the left) a bit older than the middle Grace. But it is the older Grace and Venus who now visit my dreams each month.

La Primavera, as the name implies, portrays the first spring and the beginning of love in an eternal, renewing cycle of nature. One of the things that Botticelli intended for this painting was for it to serve as a pedagogical device to stimulate conversation and discussion on the nature of love, on its relation to the multifaceted concept of *charis,* and on beauty in fifteenth-century Florentine society.

Venus presides over a beautiful glade shaded by fruit trees, and at her feet is a carpet of spring flowers. To her right the Three Graces join hands to form an unbroken chain and circle to unheard music. It is almost as if I can feel the wind moving across their transparent garments. Although there are other figures in the painting, I am drawn to these women. As in 1977, for me they are the emotional embodiment of love, grace, magnanimity, and passion, and not merely the intellectual representation of these powerful feelings.

As goddess of reproduction, sexuality, nature, and harmony, Venus is always present when the Graces dance. The erotic, the whole bodied self is apparent in this first spring, and it is this deeply felt, vital (sexual) energy that underlies the "giving, receiving, and returning" that Italian Renaissance scholar Charles Dempsey (1992, 35), sees in the dancers' hand and body movements. Venus is young and virginal, yet her rounded belly makes clear that a spring birth is imminent. In contrast to the Graces, her head is covered in modesty. She wears the red and blue mantle of a woman who would be cloistered in a "monastery" or "of relatively advanced age" (Dempsey 1992, 69), certainly a woman beyond childbearing age or disposition. Yet she presides over the recurring cycle of time (and of fertility) portrayed in the painting. The Three Graces, the Charities, attend Venus and also represent her attributes: manifestations of uninhibited generosity, of good deeds and of sage advice freely given, received, returned, and suffused with love. They seem to me a stunning visual metaphor for authentic, regenerative teaching: for the interdependent cycle of knowing, teaching, and learning.

Knowledge, like the first spring, is eternally renewed each school year since each new learner experiences it for the first time. Every semester offers a fresh start; the material may be familiar to the experienced teacher, but the mix of student input and one's own shifting life experience mean that if we teach authentically, each class brings the potential for making new sense and new meaning from old texts and issues. In each new teaching year we can revisit our younger intellectual self where we had our own "first spring," our first encounter with the excitement of a now-familiar area or problem. New teachers might wonder if they will get bored teaching the same subject area during their careers. And I know that some of us are burned out as we face another year of teaching. Yet each spring (and fall) can bring renewal; each teaching experience might be different; each class mix unique; each teaching self different. As our bodies ripen and mature, experience changes the steps we take around the circle.

I know that my movements have not always been in harmony with the Graces; I have had many missteps and still must listen hard as I continue to perfect my place in the dance. I still dance too self-consciously at times. I also try to quiet that remnant of my younger teaching self that whispers, "This is a too romantic view of the teaching life. Students don't dance: they smirk, they sleep, they goof off. Colleagues can be a pain, filled with jealousy, with overblown egos and with their own life pain." My inner voice warns me, "Guard yourself by teaching from the outer you. Don't let any of them get too close to your inner self. Teach, speak, and write only from your head or students (or administrators or colleagues) may break your heart." This kind of sentiment is based on an old fear of being too vulnerable to hurt and to ridicule for not measuring up to the academic ideal (Palmer 1998). Yet I want to be an authentic teacher, and that means facing down this inner voice that counsels caution. I don't want merely to try to dazzle students with my erudition and classroom skills or only to fill up their notebooks with my words, as Jane Tompkins (1991) reminds me. My allegiance is to my discipline, of course, but at midlife it is most certainly to my real self, too. And this authentic self (Palmer's "inner teacher," 32) wants to be connected to a dynamic community of seekers. I want to connect fully to this teaching life, to my student's inner selves, and yes, even to the hearts of my colleagues, if possible. I don't think this is romantic. Or if it is, it is romance based on a kind of courage. Certainly many of my colleagues fear this sort of connection to their peers and to their students. But at midlife I am ready to say to myself, "Risk it!"

I teach subjects that lead me to lecture more often than if I taught something else: undergraduate and graduate courses in experimental design and analysis, in sensation and perception, and in health psychology. But in class I now try to wait for students' own stories that reveal their inner selves. Recently, after our detailed look at the immune system, a student described her mother's battle with lupus and another his struggle with the pain of rheumatoid arthritis. Students in this class responded with great care and concern to these speakers. During a particularly challenging unit on factorial designs in experimental psychology, an international student who is not a native speaker of English explained how she much preferred the statistics portion of the class, where she felt on an equal footing with other students. Later, other students felt free to voice where they felt like strangers in class, too. I try to foster a community of caring in my classroom that provides opportunities for *charis*. I encourage (but don't require) students to seek out and then acknowledge in their papers any help they receive from other members of the class on their lab reports, on homework, and on examination preparation. This opportunity for offering advice, care, knowledge, and attention to one other and then acknowledging the benefit seems to me consistent with Botticelli's vision of the Charities in *Primavera* as well as my own conception of grace as gratitude and reciprocity.

Who am I after twenty-five years of teaching? I remain a demanding teacher, but now I am also one who is more patient with my students. I still work very hard at my craft, but I am also learning to listen to and to honor the hard-worn lessons of my own life as well. I try to laugh at myself more often in class than in past years. I can't be the perfect teacher/psychologist, and now I have accepted that I need not be. Have I, at last, gained the confidence to be a whole-bodied teacher?

Teaching and learning *can* be whole-bodied experiences for the midlife teacher as well as for her students. Teaching is an act of love, love of subject matter, and love of students, who must be honored as other women's sons and daughters. The allegory in the painting points me to see students and teachers joined each to the other, linked, changed, and renewed by dialogue. "Come dance with us!" we might proclaim to each new class of students. "Come join the eternal cycle of knowledge."

Botticelli's Venus appears to me the perfect embodiment of the mature woman teacher. Her attributes, the circling Graces, evoke the renewing cycle of feminine life that links us to one another: mothers who are daughters and daughters who become mothers; and the shared bodily manifestations of our maturing lives—youth and adolescence, menopause and old age.

Like many other privileged middle-class women, I have achieved much, yet also suffered losses. I am a woman who feels rooted in my aging, disabled body and confident in my intellectual capabilities. Yet I mourn the loss of my youthful energy and moon-tied cycles. I am a woman who both fears and embraces the future knowing that change is inevitable. The circling Sisters affirm in me the cycle of my many lives: the woman I was, am now, and will be.

The woman who chooses to make her way in this world as a teacher.

Notes and References

PREFACE

Lock, M. 1993. *Encounters with Aging: Mythologies of Menopause in Japan and North America*. Berkeley: University of California Press.

INTRODUCTION

Apter, T. 1995. *Secret Paths: Women in the New Midlife*. New York: W. W. Norton.

Banner, J. M., and H. C. Cannon. 1997. *The Elements of Teaching*. New Haven: Yale University Press.

Baxter-Magolda, M. B. 1992. *Knowing and Reasoning in College: Gender-Related Patterns in Students' Intellectual Development*. San Francisco: Jossey-Bass.

Beauvoir, S. de. 1952. *The Second Sex*. Translated by H. M. Parshley. New York: Bantam. (Originally published 1949.)

Belenky, M. F. 1996. "Public Homeplaces: Nurturing the Development of People, Families and Communities." Pp. 393–430 in N. R. Goldberger, J. M. Tarule, B. Clinchy, and M. F. Belenky, eds., *Knowledge, Difference, and Power: Essays Inspired by "Women's Ways of Knowing."* New York: Basic Books..

Belenky, M. F., B. M. Clinchy, N. R Goldberger, and J. M. Tarule. 1986. *Women's Ways of Knowing: The Development of Self, Voice, and Mind*. New York: Basic Books.

Chawaf, C. 1980. "Linguistic Flesh." In E. Marks and I. de Courtrivron, eds., *New French Feminisms: An Anthology*. Amherst, Mass.: University of Massachusetts Press.

Chickering, A. W., and R. J. Havinghurst. 1981. "The Life Cycle." Pp. 16–50 in A. W. Chickering and Associates, eds., *The Modern American College*. San Francisco: Jossey-Bass.

Deutsch, H. 1945. *The Psychology of Women*. Vol 2. New York: Grune and Stratton.

Downing, C. 1987. *Journey through Menopause: A Personal Rite of Passage*. New York: Crossroad.

Gendlin, E. T. 1981. *Focusing*. New York: Bantam.

Greer, G. 1992. *The Change: Women, Aging and the Menopause*. New York: Alfred A. Knopf.

Grumet, M. R. 1988. *Bitter Milk: Women and Teaching*. Amherst, Mass: University of Massachusetts Press.

Haddon, G. P. 1991. "Body Metaphors" (an excerpt). In D. Taylor and A. C. Sumrall, eds., *Women of the 14th Moon: Writings on Menopause*. Freedom, Calif.: Crossing Press.

Hampl, P. 1993. "Memory and Imagination." Pp. 671–82 in D. Hunt and C. Perry, eds., *The Dolphin Reader*. 3d. ed. Boston: Houghton Mifflin.

Lorde, A. 1980. *The Cancer Journals*. San Francisco: Spinster/Aunt Lute.

Perry, W. G. 1970. *Forms of Intellectual and Ethical Development in the College Years*. Troy, Mo.: Holt, Rinehart & Winston.

Tilt, E. J. 1870. *The Change of Life in Health and Disease: A Practical Treatise on the Nervous and Other Affections Incidental to Women at the Decline of Life.* London: John Churchill and Sons.

Wilson, R. A. 1966. *Feminine Forever.* New York: M. Evans and Company.

CHAPTER 2

Dunn, S. "Tenderness." In *New and Selected Poems.* New York: W. W. Norton.

CHAPTER 4

Ashton-Warner, S. 1963. *Teacher.* New York: Simon & Schuster.

Chawaf, C. 1981. "Linguistic Flesh." In E. Marks and I. de Courtivron, eds., *New French Feminisms: An Anthology.* Brighton, Sussex: Harvester.

Gendlin, E. 1978. *Focusing.* New York: Bantam.

Greer, G. 1992. *The Change: Women, Aging and the Menopause.* New York: Knopf.

Heilbrun, C. G. 1997. *The Last Gift of Time: Life beyond Sixty.* New York: Dial.

Luke, H. 1995. *The Way of Woman: Awakening the Perennial Feminine.* New York: Doubleday.

Morton, N. 1985. *The Journey Is Home.* Boston: Beacon Press.

Schiwy, M. 1996. *A Voice of Her Own: Women and the Journal Writing Journey.* New York: Simon & Schuster.

Wolf, C. 1984. *Cassandra: A Novel and Four Essays.* Translated by J. van Heurck. New York: Farrar, Straus and Giroux.

Woodman, M. 1990. "Conscious Femininity: Mother, Virgin, Crone." In C. Zweig, ed., *To Be a Woman: The Birth of the Conscious Feminine.* New York: J. P. Tarcher/Putnam.

Woodman, M., K. Danson, M. Hamilton, and R. G. Allen. 1992. *Leaving My Father's House: A Journey to Conscious Femininity.* Boston: Shambhala.

CHAPTER 5

Ballard, J. G. 1971. *Chronopolis and Other Stories.* New York: Putnam.

Certeau, M. de. 1985. "Practices of Space." In M. Blonsky, ed., *On Signs.* Baltimore: Johns Hopkins University Press.

Deutsche, R. 1996. *Evictions: Art and Spatial Politics.* Cambridge: MIT Press.

Hamilton, A. 1991. "An Interview with Sarah Rogers-Lafferty." In *Breakthroughs: Avant-Garde Artists in Europe and America, 1950–1990.* Wexner Center for the Arts, Ohio State University. New York: Rizzoli International Publications.

Walker Art Center. 1986. *Daniel Buren: 42e biennale de Venise pavillion francaise des Giardini.* Paris: Association Francaise d'Action Artistique.

Wilson, E. 1991. *The Sphinx and the City: Urban Life, the Control of Disorder, and Women.* Berkeley: University of California Press.

CHAPTER 11

Astrov, M., ed. 1946. *American Indian Prose and Poetry: An Anthology.* New York: Capricorn.

Ozick, C. 1998. "The Impious Patience of Job." *American Scholar* (autumn): 15–24.

CHAPTER 12

1. The letter is from Sara Quinn Rivara, a remarkable member of the Kalamazoo College class of 1999. It is quoted with her permission, and with my gratitude. How she came to be "Ramona" is another story.

2. I borrow from the title of Carolyn Heilbrun's landmark book, *Writing a Woman's Life* (New York: Ballantine, 1988).
3. These are the first lines of, respectively, *Jane Eyre* and *The Bluest Eye*.

Griffin, G. B. 1992 *Calling: Essays on Teaching in the Mother Tongue*. Pasadena, Calif: Trilogy Books.

Griffin, G. B. 1995 "On Not Knowing What We're Doing: Teaching as the Art of Faithful Failure." in *Season of the Witch: Border Lines, Marginal Notes*. Pasadena, Calif: Trilogy Books.

CHAPTER 14

Portions of this manuscript were presented at the Symposium on Eminent Women held at the Annual Meeting of the American Psychological Association, San Francisco, Calif., August 1998.

CHAPTER 15

1. As Lonnie Barbach notes in *The Pause* (Dutton, 1993), memory loss is a common symptom of menopause, due to the effects of lower estrogen levels. On the Internet support group I belonged to in the early nineties, we referred to it as CRS: Can't Remember Shit.

CHAPTER 17

1. Anne Marie Dannenberg, " 'Where Then, Shall We Place the Hero of the Wilderness?': William Apess's Eulogy on King Phillip and Doctrines of Racial Destinies," in Helen Jaskoski, ed., *Early Native American Writing: New Critical Essays* (Cambridge: Cambridge University Press, 1996), 72.
2. Ibid., 70. A fine reference on William Apess is Barry O'Connell, ed., *On Our Own Ground: The Complete Writings of William Apess, a Pequot* (Amherst, Mass.: University of Massachusetts Press, 1992).

CHAPTER 18

1. I teach management, broadly speaking. Therefore, what follows emerges from my efforts to teach management. However, I have not constructed myself in this article as a "management teacher" nor considered the art of teaching management as something separate and apart from teaching in other disciplines. I often think we construct ourselves too narrowly as management teachers, honing our gaze to disciplinary knowledge to be "taught" and not thinking more broadly about the act, and the art, of teaching.
2. This essay is full of echoes from Dillard's (1989) text, and a few passages have been quoted directly. At an Organizational Behavior Teaching Conference session in Windsor, Ontario, in 1993, I presented a series of passages from Dillard's *The Writing Life* and they sparked a cascade of ideas from participants (which I did not have the foresight to capture!). I thank the participants for their enthusiastic response, which encouraged me to write this article.
3. This and following quoted material is taken from *The Writing Life* by Annie Dillard. Copyright © 1989 by Annie Dillard. Reprinted by permission of HarperCollins Publishers, Inc.

Boyce, M. 1996. "Teaching Critically As an Act of Praxis and Resistance." *Electronic Journal of Radical Organisation Theory* 2 (2).

Butler, R. 1992. "The Trip Back." Pp. 29–43 in R. Butler, ed., *A Good Scent from a Strange Mountain*. New York: Penguin.

Dillard, A. 1984. "Saving Face." Pp. 49–50 in A. Dillard, ed., *Encounters with Chinese Writers*. Middletown, Conn.: Wesleyan University Press.

———. 1989. *The Writing Life*. New York: Harper & Row.

Fawcett, B. 1986. "A Small Committee." Pp. 15–31 in B. Fawcett, ed., *Cambodia: A Book for People Who Find Television Too Slow*. New York: Collier.

hooks, b. 1994. *Teaching to Transgress: Education As the Practice of Freedom*. New York: Routledge.

CHAPTER 21

Bateson, M. C. 1990. *Composing a Life*. New York: Plume.

Belenky, M. E., B. M. Clinchy, N. R. Goldberger, and J. M. Tarule. 1986. *Women's Ways of Knowing: The Development of Self, Voice, and Mind*. New York: Basic Books.

Brookfield, S. D. 1990. *The Skillful Teacher: On Technique, Trust, and Responsiveness in the Classroom*. San Francisco: Jossey-Bass.

Crosby, F. J. 1984. "The Denial of Personal Discrimination." *American Behavioral Scientist* 27: 371–86.

Freire, P. 1970. *Pedagogy of the Oppressed*. New York: Continuum.

CHAPTER 22

1. See my "Black Women and the Constitution: Finding Our Place, Asserting Our Rights," *Harvard Civil Rights–Civil Liberties Law and Review* 24 (1989): 9–44.
2. See my "Commonalities: On Being Black and White, Different, and the Same," *Yale Journal of Law and Feminism* 2 (1990): 305–27, reprinted in my *Notes of a White Black Woman: Race, Color, Community* (University Park, Penn.: Pennsylvania State University Press, 1995).
3. See Masani Alexis DeVeaux and Judy Scales-Trent, "Ceremony: A Conversation on Changing Names," *SAGE* 8 (summer 1991): 50–57
4. See my "Using Literature in Law School: The Importance of Reading and Telling Stories," *Berkeley Women's Law Journal* 7 (1992): 90–124.
5. For further discussion of the role food played in one seminar, see my "Kindred and Kin: One Story from a Seminar on Literature and Law," in Jacqueline St. Joan and Annette McElhiney, eds. *Beyond Portia: A Feminist Reader on Law and Literature* (Boston: Northeastern University Press, 1997), pp. 303–9.
6. See "Using Literature in Law School," note 5, at 90–96.
7. I found this information at http://www.poets.org/apl/daily.

CHAPTER 23

1. For example, Hong Kong's colonization by the United Kingdom and the British domination and exploitation there were basically taboo subjects for class discussion.
2. Special thanks to Gang-Hua Fan, Chad Fleck, Jamie Kamin, Deanna Lyter, and Kay W. Silver for giving me permission to include their voices addressing the usefulness of the DEP teaching approach. I am also indebted to Elaine Stahl Leo, whose editing helps me articulate my own voice in writing

3. The dialogic approach to education is not at all a new way of teaching but one with international philosophical roots in the work of the Greeks Socrates and Plato, Chinese Confucian teaching and Mao Zedong's "speak-bitterness" technique used in the Communist and cultural revolutions, and the expositions of the Russian Mikhail Bahktin on dialogic imagination and the Brazilian Paulo Freire on critical literacy for adult education.
4. After three years of college teaching, I came to realize that my race, gender, working-class origin, nationality (perceived as a foreigner in the U.S.), language accent, and culture constituted six major jeopardies that sometimes worked to my disadvantage in teaching, as reflected in teaching evaluations I received from students and even from some colleagues.
5. The experimentation with the DEP approach is an ongoing process. Several interested students and I are assessing this teaching/learning approach in terms of its advantages and disadvantages in actual practice in order to explore ways of improving it.

Chow, E. N.-ling. 1985. "Teaching Sex and Gender in Sociology: Incorporating the Perspective of Women of Color." *Teaching Sociology* 12: 299–311.
Foucault, M. 1980. *Power/Knowledge: Selected Interviews and Other Writings, 1972–1977.* Edited by C. Gordon. New York: Pantheon.
Freire, P. 1970. *Pedagogy of the Oppressed.* New York: Continuum.
———. 1985. *The Politics of Education: Culture, Power and Liberation.* South Hadley, Mass.: Bergin Garvey.
Giroux, H. 1983. *Theory and Resistance in Education.* London: Heineman.
Gore, J. 1992. "What We Can Do for You! What Can 'We' Do for 'You'? Struggling over Empowerment in Critical and Feminist Pedagogy." Pp. 54–73 in C. Luke and J. Gore, eds., *Feminisms and Critical Pedagogy.* New York: Routledge.
Gramsci, A. 1971. *Selections from Prison Notebooks.* Edited and translated by Q. Hoare. New York: International Publishers.
Haraway, D. 1988. "Situated Knowledge: The Science Question in Feminism and the Privilege of Partial Perspective." *Feminist Studies* 14: 575–600.
Hartsock, N. C. M. 1987. "The Feminist Standpoint: Developing the Ground for a Specific Feminist Historical Materialism." Pp. 157–80 in S. Harding, ed., *Feminism and Methodology.* Bloomington, Ind.: Indiana University Press.
Krueger, R. A. 1994. *Focus Groups: A Practical Guide for Applied Research.* 2d ed. Thousand Oaks, Calif.: Sage.
Luke, C. 1992. "Feminist Politics in Radical Pedagogy." Pp. 25–53 in C. Luke and J. Gore, eds., *Feminisms and Critical Pedagogy.* New York: Routledge.
Smith, D. E. 1987. "Women's Perspective As a Radical Critique of Sociology." Pp. 84–96 in S. Harding, ed., *Feminism and Methodology.* Bloomington, Ind.: Indiana University Press.

CHAPTER 24
Dill, B. T. 1983. "Race, Class, and Gender: Prospects for an All-Inclusive Sisterhood." *Feminist Studies* 9 (1).
Light, R. 1990. *Explorations with Students and Faculty about Teaching, Learning, and Student Life.* Cambridge: Harvard University Press.
Rosser, S. V. 1986. *Teaching Science and Health from a Feminist Perspective: A Practical Guide.* Elmsford, N.Y.: Pergamon.
———. 1990. *Female Friendly Science.* Elmsford, N.Y.: Pergamon.

———. 1998. "Group Work: The Consequences of Ignoring Race and Gender." *College Teaching* 46 (3): 82–88.

———. Forthcoming. *Women's Studies, Women Scientists and Physicians: The Crucial Union for the Next Millennium.* New York: Teachers College Press.

———. Forthcoming. "When Body Politics of Partial Identifications Collide with Multiple Identities of Real Academics: Limited Understanding of Research and Truncated Collegial Interactions." In Debra Walker King, ed., *Body Politics.*

Chapter 26

Barrows, A. 1996. "The Light of Outrage: Women, Anger, and Buddhist Practice." Pp. 51–56 in M. Dresser, ed., *Buddhist Women on the Edge.* Berkeley: North Atlantic Books.

Brown, L. M., and C. Gilligan. 1992. *Meeting at the Crossroads: Women's Psychology and Girls' Development.* Cambridge: Harvard University Press.

Dorney, J. 1991. "The Courage to Act in a Small Way: Clues toward Community and Change among Women Teaching Girls." Ph.D. diss., Harvard University.

———. 1995. "Teaching toward Resistance: A Task for Women Teaching Girls." *Youth and Society,* 27 (1): 55–72.

Dorney, J., and C. Flood. 1997. "Breaking Gender Silences in the Curriculum: A Retreat Intervention with Middle School Educators." *Educational Action Research Journal* 5 (1): 71–86.

Gilligan, C. 1990. "Joining the Resistance: Psychology, Politics, Girls, and Women." *Michigan Quarterly Review* 29: 501–36.

Grumet, M. R. 1988. *Bitter Milk: Women and Teaching.* Amherst, Mass.: University of Massachusetts Press.

Harris, M. 1988. *Women and Teaching.* New York: Paulist Press.

Harrison, B. 1985. "The Power of Anger in the Work of Love: Christian Ethics for Women and Other Strangers." Pp. 3–21 in *Making the Connections: Essays in Feminist Social Ethics.* Boston: Beacon.

Jagger, A. 1989. "Love and Knowledge: Emotion in Feminist Epistemology." In A. Jagger and Bordo, eds., *Gender/Body/Knowledge: Feminist Reconstructions of Being and Knowing.* New Brunswick, N.J.: Rutgers University Press.

Lorde, A. 1984. "Uses of the Erotic: The Erotic As Power." Pp. 53–59 in *Sister Outsider.* Trumansburg, N.Y.: Crossing Press.

Chapter 27

Banner, J. M., and H. C. Cannon. 1997. *The Elements of Teaching.* New Haven, Conn.: Yale University Press.

Dempsey, C. 1992. *The Portrayal of Love: Botticelli's* Primavera *and Humanist Culture at the Time of Lorenzo the Magnificent.* Princeton, N.J.: Princeton University Press.

MacLachlan, B. 1993. *The Age of Grace: Charis in Early Greek Poetry.* Princeton, N.J.: Princeton University Press.

Palmer, P. J. 1998. *The Courage to Teach: Exploring the Inner Landscape of a Teacher's Life.* San Francisco: Jossey-Bass.

Tompkins, J. 1991. "Pedagogy of the Distressed." *College English* 52: 653–70.

Selected Bibliography

Adair, J., and H. Gregory. 1996. *Menopause Country.* Sedro Woolley, Wash.: Pinstripe Publishing.

Aisenberg, N., and M. Harrington. 1988. *Women of Academe: Outsiders in the Sacred Grove.* Amherst, Mass.: University of Massachusetts Press.

Allaz, A–F., M. Bernstein, P. Rouget, M. Archinard, and A. Morabia. 1998. "Body Weight Preoccupation in Middle-Age and Ageing Women: A General Population Survey." *International Journal of Eating Disorders* 23: 287–94.

Allen, P. G. 1986. *The Sacred Hoop: Recovering the Feminine in American Indian Traditions.* Boston: Beacon.

Allende, I. 1994. *Paula.* New York: HarperCollins.

———. 1998. *Aphrodite: A Memoir of the Senses.* Translated by M. S. Peden. New York: HaperCollins.

Andrews, L.V. 1993. *Woman at the Edge of Two Worlds: The Spiritual Journey of Menopause.* New York: HarperCollins.

Apter, T. 1985. *Why Women Don't Have Wives: Professional Success and Motherhood.* New York: Schocken.

———. 1995. *Secret Paths: Women in the New Midlife.* N.Y.: W. W. Norton.

Ascher, C., L. DeSalvo, and S. Ruddick. 1984. *Between Women: Biographers, Novelists, Critics, Teachers, and Artists Write about Their Work on Women.* Boston: Beacon.

Ashton-Warner, S. 1963. *Teacher.* New York: Simon & Schuster.

———. 1967. *Myself.* New York: Simon & Schuster.

Avis, N. E., and S. M. McKinlay. 1991. "Longitudinal Analysis of Women's Attitudes towards the Menopause." *Maturitas* 13 (1): 65–79.

Bagilhole, B. 1993. "Survivors in a Male Preserve: A Study of British Women Academics' Experiences and Perceptions of Discrimination in a UK University." *Higher Education* 26: 431–47.

Ballinger, C. B. 1990. "Psychiatric Aspects of the Menopause." *British Journal of Psychiatry* 156: 773–87.

Banner, J. M., and H. C. Cannon. 1997. *The Elements of Teaching.* New Haven, Conn.: Yale University Press.

Barbach, L. 1993. *The Pause: Positive Approaches to Menopause.* New York: Dutton.

Barnett, R. C., and G. K. Baruch. 1978. "Women in the Middle Years." *Psychology of Women Quarterly* 3: 187–97.

Baruch, G. K., and J. Brooks Gunn. 1984. *Women in Midlife.* New York: Plenum.

Baxter-Magolda, M. B. 1992. *Knowing and Reasoning in College: Gender-Related Patterns in Students' Intellectual Development.* San Francisco: Jossey-Bass.

Bateson, M. C. 1989. *Composing a Life.* New York: Atlantic Monthly Press.

Beauvoir, S. de. 1952. *The Second Sex.* Translated by H. M. Parshley. New York: Bantam. (Originally published 1949.)

Belenky, M. F., B. M. Clinchy, N. R. Goldberger, and J. M. Tarule. 1986. *Women's Ways of Knowing: The Development of Self, Voice, and Mind.* New York: Basic Books.

Bemesderfer, S. 1996. "A Revised Psychoanalytic View of Menopause." *Journal of the American Psychoanalytic Association* 44 (Suppl.): 351–69.

Benjamin, L., ed. 1997. *Black Women in the Academy: Promises and Perils.* Gainesville, Fla.: University Press of Florida.

Berger, M. M., ed. 1994. *Women beyond Freud: New Concepts of Feminine Psychology.* New York: Brunner/Mazel.

Beyene, Y. 1989. *From Menarche to Menopause: Reproductive Lives of Peasant Women in Two Cultures.* Albany, N.Y.: SUNY Press.

Blanchard-Fields, F., and T. M. Hess, eds. 1996. *Perspectives on Cognitive Change in Adulthood and Aging.* New York: McGraw-Hill.

Bolen, J. S. 1996. *Close to the Bone: Life-Threatening Illness and the Search for Meaning.* New York: Scribner.

Bordo, S. 1993. *Unbearable Weight: Feminism, Western Culture and the Body.* Berkeley: University of California Press.

Bowles, G. 1994. "Going Back through My Journals: The Unsettled Self, 1961–1986." *NWSA Journal* 6: 255–75.

Boyer, E. 1990. *Scholarship Reconsidered: Priorities of the Professoriate.* Princeton, N.J.: Carnegie Foundation for the Advancement of Teaching.

Brady, M. 1995. *Midlife: Meditations for Women.* San Francisco: Harper.

Brookfield, S. D. 1990. *The Skillful Teacher: On Technique, Trust, and Responsiveness in the Classroom.* San Francisco: Jossey-Bass.

———. 1995. *Becoming a Critically Reflective Teacher.* San Francisco: Jossey-Bass.

Brown, L. M, and C. Gilligan. 1992. *Meeting at the Crossroads: Women's Psychology and Girls' Development.* Cambridge: Harvard University Press.

Buss, D. M. 1995. "Psychological Sex Differences: Origins through Sexual Selection." *American Psychologist* 50: 164–68.

Callahan, J. C., ed. 1993. *Menopause: A Midlife Passage.* Bloomington, Ind.: Indiana University Press.

Caplan, P. J. 1993. *Lifting a Ton of Feathers: A Woman's Guide to Surviving in the Academic World.* Toronto: University of Toronto Press.

Carlson, E. S., S. Li, and K. Holm. 1997. "An Analysis of Menopause in the Popular Press." *Health Care for Women International* 18: 557–64.

Castillejo, I. C. de. 1973. *Knowing Woman: A Feminine Psychology.* New York: Putnam.

Charney, D. A. 1996. "The Psychoendocrinology of Menopause in Cross-Cultural Perspective." *Transcultural Psychiatric Research Review* 33: 413–34.

Chickering, A. W., and Z. F. Gamson. 1987. "Seven Principles for Good Practice in Undergraduate Education." *American Association of Higher Education Bulletin* 45 (8): 3–7.

Chickering, A. W., and R. J. Havinghurst. 1981. "The Life Cycle." In A.W. Chickering and Associates, eds., *The Modern American College.* San Francisco: Jossey-Bass.

Chodorow, N. 1978. *The Reproduction of Mothering: Psychoanalysis and the Sociology of Gender.* Berkeley: University of California Press.

Christian-Smith, L. K., and K. S. Kellor, eds. 1998. *Everyday Knowledge and Uncommon Truths: Women of the Academy.* Boulder, Colo.: Westview Press.

Claman, E., ed. 1994. *Each in Her Own Way: Women Writing on the Menopause.* Eugene, Ore.: Queen of Swords Press.

Cobb, J. O. 1998. "Reassuring the Woman Facing Menopause: Strategies and Resources." *Patient Education and Counseling* 33: 281–88.

Cole, T. R., and S. A. Gadow, eds. 1986. *What Does it Mean to Grow Old? Reflections from the Humanities.* Durham, N.C.: Duke University Press.

Coles, R. 1989. *The Call of Stories: Teaching and the Moral Imagination.* Boston: Houghton Mifflin.

Collay, M. 1998. "Recherche: Teaching Our Life Histories." *Teaching and Teacher Education* 14: 245–55.

Collins, P. H. 1990. *Black Feminist Thought: Knowledge, Consciousness, and the Politics of Empowerment.* New York: Routledge.

Cornman, J. M., and E. R. Kingston. 1996. "Trends, Issues, Perspectives, and Values for the Aging of the Baby Boom Cohorts." *Gerontologist* 36: 15–26.

Cross, K. P., and M. Steadman. 1996. *Classroom Research: Implementing the Scholarship of Teaching.* San Francisco: Jossey-Bass.

Culley, M. 1985. *A Day at a Time: The Diary Literature of American Women from 1764 to the Present.* New York: Feminist Press.

Culley, M., and C. Portuges, eds. 1985. *Gendered Subjects: The Dynamics of Feminist Teaching.* Boston: Routledge.

Dalke, A. F. 1995. "From Teaching Texts to Teaching Students: A Journal of my Instruction." *JGE: The Journal of General Education* 44: 140–70.

Daly, J. 1995. "Caught in the Web: The Social Construction of Menopause as a Disease." *Journal of Reproductive and Infant Psychology* 13: 115–26.

Davis, D. L. 1997. "Blood and Nerves Revisited: Menopause and Privatization of the Body in a Newfoundland Postindustrial Fishery." *Medical Anthropology Quarterly* 11 (1): 3–20.

Defey, D., E. Storch, S. Cardozo, O. Diaz, and G. Fernandez. 1996. "The Menopause: Women's Psychology and Healthcare. *Social Science & Medicine* 42: 1447–56.

Delaney, J., M. J. Lupton, and E. Toth. 1976. *The Curse: A Cultural History of Menstruation.* New York: Dutton.

DeNeef, A. L., and C. D. Goodwin, eds. 1995. *The Academic's Handbook.* 2d ed. Durham, N.C.: Duke University Press.

Dennerstein, L., J. Shelley, and J. Shelly, eds. 1998. *A Woman's Guide to Menopause and Hormone Replacement Therapy.* Washington, D.C.: American Psychiatric Press.

Deutsch, H. 1945. *The Psychology of Women.* Vol 2. New York: Grune and Stratton.

Downing, C. 1987. *Journey through Menopause: A Personal Rite of Passage.* New York: Crossroad.

Downing, C. 1992. *Women's Mysteries: Towards a Poetics of Gender.* New York: Crossroad.

Eccles, J. S. 1994. "Understanding Women's Educational and Occupational Choices: Applying the Eccles et al. Model of Achievement-Related Choices." *Psychology of Women Quarterly* 18: 585–609.

England, J., and J. Finch. 1991. "Rural Women: A Thematic Perspective on Midlife." *Canadian Journal of Counselling* 25: 594–602.

Enos, T. 1996. *Gender Roles and Faculty Lives in Rhetoric and Composition.* Carbondale, Ill.: Southern Illinois University Press.

Erikson, E. H. 1997. *The Life Cycle Completed.* Extended version. New York: W. W. Norton.

Fausto-Sterling, A. 1985. *Myths of Gender.* New York: Basic Books.

Fee, E., and N. Krieger, eds. 1994. *Women's Health, Politics and Power: Essays on Sex/Gender, Medicine, and Public Health.* New York: Baywood.

Field, J. 1981. *A Life of One's Own.* Los Angeles: J. P. Tarcher.

Fine, M., and A. Asch, eds. 1988. *Women with Disabilities: Essays in Psychology, Culture and Politics.* Philadelphia: Temple University Press.

Fisher, S. 1994. *Stress in Academic Life: The Mental Assembly Line.* Bristol, Pa.: Open University Press.

Flint, M., F. Kronenberg, and W. Utian. 1990. *Multidisciplinary Perspectives on Menopause.* New York: New York Academy of Sciences.

Formanek, R., ed. 1990. *The Meanings of Menopause: Historical Medical and Clinical Perspectives.* Hillsdale, N.J.: Analytic Press.

Freire, P. 1986. *Pedagogy of the Oppressed.* Translated by M. B. Ramos. New York: Continuum. (Original work published 1970.)

Frey, K. A. 1981. "Middle-Aged Women's Experience and Perceptions of Menopause." *Women & Health* 6 (1–2): 25–36.

Frost, P. J., and M. S. Taylor, eds. 1996. *Rhythms of Academic Life: Personal Accounts of Careers in Academia.* Thousand Oaks, Calif.: Sage.

Frye, N., and J. S. Panger. 1994. *Reflections of a Schoolmistress.* St. Cloud, Minn: Aurinko Publications.

Fuchs, E. 1977. *The Second Season: Life, Love, and Sex: Women in the Middle Years.* Garden City, N.Y.: Anchor.

Furman, S. C., and C. S. Furman. 1997. *Turning Point: The Myths and Realities of Menopause.* Oxford: Oxford University Press.

Gannett, C. 1994. "Unlocking the Journal: Response and Responsibility." *NWSA Journal* 5: 276–90.

Gannon, L., and B. Ekstrom. 1993. "Attitudes toward Menopause: The Influence of Sociocultural Paradigms." *Psychology of Women Quarterly* 17: 275–88.

Gannon, L., and J. Stevens. 1998. "Portraits of Menopause in the Mass Media." *Women & Health* 27 (3): 1–15.

Gardner, H. 1983. *Frames of Mind.* New York: Basic Books.

———. 1993. *Multiple Intelligences.* New York: Basic Books.

Gendlin, E. T. 1981. *Focusing.* New York: Bantam.

Genia, V., and B. A. Cook. 1998. "Women at Midlife: Spiritual Maturity and Life Satisfaction." *Journal of Religion and Health* 37: 115–23.

Gilligan, C. 1982. *In a Different Voice:Psychological Theory and Women's Development.* Cambridge: Harvard University Press.

Glazer-Raymo, J. 1999. *Shattering the Myths: Women in Academe.* Baltimore: Johns Hopkins University Press.

Goldberger, N. R., J. M. Tarule, B. Clinchy, and M. F. Belenky, eds. 1996. *Knowledge, Difference and Power: Essays Inspired by "Women's Ways of Knowing."* New York: Basic Books.

Gonyea, J. G. 1996. "Finished at Fifty: The Politics of the Menopause and Hormone Replacement Therapy." *American Journal of Preventive Medicine* 12: 415–19.

Goodson, I., ed. 1992. *Studying Teachers' Lives.* London: Routledge.

Gordon, P. A., and D. Feldman. 1998. "Impact of Chronic Illness: Differing Perspectives of Younger and Older Women." *Journal of Personal and Interpersonal Loss* 3: 239–56.

Gosden, R. G. 1985. *Biology of Menopause: The Causes and Consequences of Ovarian Ageing.* New York: Academic Press.

Gray, F. du Plessix. "The Third Age." *New Yorker,* Feb. 26 and Mar. 4, 186–92.

Greer, G. 1992. *The Change: Women, Aging and the Menopause.* New York: Alfred A. Knopf.

Gregory, S. T. 1995. *Black Women in the Academy: The Secrets to Success and Achievement.* Lanham, Md.: University Press of America.

Griffin, G. B. 1992. *Calling: Essays on Teaching in the Mother Tongue.* Pasadena, Calif.: Trilogy Books.

———. 1995. *Season of the Witch: Border Lines, Marginal Notes.* Pasadena, Calif.: Trilogy Books.

Grumet, M. R. 1988. *Bitter Milk: Women and Teaching.* Amherst, Mass.: University of Massachusetts Press

Gullette, M. M. 1996. "Midlife Heroines, 'Older and Freer.' " *Kenyon Review* 18 (2): 10–31.

———. 1997. *Declining to Decline: Cultural Combat and the Politics of Midlife.* Charlottesville, Va.: University Press of Virginia.

Halpern, D. F. 1992. *Sex Differences in Cognitive Abilities.* Hillsdale, N.J.: Erlbaum.

Hampl, P. 1993. "Memory and Imagination." Pp. 671–82 in D. Hunt and C. Perry, eds., *The Dolphin Reader.* 3d ed. Boston: Houghton Mifflin.

Harris, M. 1988. *Women and Teaching: Themes for a Spirituality of Pedagogy.* New York: Paulist Press.

Haynes, D. J., ed. 1998. "Identity, the Body, and the Menopause." Special issue. *Frontiers* 19 (1).

Heilbrun, C. 1988. *Writing a Woman's Life.* New York: Ballantine.

———. 1997. *The Last Gift of Time: Life beyond Sixty.* New York: Dial.

Herrmann, A. 1997. *A Menopausal Memoir: Letters from Another Climate.* New York: Haworth Press.

Hillyer, B. 1993. *Feminism and Disability.* Norman, Okla.: University of Oklahoma Press.

Horney, K. 1926. "The Flight from Womanhood." *International Journal of Psychoanalysis* 7: 324–39.

hooks, b. 1994. *Teaching to Transgress: Education as the Practice of Freedom.* New York: Routledge.

———. 1997. *Wounds of Passion.* New York: Holt

Horrigan, B. 1996. *Red Moon Passage: The Power and Wisdom of Menopause.* New York: Crown.

Huberman, M. 1993. *The Lives of Teachers.* Translated by J. Neufeld. New York: Teachers College Press. (Originally published 1989.)

Hunter, M. S. 1993. "Predictors of Menopausal Symptoms: Psychosocial Aspects." *Balliere's Clinical Endocrinology and Metabolism* 7: 33–45.

Jackson, J. S., L. M. Chatters, and R. J. Taylor. 1986. *Aging in Black America.* Newbury Park, Calif: Sage.

James, J., and R. Farmer, eds. 1993. *Spirit, Space and Survival: African American Women in (White) Academe.* New York: Routledge.

Jones, A. 1996. "Desire, Sexual Harassment, and Pedagogy in the University Classroom." *Theory into Practice* 35: 102–09.

Jones, J. 1994. "Embodied Meaning: Menopause and the Change of Life." *Social Work in Health Care* 19 (3–4): 43–65.

Jones, J. B. 1997. "Representations of Menopause and Their Health Care Implications: A Qualitative Study." *American Journal of Preventive Medicine* 13: 58–65.

Jordan, J. V. , A. Kaplan, J. B. Miller, I. P Stiver, and J. Surrey, eds. 1991. *Women's Growth in Connection: Writings from the Stone Center.* New York: Guilford Press.

Josselson, R. 1987. *Finding Herself: Pathways to Identity Development in Women.* San Francisco: Jossey-Bass.

Kaplan, A. 1993. *French Lessons: A Memoir.* Chicago: University of Chicago Press.

Katz, J., and M. Henry. 1988. *Turning Professors into Teachers.* New York: Macmillan.

Kaufert, P. A. 1996. "The Social and Cultural Context of Menopause." *Maturitas* 23: 169–180.

Kaufert, P. A., and P. Gilbert. 1986. "Women, Menopause, and Medicalization." *Culture, Medicine and Psychiatry* 10: 7–21.

Kember, D. 1997. "A Reconceptualisation of the Research into University Academics' Conceptions of Teaching." *Learning and Instruction* 7: 255–85.

Kerns, V., and J. K. Brown, eds. 1992. *In Her Prime: New Views of Middle-Aged Women.* 2d. ed. Urbana, Ill.: University of Illinois Press.

Kirsch, G. E. 1993. *Women Writing in the Academy: Audience, Authority, and Transformation.* Carbondale, Ill.: Southern Illinois University Press.

Lachman, M. E., and J. B. James, eds. 1997. *Multiple Paths of Midlife Development.* Chicago: University of Chicago Press.

LaPaglia, N. 1994. *Storytellers: The Image of the Two-Year College in American Fiction and in Women's Journals.* DeKalb, Ill.: LEPS Press.

Lee, M. 1978. *Memories beyond Bloomers (1924–1954).* Washington, D.C.: American Alliance for Health, Physical Education, and Recreation.

Leidy, L. E. 1994. "Biological Aspects of Menopause: Across the Lifespan." *Annual Review of Anthropology* 23: 231–53.

Levine, S. B. 1998. *Sexuality in Mid-Life.* New York: Plenum.

Lewis, M. G. 1993. *Without a Word: Teaching beyond Women's Silence.* New York: Routledge.

Lewis, V. G., and L. D. Borders. 1995. "Life Satisfaction of Single Middle-Aged Professional Women." *Journal of Counseling & Development* 74: 94–100.

Lie, S. S., and V. E. O'Leary, eds. 1990. *Storming the Tower: Women in the Academic World.* London: Kogan Page.

Lifshin, L., ed. 1982. *Ariadne's Thread: A Collection of Contemporary Women's Journals.* New York: Harper.

Lock, M. 1993. *Encounters with Aging: Mythologies of Menopause in Japan and North America.* Berkeley: University of California Press.

Lorde, A. 1980. *The Cancer Journals.* San Francisco: Spinster/Aunt Lute.

Love, S. M. 1997. *Dr. Susan Love's Hormone Book.* New York: Random House.

Luke, C., and J. Gore, eds. 1992. *Feminisms and Critical Pedagogy.* New York: Routledge.

Lynch, L. and A. Woods. 1991. *Off the Rag: Lesbians Writing on Menopause.* Norwich, Vt.: New Victoria Publishers.

Macpherson, K. I. 1995. "Going to the Source: Women Reclaim Menopause." *Feminist Studies* 21 (2): 347–58.

Mansfield, P. K., P. B. Koch, and A. M. Voda. 1998. "Qualities Midlife Women Desire in Their Sexual Relationships and Their Changing Sexual Response." *Psychology of Women Quarterly* 22: 285–303.

Mankowitz, A. 1984. *Change of Life: A Psychological Study of Dreams and the Menopause.* Toronto: Inner City Books.

Martin, E. 1992. *The Woman in the Body: A Cultural Analysis of Reproduction.* Boston: Beacon.

———. 1994. "Medical Metaphors of Women's Bodies: Menstruation and Menopause." Pp. 213–32 in E. Fee and N. Krieger, eds., *Women's Health, Politics and Power: Essays on Sex/Gender, Medicine and Public Health.* New York: Baywood Publishing Company.

Martin, J. R. 1992. *The Schoolhome: Rethinking Schools for Changing Families.* Cambridge: Harvard University Press.

Matthews, K. 1992. "Myths and Realities of Menopause." *Psychosomatic Medicine* 54 (1): 1–9.

McCain, M. van Eyk. 1991. *Transformation through Menopause.* New York: Bergin & Garvey.

McCrea, F. 1983. "The Politics of Menopause: The 'Discovery' of a Deficiency Disease." *Social Problems* 31: 111–23.

McLaughlin, D., and W. G. Tierney, eds. 1993. *Naming Silenced Lives: Personal Narratives and Processes of Educational Change.* New York: Routledge.

McMaster, J., M. Pitts, and G. Poyah. 1997. "The Menopausal Experience of Women in a Developing Country: 'There Is a Time for Everything: To Be a Teenager, a Mother and a Granny.'" *Women & Health* 26 (4): 1–13.

McQuaide, S. 1996. "Keeping the Wise Blood: The Construction of Images in a Mid-Life Women's Group." *Social Work with Groups* 19: 131–44.

McWilliam, E. 1996. "Seductress or Schoolmarm: On the Improbability of the Great Female Teacher." *Interchange* 27: 1–11.

Meinz, E. J., and T. A. Salthouse. 1998. "Is Age Kinder to Females Than to Males?" *Psychonomic Bulletin & Review* 5 (1): 56–70.

Middleton, S. 1993. *Educating Feminists: Life Histories and Pedagogy.* New York: Teachers College Press.

Miller, N. K. 1991. *Getting Personal: Feminist Occasions and Other Autobiographical Acts.* New York: Routledge.

Minnich, E. 1990. *Transforming Knowledge.* Philadelphia: Temple University Press.

Mintz, B., and E. D. Rothblum, eds. 1997. *Lesbians in Academia.* New York: Routledge.

Morgan, D. L., ed. 1998. "The Baby Boom and Beyond." Special issue. *Generations* 22 (1) spring.

Morley, L., and V. Walsh, eds. 1996. *Breaking Boundaries: Women in Higher Education.* Bristol, Pa.: Taylor & Francis.

Nemiroff, G. H. 1992. *Reconstructing Education: Toward a Pedagogy of Critical Humanism.* New York: Bergin & Garvey.

Neugarten, B. L., ed. 1968. *Middle Age and Aging.* Chicago: University of Chicago Press.

———. 1996. *The Meanings of Age: Selected Papers of Bernice L. Neugarten.* Chicago: University of Chicago Press.

Neumann, E. 1963. *The Great Mother: An Analysis of the Archetype.* Princeton, N.J.: Princeton University Press.

Newman, J. M. ed. 1990. *Finding Our Way: Teachers Exploring Their Assumptions.* Portsmouth, N.H.: Heinemann Educational Books.

————. 1991. *Interwoven Conversations: Learning and Teaching through Critical Reflection.* Toronto: Ontario Institute for Studies in Education Press.

Noddings, N. 1984. *Caring: A Feminist Approach to Ethics and Moral Education.* Berkeley: University of California Press.

Oates, J. C. 1983. *First Person Singular: Writers on the Craft.* Princeton, N.J.: Ontario Review Press.

Olsen, T. 1978. *Silences.* New York: Delacorte.

Palmer, P. J. 1983. *To Know As We Are Known: Education As a Spiritual Journey.* San Francisco: Harper & Row.

————. 1998. *The Courage to Teach: Exploring the Inner Landscape of a Teacher's Life.* San Francisco: Jossey-Bass.

Pearsall, M, ed. 1997. *The Other within Us: Feminist Explorations of Women and Aging.* New York: Westview Press/HarperCollins.

Perkins, D. 1992. *Smart Schools: From Training Memories to Educating Minds.* New York: Free Press.

Perry, W. G. 1970. *Forms of Intellectual and Ethical Development in the College Years.* Troy, Mo.: Holt, Rinehart & Winston.

Personal Narratives Group. 1989. *Interpreting Women's Lives: Feminist Theory and Personal Narratives.* Bloomington, Ind.: Indiana University Press.

Peters, C. 1997. "Single Women in Early Modern England: Attitudes and Expectations." *Continuity and Change* 12: 325–45.

Richards, L., C. Seibold, and N. Davis, eds. 1999. *Intermission: Women, Menopause, and Midlife.* Oxford: Oxford University Press.

Robinson, G. 1996. "Cross-Cultural Perspectives on Menopause." *Journal of Nervous and Mental Disease* 184: 453–58.

Rostosky, S. S., and C. B. Travis, 1996. "Menopause Research and the Dominance of the Bio-Medical Model, 1984–1994." *Psychology of Women Quarterly* 20: 285–312.

Ruddick, S. 1989. *Maternal Thinking: Toward a Politics of Peace.* Boston: Beacon.

Rosser, S. V. 1986. *Teaching Science and Health from a Feminist Perspective: A Practical Guide.* New York: Pergamon.

Roundtree, C. 1993. *On Women Turning 50.* New York: HarperCollins.

Rousseau, M. E., and W. F. McCool. 1997. "The Menopausal Experience of African American Women: Overview and Suggestions for Research." *Health Care for Women International,* 18: 233–50.

Ryan, J. and C. Sackrey. 1996. *Strangers in Paradise: Academics from the Working Class.* Lanham, Md.: University Press of America.

Sang, B., J. Warshow, and A. J. Smith, eds. 1991. *Lesbians at Midlife: The Creative Transition. An Anthology.* San Francisco: Spinsters Book Company.

Sankowsky, D. 1997. "To Share or Not to Share: The Place of Personal Disclosure in Scholarly Writing." *Journal of Adult Development* 4: 237–45.

Sarton, M. 1973. *Journal of a Solitude.* New York: W. W. Norton.

Schaie, K. W. 1996. *Intellectual Development in Adulthood: The Seattle Longitudinal Study.* Cambridge: Cambridge University Press.

Sherwin, B. B. 1997. "Estrogen Effects on Cognition in Menopausal Women." *Neurology* 48 (suppl.): S21–S26.

Schiwy, M. A. 1994. "Taking Things Personally: Women, Journal Writing, and Self-Creation." *NWSA Journal* 6: 234–54.

———.1996. *A Voice of Her Own: Women and the Journal Writing Journey.* New York: Simon & Schuster.

Schmidt, J. Z., ed. 1998. *Women/Writing/Teaching.* Albany, N.Y.: SUNY Press.

Schmidt, P. A. 1997. *Beginning in Retrospect: Writing and Reading a Teacher's Life.* New York: Teachers College Press.

Schonbaum, E., ed. 1991. *The Climacteric Hot Flush.* Basel: Karger.

Sefcovic, E. M. I. 1996. "Stuck in the Middle: Representations of Middle-Aged Women in Three Popular Books about Menopause." *Women's Studies in Communication* 19: 1–27.

Selman, G. 1994. *Felt along the Heart: A Life in Adult Education.* Vancouver: University of British Columbia.

Sheehy, G. 1976. *Passages: Predictable Crises of Adult Life.* New York: Dutton.

———. 1992. *The Silent Passage: Menopause.* New York: Random House.

Shor, I., and P. A. Freire. 1987. *A Pedagogy for Liberation: Dialogues on Transforming Education.* South Hadley, Mass.: Bergin & Garvey.

Smedley, S. 1995. "One Story amongst Many." *Early Child Development and Care* 110: 101–12.

Smelser, N.J., and E. H. Erikson, eds. 1980. *Themes of Work and Love in Adulthood.* Cambridge: Harvard University Press.

Smith-Rosenberg, C. 1973. "Puberty to Menopause: The Cycle of Femininity in Nineteenth-Century America." *Feminist Studies* 1 (3/4): 58–72.

Steedman, C. 1986. *Landscape for a Good Woman.* London: Virago.

Stewart, A. J., and E. A. Vandewater. 1999. " 'If I had it to do over again . . .': Midlife Review, Midcourse Corrections, and Women's Well-Being in Midlife." *Journal of Personality and Social Psychology* 76: 270–83.

Svinicki, M. D., ed. 1990. *The Changing Face of College Teaching: New Directions for Teaching and Learning.* No. 42. San Francisco: Jossey-Bass.

Swindells, J., ed. 1995. *The Uses of Autobiography: Gender and Society: Feminist Perspectives on the Past and Present.* Bristol, Pa.: Taylor & Francis.

Tang, J., and E. Smith, eds. 1996. *Women and Minorities in American Professions.* Albany, N.Y.: SUNY Press.

Tavis, C. 1992. *The Mismeasure of Woman: Why Women Are Not the Better Sex, the Inferior Sex, or the Opposite Sex.* New York: Simon & Schuster.

Taylor, D. 1988. *Reflower: Rethinking Menstruation.* Watsonville, Calif.: Crossing Press.

Taylor, D., and A. C. Sumrall, eds. 1991. *Women of the 14th Moon: Writings on Menopause.* Freedom, Calif.: Crossing Press.

Taetzsch, L., ed. 1995. *Hot Flashes: Women Writers on the Change of Life.* Boston: Faber and Faber.

Tennant, M, and P. Pogson. 1995. *Understanding Learning and Change in Adulthood: A Developmental Perspective.* San Francisco: Jossey-Bass.

Thomas, A. G. 1997. *The Women We Become: Myths, Folktales, and Stories about Growing Older.* Rocklin, Calif.: Prima.

Thompson, C. J., and E. L. Dey. 1998. "Pushed to the Margins: Sources of Stress for African American College and University Faculty." *Journal of Higher Education* 69: 324–45.

Tilt, E. J. 1870. *The Change of Life in Health and Disease: A Practical Treatise on the Nervous and Other Affections Incidental to Women at the Decline of Life.* London: John Churchill and Sons.

Tompkins, J. 1996. *A Life in School: What the Teacher Learned.* Reading, Mass.: Addison-Wesley.

Tokarczyk, M. M., and E. A. Fay. 1993. *Working-Class Women in the Academy: Laborers in the Knowledge Factory.* Amherst, Mass.: University of Massachusetts Press.

Truitt, A. 1982. *Daybook: The Journal of an Artist.* New York: Pantheon.

———. 1996. *Prospect: The Journey of an Artist.* New York: Penguin.

Tseelon, E. 1995. *The Masque of Femininity: The Presentation of Woman in Everyday Life.* London: Sage.

Twombly, S. B. 1998. "Women Academic Leaders in a Latin American University: Reconciling the Paradoxes of Professional Lives." *Higher Education* 35: 367–97.

Vasil, L. 1996. "Social Process Skills and Career Achievement among Male and Female Academics." *Journal of Higher Education* 67: 103–14.

Vertinsky, P. 1998. " 'Run, Jane, Run': Central Tensions in the Current Debate about Enhancing Women's Health through Exercise." *Women & Health* 27 (4): 81–111.

Vickers, J. F., and B. L. Thomas. 1993. *No More Frogs, No More Princes: Women Making Creative Choices in Midlife.* Freedom, Calif.: Crossing Press.

Voda, A. M., M. Dinnerstein, and S. R. O'Donnell. 1982. *Changing Perspectives on Menopause.* Austin, Tex.: University of Texas Press.

Wager, M. 1998. "Women or Researchers? The Identities of Academic Women." *Feminism & Psychology* 8(2): 236–44.

Wax, J. 1979. *Starting in the Middle.* New York: Holt, Rinehart & Winston

Weiler, K. 1988. *Women Teaching for Change: Gender, Class and Power.* South Hadley, Mass.: Bergin & Garvey.

Wendell, S. 1996. *The Rejected Body: Feminist Philosophical Reflections on Disability.* New York: Routledge.

West, M. S. 1995. "Women Faculty: Frozen in Time." *Academe* 81: 26–29.

Wilk, C. A., and M. A. Kirk. 1995. "Menopause: A Developmental Stage, Not a Deficiency Disease." *Psychotherapy* 32: 233–41.

Williams, P. J. 1991. *The Alchemy of Race and Rights: Diary of a Law Professor.* Cambridge, Mass.: Harvard University Press.

Willis, S. L., and J. D. Reid, eds. 1999. *Life in the Middle: Psychological and Social Development in Middle Age.* San Diego, Calif.: Academic Press.

Wilson, R. A. 1966. *Feminine Forever.* New York: M. Evans and Company.

Wind, L. H. 1997. *Grandmothers of the Wind: Menopause, Wisdom and Power.* Fishers, N.Y.: Heron Press.

Winnicott, D. W. 1965. T*he Maturational Process and the Facilitating Environment: Studies in the Theory of Emotional Development.* New York: International Universities Press.

Wolszon, L. R. 1998. "Women's Body Image Theory: A Hermeneutic Critique." *American Behavioral Scientist* 41: 542–57.

Wrightsman, L. S. 1994. *Adult Personality Development: Theories and Concepts.* Newbury Park, Calif.: Sage.

Woolf, V. 1942/1970. *The Death of the Moth and Other Essays.* New York: Harcourt, Brace, Jovanovich.

Wyatt-Brown, A. M. 1989. "Creativity in Midlife: The Novels of Anita Brookner." *Journal of Aging Studies* 3: 175–81.

Contributors

JULIA ALVAREZ is a poet, essayist, and fiction writer who spent her early childhood in the Dominican Republic. In 1991 she published *How The Garcia Girls Lost Their Accents,* which won a Pen Oakland Award for works that present a multicultural viewpoint, and was selected a Notable Book by the *New York Times* and an American Library Notable Book, 1992. Her second novel, *In the Time of the Butterflies,* was a finalist for the National Book Critics' Award in fiction in 1995. She also has published two books of poems: *The Other Side/El Otro Lado* and *Homecoming: New and Collected Poems,* and her work was selected by the New York Public Library for its 100th anniversary exhibit in 1996, *The Hand of the Poet: Original Manuscripts by 100 Masters, from John Donne to Julia Alvarez.* A third novel, *¡YO!* was published in January 1997; a collection of essays, *Something to Declare,* was published in 1998. She has just sold her first children's book, *The Secret Footprints,* and currently is working on a new novel.

ESTHER NGAN-LING CHOW is Professor of Sociology at the American University in Washington, D.C. As a feminist scholar, researcher, and community activist she has conducted research and published extensively on the intersection of race, class, and gender; social inequality; work and family; gender and international development; global feminism; migration; and Asian American and policy analysis. Her recent book is *Race, Class and Gender: Common Bonds, Different Voices;* forthcoming is *Transforming Gender and Development in East Asia.*

DONA LEE DAVIS is Professor of Anthropology at the University of South Dakota in Vermillion, where she has been since 1980. She also is a Visiting Professor of Social Anthropology at the University of Tromsø in northern Norway. Her areas of research and publication include women and health, gender and sexuality, medical and psychological anthropology, North Atlantic fishing cultures (Newfoundland and Norway), and anthropological methods and ethics. Her publications include *Blood and Nerves: An Ethnographic Focus on Menopause* and *To Work and to Weep: Women in Fishing Economies* (coedited with Jane Nadel-Klein), as well as four edited collections on the nature of nerves and numerous articles in medical and psychological anthropology. Her most recent publication on menopause is "Blood and Nerves Revisited: Menopause and the Privatization of the Body in a Newfoundland Post-industrial Fishery."

JUDITH A. DORNEY is an Associate Professor in the Department of Educational Studies at SUNY New Paltz. Teaching is one of her passions. Prior to her doctorate and college teaching, she was a high school teacher for fifteen years. She has facilitated workshops and retreats with teachers across the country, helping them to reflect on how gender socialization has influenced their teaching and their relationships to knowledge. Her publications deal with the development of voice in teachers and the import of community on their work.

JEAN BETHKE ELSHTAIN is the Laura Spelman Rockefeller Professor of Social and Political Ethics at the University of Chicago and the author of many works, beginning with *Public Man, Private Woman: Women in Social and Political Thought*. Other titles include *Women and War; Democracy on Trial; Power Trips and Other Journeys; Meditations on Modern Political Thought; Real Politics: At the Center of Everyday Life;* and *Augustine and the Limits of Politics.*

DEAN FALK, a paleoanthropologist, is currently a Professor of Anthropology at the State University of New York at Albany. Her research focuses on the evolution of the brain and cognition, hominid systematics, and the evolution of cranial blood flow. Falk is also involved in applying medical imaging technology to research on skulls of fossilized middle Pleistocene hominids. In collaboration with colleagues from the University of Vienna, she formulated the "radiator" theory of hominid brain evolution and has published a book entitled *Braindance.*

PHYLLIS R. FREEMAN, an Associate Professor of Psychology and Acting Dean of the Graduate School at the State University of New York at New Paltz, has been a college teacher for twenty-five years; and she was the Coordinator of the Psychology Graduate Program at SUNY New Paltz for eleven years. She teaches courses in health psychology, psychology of perception, and research design and analysis. She has lectured, published, and received grants and awards in the areas of prenatal drug effects on behavior, alcoholism, post-secondary pedagogy, and the history of psychiatry. She has held a summer NEH grant in humanities and medicine and a summer postdoctoral fellowship in behavioral genetics, and was a visiting scholar at the Hastings Center for the Study of Ethics. In 1996 she was awarded the first SUNY New Paltz College of Liberal Arts and Sciences Teacher of the Year Award.

TIKVA SIMONE FRYMER is Professor of Hebrew Bible at the Divinity School at the University of Chicago. Frymer-Kensky's areas of specialization include Assyriology and Sumerology, biblical studies, Jewish studies, and women and religion. Her most recent books are *In the Wake of the Goddesses: Women, Culture and the Biblical Transformation of Pagan Myth* and *Motherprayer: The Pregnant Woman's Spiritual Companion*. In progress are a book on women in the Bible, the Judicial Ordeal in the ancient Near East, and commentaries on Ruth and on Exodus.

DIANE GLANCY is Professor of English at Macalester College in St. Paul, Minnesota, where she teaches poetry, fiction, creative nonfiction, scriptwriting, and Native American literature. She is the author of several volumes of poetry (*Iron Woman, Lone Dog's Winter Count, Boom Town,* and *Asylum in the Grasslands*); novels (*Fuller Man, Flutie,* and *Pushing the Bear: A Novel of the Trail of Tears*); plays (*War Cries: A Collection of Plays*); essays (*The West Pole*); and autobiography (*Claiming Breath*). Her work has been anthologized in many collections of Native American literature, contemporary women's fiction, and poetry, and has been included in the Pushcart Prize series. Awards for her work include the Capricorn Prize, given by the Writers Voice, New York; the Charles and Mildred Nilon Fiction Award for *Trigger Dance*; and the American Book Award from the Before Columbus Foundation for *Claiming Breath*.

MARY GORDON holds the McIntosh Chair as Professor of English at Barnard College. A prolific writer, she has authored many works, including an autobiographical memoir about her father, *Shadow Man;* a collection of essays, *Dead Girls and Bad Boys and Other Essays;* several novels (*Final Payments, The Company of Women, Men and Angels,* and *The Other Side*); a book of novellas, *The Rest of Life;* and a collection of short stories, *Temporary Shelter.* Her latest work, *Spending,* appeared in 1998. She has received the Lila Acheson Wallace Reader's Digest Writer's Award and a Guggenheim Fellowship. Currently she is working on another collection of autobiographical essays and a novel.

GAIL B. GRIFFIN, Professor of English at Kalamazoo College since 1977, has directed the Women's Studies Program there since 1980. She is the author of articles on nineteenth-century literature and the pedagogical dynamics of whiteness, as well as poetry that has appeared in *Passages North, Calyx, New Delta Review,* and *Contemporary Michigan Poets: The Third Coast.* But her real love is creative nonfiction, represented by two collections, *Calling: Essays on Teaching in the Mother Tongue* and *Season of the Witch: Border Lines, Marginal Notes.* She has won Kalamazoo College's awards for teaching, creative work, and involvement in student life, and in 1995 she was chosen C.A.S.E./Carnegie Michigan Professor of the Year.

PAULA GUNN ALLEN is Professor Emeritus of English, American Indian Studies, and Creative Writing at UCLA. Previous to her tenure there, she was the director of the Native American Studies Program at the University of California at Berkeley, where she was Professor of Native American Literature and Ethnic Studies. Her many influential works in the field of Native American literature include *Spider Woman's Granddaughters: Traditional Tales and Contemporary Writing by Native American Women; The Sacred Hoop: Recovering the Feminine in American Indian Traditions;* and *Off the Reservation: Contemporary Native American Women's Literature.* Her volumes of poetry include *Skins and Bones: Poems, 1979–1987* and *Life Is a Fatal Disease: Collected Poems 1968–1995.* Her work has appeared in numerous anthologies of Native American literature and women's writing. She received the American Book Award from the Before Columbus Foundation in 1990 for *Spider Woman's Granddaughters* and the Native American Prize for Literature. Her recent collection of essays, *Off Reservation: Reflections on Boundary-Busting, Border-Crossing Loose Canons,* was released in the fall of 1998.

DIANE F. HALPERN is Chair and Professor of Psychology at California State University, San Bernardino. She is the author of several books in the area of cognition and instruction: *Thought and Knowledge: An Introduction to Critical Thinking; Thinking Critically about Critical Thinking Instruction; Sex Differences in Cognitive Abilities; Enhancing Thinking Skills in the Sciences and Mathematics; Changing College Classrooms;* and *Student Outcomes Assessment.* In addition, she has won many awards for her teaching and research, including the 1998 Distinguished Teaching Award from the Psychological Foundation, the 1997 Career Contributions to Education Award from the American Psychological Association, and California State University's State-Wide Outstanding Professor Award. Recently Professor Halpern received a Fulbright Award, which allowed her to become the first American psychologist to teach her own courses at Moscow State University.

PATRICIA HAMPL is Professor of English at the University of Minnesota, where she teaches creative writing (poetry and prose), memoir and autobiography, and contemporary American poetry and fiction. Her many publications include autobiographical works (*A Romantic Education*), creative nonfiction (*Spillville* and *Virgin Time*), and poetry (*Resort and Other Poems*). Her prose and poetry have been anthologized in many magazines and journals, including the *Graywolf Annual; The Best American Short Stories;* the *New Yorker; Iowa Review; Kenyon Review; Granta;* and the *American Poetry Review.* She is the recipient of National Endowment for the Arts Fellowships, Guggenheim Fellowships, and, most recently, the prestigious MacArthur Fellowship. Hampl also has been given the CLA Distinguished Teacher of the Year Award. Her most recent collection of essays is *I Could Tell You Stories: Sojourns in the Land of Memory* (1999).

BELL HOOKS is Distinguished Professor of English at City College in New York. A prominent cultural critic and feminist theorist and artist, she is the author of many works, including two volumes of autobiography (*Bone Black* and *Wounds of Passion*); several works of cultural criticism (for example, *Outlaw Culture; Resisting Representations; Yearning: Race, Class and Cultural Politics*); and feminist theory (for example, *Ain't I a Woman: Black Women and Feminism; Talking Back: Thinking Feminist, Thinking black*). Her most recent work, *remembered rapture: the writer at work,* is a study of contemporary women's African American literature and the writing life.

MARGARET MATLIN holds the title of Distinguished Teaching Professor of Psychology at the State University of New York at Geneseo, where she has taught for twenty-eight years. She is the author of four current textbooks in introductory psychology, the psychology of women, cognitive psychology, and sensation and perception. Professor Matlin also has won several national teaching awards, including the American Psychological Association Teaching of Psychology Award and the American Psychological Foundation's Distinguished Teaching in Psychology Award. Under the auspices of the Educational Testing Service, she chairs the committee that designs the Psychology Graduate Record Examination.

JEAN F. O'BARR is the Margaret Taylor Smith Director of Women's Studies at Duke University. A political scientist by training, she became director in 1983 at the program's founding. She is the author of numerous books, including *Feminism in Action: Building Community and Institutions through Women's Studies* and *Women Imagine Change: A Global Anthology of Women's Resistance 600 BCE to the Present*. She won the Lubin Award for Excellence in Teaching from Duke University in 1997 and the Distinguished Alumni Award from Northwestern University in 1999. Dr. O'Barr is a frequent popular speaker on women's issues and a frequent program reviewer in women's studies.

GAYLE PEMBERTON is the William R. Kenan Professor of the Humanities and Chair of African American Studies at Wesleyan University, where she teaches American and African American fiction, film, and nonfiction. She is the author of *The Hottest Water in Chicago: Notes of a Native Daughter; And I Am Not Resigned*, a play; and numerous essays on American culture, higher education, and teaching. *And the Colored Girls Go...Black Women and American Cinema* is forthcoming from W. W. Norton. Her awards include a Guggenheim Fellowship and a W. E. B. Du Bois Fellowship at Harvard University.

PATRICIA C. PHILLIPS is Dean of the School of Fine and Performing Arts at the State University of New York at New Paltz and an independent art critic. Her writing concerns public art, architecture, design, and sculpture—and the intersection of these areas. Her articles and essays have been published by *Artforum, Art in America, Flash Art, Rizzoli International Publications, MIT Press, Princeton Architectural Press,* and *Actar Press,* as well as other publications. In 1996 she curated the exhibitions *Making Sense: Five Installations on Sensation* at the Katonah Museum of Art and *City Speculations* at the Queens Museum of Art. She is editor of *City Speculations,* which was published by Princeton Architectural Press in 1996. Recently she has published essays and texts on Ann Hamilton, Alfredo Jaar, Rimer Cardillo, Morphosis (architects), contemporary landscapes, and public art for a number of books and publications.

SUE V. ROSSER is Dean of the Ivan Allen College of the Georgia Institute of Technology. Prior to this appointment, Rosser served as Professor of Anthropology at the University of Florida at Gainesville, where she also directed the Center for Women's Studies and Gender Research. From 1994 to 1995 Rosser was also Senior Program Officer for Women's Programs at the National Science Foundation. Rosser has edited collections and written approximately eighty journal articles on the theoretical and applied problems of women and science and women's health. Among her books are *Teaching Science and Health from a Feminist Perspective: A Practical Guide; Feminism within the Science and Health Care Professions; Overcoming Resistance; Female Friendly Science; Feminism and Biology: A Dynamic Interaction; Women's Health: Missing from U.S. Medicine; Teaching the Majority;* and, most recently, *Re-engineering Female Friendly Science.* She also served as the Latin and North American Coeditor of Women's Studies International Forum from 1989 to 1993 and currently serves on the editorials boards of *NWSA Journal, Journal of Women and Minorities in Science and Engineering,* and *Women's Studies Quarterly.*

JUDY SCALES-TRENT is Professor of Law at the State University of New York at Buffalo and author of *Notes of a White Black Woman: Race, Color, Community.* She practiced law for twelve years at the Equal Employment Opportunity Commission before joining the law school community as a faculty member. Scales-Trent has written extensively on the intersection of race and gender in American law. In her most recent publication, she carried her interest in this topic beyond America's borders by addressing those legal and policy issues which affect African immigrant women in France.

MARLENE A. SCHIWY is the founder of the Women's Journal Workshop and is on the English and Women's Studies faculties at the College of Staten Island, CUNY. Her most recent work is *A Voice of Her Own: Women and the Journal Writing Journey,* and currently she is completing a new book entitled *What Matters Most: A Journal of Simple Living.*

JAN ZLOTNIK SCHMIDT is Professor of English and coordinator of the Composition Program at the State University of New York at New Paltz, where she teaches composition, creative writing, autobiography, and theories of writing courses. Her publications include *Women/Writing/Teaching,* an anthology of autobiographies of women writing teachers; *Legacies: Fiction, Poetry, Drama, Nonfiction,* coauthored with Dr. Carley Bogarad (deceased), a literature for composition textbook; and *We Speak in Tongues* (a poetry volume). An expert in autobiography studies and in writing theory and pedagogy, she has published, received grants in these fields, and has given presentations and workshops at local, regional, and national conferences. Forthcoming are a second volume of poetry, *She had this memory,* and a second edition of *Legacies.*

MIMI SCHWARTZ is Professor of Writing at Richard Stockton College of New Jersey, where she teaches autobiography, creative nonfiction, argument and persuasion, rhetoric, and composition. Her research interests in the creative process and in the ways that writers transform early scribbles into finished poems, stories, essays, and scholarship have resulted in two books on writing—*Writing for Many Roles* and *Writer's Craft, Teacher's Art*—and over thirty-five articles and presentations in national journals and conferences. Her work has appeared in the *New York Times,* the *Philadelphia Inquirer, Lear's* magazine, *Creative Nonfiction,* and *Puerto del Sol,* among others. Two of her creative nonfiction essays have received Honorable Mention in *Best American Essays* (1990. 1994).

LYNNE TAETZSCH is an Associate Professor of English at Morehead State University in Morehead, Kentucky, where she teaches creative writing. She is the editor of *Hot Flashes: Women Writers on the Change of Life,* an anthology of personal essays and poems. Her stories and essays have appeared in *Minding the Body, The Tennessee Review, Pacific Review,* and *Chiron Review,* among others. She also is a visual artist whose paintings have been exhibited in Kentucky, California, Florida, New York, New Jersey, Washington, D.C., and South Korea.

JANE TOMPKINS, formerly Professor of English at Duke University and currently Professor of Education at the University of Illinois at Chicago, has published extensively in the fields of literary theory, American literature, popular culture, and women's writing. Among her publications are *Sensational Designs: The Cultural Work of American Fiction, 1790–1860; West of Everything: The Inner Life of Westerns;* and, most recently, an autobiographical critique of the educational system, *A Life in School: What the Teacher Learned.* A teacher, writer, and workshop leader interested in a holistic approach to learning, teaching, and living, she gives lectures and workshops around the country on making the classroom a more humane environment.

CHRISTA L. WALCK is Professor of Organizational Behavior in the school of Business and Economics at Michigan Technological University. She received her Ph.D. in history from Harvard University in 1980. Her teaching and writing lives are a continuing journey to bridge the liberal arts of history and anthropology with the study and practice of management.

Acknowledgments